SPIDER WOMEN

A TAPESTRY OF CREATIVITY AND HEALING

SPIDER WOMEN

A Tapestry of Creativity and Healing

EDITED BY JOAN TURNER AND CAROL ROSE

Cover design by Terry Gallagher/Doowah Design Inc.

Published with the generous assistance of the Manitoba Arts Council and The Canada Council for the Arts.

Printed and bound in Canada

Canadian Cataloguing in Publication Data

Spider women

Includes bibliographical references.
ISBN 1-896239-44-7
     1. Canadian literature (English)—Women authors.
2. Canadian literature (English)—20th century. I. Rose, Carol, 1943-
II. Turner, Joan, 1936-

PS8235.W7S65 1999   C810.8'09287   C99-900507-3
PR9194.5.W6S65 1999

About the Cover
Into Myself: Threads of My Soul

Photo by Sheila Spence

Ten women participated in a creative quilt-making workshop at the Spider Women Retreat. For many, this was their first attempt at fibre arts. Using a collage technique, they each constructed a 6" by 12" quilt block depicting their personal thoughts and feelings. Everyone was amazed at the creativity shown. We had lots of fun. I took the blocks home (minus two — which the creators could not part with), pieced them together and quilted them. The wall hanging now is in the collection of Woman Healing for Change at Soul Seasons Counselling and Consulting, Winnipeg, MB.

Participants included: Cheryl Malmo, Edmonton; Toni Laidlaw, Halifax; Lynda Ceresne, Halifax; Mabel Somerville, Winnipeg; Hope Dawn Foltz, Winnipeg; Kathy Ewald, Sherwood Park, AB; Norma Buchan, Winnipeg; and myself, Pat Borecky, Winnipeg and Calgary.

Contents

Three: Through the Dark

Four: Art and Therapy

Five: Relationships

Seven: Singing Our Songs

Eight: Women and Spirituality

Nine: Working for Change

Ten: Afterword

Spider Women: A Story[1]

Long, long ago, at the beginning of time, so the wise women tell us, Spider Grandmother imagined the universe into being through her dreaming and singing. As she rippled and wrinkled within, the worlds came into being inside her. As she sang, the directions came to be, and also the seasons. Eventually she brought forth twin daughters, Icstsity and Nautsity, who together with her created more beings through their whirling and singing — the light, the stars, and the planets. The Earth also became a place with ripples and wrinkles and spidery lines of power, and like Spider Grandmother, held great power inside. In time there were many beings on the Earth who imitated this wrinkling: walnuts and acorns, apples and pineapples, cactuses and mountains, humans, and even oceans, honoured Spider Grandmother and her power in the wrinkling of their bodies, and in their power to bring forth new life.

Over time, many people forgot about Spider Grandmother. Other stories were told, of Arachne, a brave woman who dared to challenge the goddess Athena in a weaving contest. While Athena wove imposing scenes of the gods punishing humans for their audacity, Arachne wove eloquent images of the plight of women raped by the gods. For this daring feat, she was struck by Athena and turned into a spider. Elsewhere, the spider became Annancy, a male trickster spider who was irresponsible and fun-loving and knew how to survive. During the Burning Times in Europe, the spider was one of the signs to identify witches by, and many many women became terribly afraid of spiders and swept their houses frantically and furiously to get rid of them. We still associate brooms with witches nowadays, and many many women and particularly young girls are still deathly afraid of spiders. Our growing bodies remember this terrible time even though most of our stories have been forgotten.

In our time, women are getting together in many circles all over the world to remember the old stories and the old ways, to honour Spider Grandmother and to celebrate together women's power to dream and sing and dance and create. Because many of us have experienced violence in one form or another as women, our celebrations include remembering and healing from this violence. Because many of us have inherited family and cultural stories that include violence toward women and children, our celebrations include the collective and individual rewriting of these stories. Because many of us have lived not being able to use our full capacity for creativity and wisdom as women, our celebrations include workshops for teaching us old and new skills, and strategies for changing our lives and the world.

Spider Grandmother with her elaborate weaving reminds us that we do not have to be big in order to be strong, or have many tools in order to create beauty. She reminds us that healing and creativity are more than personal narratives; they are the very fabric out of which the living world is made. She warns us not to become narrow and selfish in our actions, or to use our will to sting and poison those around us. She challenges us to open our hearts and our vision to the creative spirit that is in us, and to learn to use our potential to serve all our relations: the two-leggeds, the four-leggeds, the wingeds, those that crawl upon the Earth, and the Mother Earth herself.

In April 1995, more than a hundred women, artists and healers, from across Canada gathered on Hecla Island for a four-day retreat, to talk with each other and to share their craft and their wisdom. Individually and together, they endeavoured to honour the creative spirit of Spider Grandmother through workshops and rituals and celebrations. Together they dreamed of becoming Spider Women: weaving their songs and dreams and fears and wishes into a shimmering web, strong enough to hold them together, intricate enough to honour each shining thread.

"revisioning heaven" by Judy Springer

"dancing women" by Edith Regier and Barbara Taylor

Chapter One

Creativity and Healing

Introduction:
A Tapestry of Creativity and Healing

Joan Turner

A gull appears overhead. I'm struck by the coincidence of my thoughts and the appearance of this serene white bird. The blue-green waves lap rhythmically over and over, lulling me. I feel the wind and the waves take the stress out of my body, lifting it to the expansive prairie sky. I am being refreshed and nurtured into wholeness. A spider web, shimmering in the morning sun, captures my attention. I remember that as a child I was fascinated by spiders, and especially by their webs. Each web seemed unique and special. In this book each paper, poem, drawing, story, musical composition, mandala, photograph or other work of art is also unique, formed by the creativity of women. As the strands are woven together, the web appears, its form, a book.

This book is about Canadian women; how we heal and create. We provide for you, the reader, a tapestry with threads of many colours, woven by many hands. We think this book is representative of the focus of many North American women as we remember, heal, and prepare for the twenty-first century. We are becoming more conscious of the delicate balance of nature and our relationship to all living things: to other women, to the smallest, most vulnerable child, to fish, animals and plants, and to insects like the spider. Our imaginations are being stretched. We reach back to understand our herstory and we envision the future. We are learning and becoming stronger. We develop alternative forms of healing and recognize that many of us have choices. We speak with heart, hand and spirit, as well as from our minds. We move through our fears and prejudices. We take courage. We share our experiences, including our pain, deepening and expanding our individual and collective wisdom.

Carol and I like the title *Spider Women: A Tapestry of Creativity and Healing* for its power and the possibilities it presents. Having passed the half-century mark, we consider ourselves crones. Together, we have connections with many women. Some of the women in this book were known to us when we started, others became known to us through women's responses to the book. The idea for this anthology came to Di Brandt, Gela Stach-Gaber and me in Winnipeg one winter night. We imagined a book that would weave together the creativity of writers, artists and healers, and other Canadian women. At the first Prairie Spring Literary Event in Winnipeg (co-sponsored by *Prairie Fire* magazine and Woman Healing for Change), we handed out 'a call for submissions' for this book. I remember feeling excited. We inserted the call into registration kits for the 1995 Spider Women Retreat. The Manitoba Writers' Guild published our call in their newsletter, and many other women learned about the book by word of mouth. Some women were approached because of their skills and reputation.

Contributors to the book are all Canadians. They live across Canada from Victoria to Newfoundland and from Norman, Oklahoma in the USA to Yellowknife, Northwest Territories, to Baker Lake in Nunavut. Author/artist Heather Spears currently resides in Denmark for most of each year. Denise Osted now lives in The Netherlands. Elizabeth Carriere is working in Indonesia. The web of connections between women is intricate. Some are friends or colleagues. Some are mothers and daughters, some are sisters. Others are involved in Woman Healing for Change (WHFC), a Manitoba organization; some met at WHFC retreats. Others will meet for the first time in this book. Contributors ranged in age from 9 1/2 to about 74 years at the time of writing. Some are professionals in their field, others are not. The subject is women's creativity and healing.

In the opening story, Spider Grandmother "reminds us that healing and creativity are more than personal narratives; they are the very fabric out of which the living world is made." West Coast writer Joanne Arnott describes the healing with courage, determination and creative writing. She outlines five stages of healing beginning with "Something's Wrong," through "Transition" in mid-phase, to "Reclaiming/Celebrating." In "Art Changes Lives," Joan Hibbert talks about creativity and art being an essential part of life. Irene E. Karpiak describes creativity and healing in the context of adult development. She encourages us to embrace life changes and transitions for their learning and for their potential to take us into our fullness. In "Remembering and Healing," Carol Stewart invites us to open and to stretch our minds. "Are your ideas about yourself, about reality, great enough, loving enough to support the flow of life force from your depths into your everyday life, so that you can live all that is in you, and live it in a way that is healing and life serving?" she asks.

We imagine you, the reader, to be a Canadian, American or European. You may have been touched, or wounded, by trauma or abuse and have participated in a healing process, or been close to someone who has. Perhaps you are a student, or you like to sing, you work as an artist or a healer, or you are interested in particular women in this book. You probably want to learn more about creativity and healing and about contemporary women's issues. Whoever you are, wherever you are, we welcome you to this anthology. We hope to engage you and to challenge you. We invite your feedback.

In this book, many women express themselves creatively, some opening themselves to public scrutiny for the first time. Others, like Joanne Arnott, Di Brandt and Governor General's Award winner Anne Szumigalski, have many published books to their credit. Some of the women, including Arnott, Hibbert, Norgang, Zeglinski and Turner, were at the Spider Women Retreat.

The Spider Women Retreat, organized by WHFC at Gull Harbour, Hecla Island, in the Interlake district of Manitoba, originated in the midst of controversy. Some women felt passionately about a gathering of women artists and healers and interested participants from across Canada. Other women spoke for a less ambitious, inexpensive model, advocating for a provincial rather than national retreat for women. The debate, sometimes emotional, sometimes filled with tension and controversy, was resolved through "weaver"-facilitated meetings. Everyone in the circle was asked to participate until consensus was achieved. Eventually, the decision was made to hold a national retreat called "Spider Women: An Exploration of Creativity and Healing" on Hecla Island in April 1995.

Hecla Island was originally settled by Icelanders, who called the area New Iceland, and left a legacy of hard work and optimism in the midst of struggle. In April each year, many migrating birds, particularly Canada geese and gulls, land for feeding and rest on their journey north. Some stay to nest and raise their young. In April, Lake Winnipeg, a huge inland lake, begins to break up, ice shifts and cracks, open blue water appears near the shore. On the Island, Mother Earth presents us with many signs that a transition is taking place. The days grow longer and winter moves into spring. The Northern Lights may appear in the night sky. It may snow, or a rainbow may follow the rain. Springtime is experienced as a time of increasing light, warming of the earth and new growth. It is a fitting time for women to gather, share their knowledge, skills and experiences, heal their wounds, explore their creativity, and expand themselves and their worlds. The weaving and extending continues long after a gathering. This book reflects that fact. For example, beautiful quilt blocks, created by eight women in a workshop with fibre artist Pat Borecky, were stitched together and became a piece entitled "Threads of My Soul," subsequently photographed by artist Sheila Spence. The quilt, a fine example of the uniqueness of individual handwork, and of an art piece accomplished by combining pieces into a creative whole, becomes the striking cover of this book.

Spider Women: A Tapestry of Creativity and Healing is organized into ten sections plus a section of art in colour. The first section, "Creativity and Healing", includes this synopsis of the book. It is followed by Joanne Arnott's poetic description of a personal healing journey. Then, in their respective papers, professors Keith Louise Fulton and Irene E. Karpiak eloquently examine the concepts of change and transition in women's lives. Joie Zeglinski portrays the pushes and pulls, frustrations and delights, of decision-making in a time of transition. The expressive arts are helpful to her in this process. Poetry by Joanne Arnott andKeith Louise Fulton, and drawings by Judy Springer establish the themes of creativity, healing and change.

In the second section, "Spiders in Our Lives," we find two pieces by Toronto poet Libby Scheier: "White Spider" and "The Onset of Day." We have noticed that, in these times, a number of contemporary women artists and writers have chosen spiders as their theme. Cassie Williams Aitchison studied spiders as a doctoral student and now works as a healer. At our request, she wrote a professional, yet personal paper, called "Spiders in My Life" accompanied by line drawings of spiders and their webs.

Carol and I were delighted when our publisher, agreed to include art in colour, as well as in black and white. The colour plates begin with two incredibly beautiful spider webs photographed by Lillian Allen, whose work centres on an intimate connection with the natural world. This connection also appears in Mar Louisee Chown's paintings of a large white spider and of a "Mourning Cloak" butterfly which the artist painted while healing through the grief of her mother's death. Rae Harris's drawing "Waiting Women I" deAls with the need of women to redefine their lives following separAtion and divorce. "Big Pink Woman" by Sophia Rosenberg of Victoria is a richly coloured work that depicts a woman embodied in her fullness. Janet Kigusiuq of Baker Lake, a grandmother who has had many experiences with birth and mothering, shares with us "Birthing Scene" and "Mother and Child." Germaine Arnaktauyok of Yellowknife depicts "Sedna — Sea Goddess," and important figure in Inuit culture, as a woman with a huge rope of hair.

Well-known Canadian artist Esther Warkov's complex and many-layered paper creations include "House of Tea," a social commentary on the lives of creative women in an earlier era. Aliana Au blends her memories from China, including her sense of loss and change, with her experience of life on the Canadian prairies in "The Warrior & the Woman Warrior IV" and "My Mother's Silver Bridal Head Piece." Maureen Stefaniuk's roots are in the Ukraine and she draws from the heritage and her spirituality to provide for us a "Ukrainian Matriarchal Earth Trinity." The weaving of one's culture into one's creativity is further represented by Val T. Vint, who draws upon her Métis heritage and gifts us with her beaded piece, "The Moon," a symbol that is often a source of strength and power for women. "Rubedo/Sacrifice" by Trudy Golley takes the architecture of the empowered female as its subject. In a mandala, peace-seeker Gloria Norgang brings several spiritual traditions together, weaving and interweaving images and words. "Respect for Life" by Germaine Arnaktauyok brngs us back to the circle, to an appreciation of all life. The art in this book clearly provides us with a sense of the rich array of multicultural, multi-dimensional images being created by Canadian women.

"Through the Dark," the third section, takes us into the pain and darkness of healing work. Lilita Klavins establishes the theme in a piece called "Pain." Lilita and Donna F. Johnson write about domestic violence towards women, Irene Heaman, Arlo Raven and Val T. Vint about surviving sexual and child abuse. The vulnerability *and* strength of survivors is apparent. Particular experiences with the darkness, and with fear, are described by Di Brandt, Isabel Wendell, Carol Rose, Denise Osted and Cecile Brisebois Guillemot. A provocative photograph by artist Diana Thorneycroft and a drawing by Heather Spears complete this section. In all these pieces, it is the creativity of the author that shines through, taking her and the reader through pain and darkness, fear and anger, towards empowerment and healing.

Section Four focuses on "Art and Therapy." Poetry by Margo Reimer, Gwen Satran, Robyn Maharaj and Carol Rose together with writing by Sophia Rosenberg and art by Joan Hibbert, Heather Spears and Veronica G. Green, provide us with fine examples of women's artistic expression. In "Remembering and Healing," Carol Stewart invites us to learn to sing our Soul's song, to remember who we are and the Great Mystery of which we are a part. "The Art of Therapy: Using an Artist's Tools," written in dialogue by Lynne Mitchell-Pedersen and Susan Curtis, brings the art of therapy into focus. Some difficult issues in therapy are examined, and the importance of flexibility and creativity articulated. In an interview with Joan Turner, Joan Hibbert, a woman moving into retirement, describes art as an important component of life. She talks about using art to help people identify and work on their issues, and to communicate love to grandchildren. In "Dried Flowers," Judy Bancroft describes a craft activity that helped her cope with loneliness and change. In "Harnessing the Imagination," my co-editor Carol Rose, a student of Colette Aboulker-Muscat of Jerusalem, writes about the use of imagery for healing. Youthful Adira Rose provides an example of healing through imagery.

Section Five, "Relationships", begins with poetry by Anne Szumigalski about the painful loss of an infant. "Olivia & after the rain" by Gloe Cormie offers a tender and loving view of a relationship with a breast-feeding baby. M. Joan Baragar's "Reflections from the Middle of the Mattress," about separation after a long marriage, is both funny and sad. Singing, wood-working and therapy are tools for healing which Baragar describes. We learn, too, that a sense of humour is important. There are many painfully moving pieces in this section. See, for example, "Writing My Way to Recovery" by Anna

Olson and "Letting Go" by Marj Heinrichs. Olson uses writing as a way to heal after the death of her young daughter. With tenderness and pain, Heinrichs describes her family's sensitive response to the accidental death of her teenaged son. Deborah Gabinet writes about singing with her father as he nears death. Mary Toombs tenderly cares for her mother in an nursing home in "this is the way you visit your mother". The significance of friendship is also represented in this section. Long-time friends Helen Levine and Eva Kenyon dialogue about "Revisiting a Very Old Friendship." Levine also provides us with "Yellow Roses," about the importance of gifting ourselves and others especially in times of vulnerability. "My Cotton Blue/Mauve Coat," also by Levine, reminds us how comfortable old and familiar clothing can be. In this section there is also heartfelt writing about mothers, daughters and sisters.

One can see that relationships are of central importance in women's lives. Those of us who are therapists know how important the support of other women and friends and family is to the healing process. We know too how difficult and lonely it can be for a woman who does not have those supports. My personal life and my work as a therapist has demonstrated to me that women need women friends. Sophia Rosenberg's art, entitled "We Are Stones in the Same River," portrays the warmth and depth of a woman in relationship with another woman. In poetry entitled "i'm thinking about her again" by Allyson Donnelly, and "the telling is my daughter's" by Keith Louise Fulton, we learn about love between women.

Women have always told stories to share wisdom and experiences. The sixth section is called "Telling Our Stories". Drama educator Raye Anderson raises our awareness about how traditional stories depict women. "George" by Kathryn Countryman and "Threading My Way" by Katherine Martens are about menstruation, from onset through menopause. Katherine also describes counselling and body work, and recovery from a near-drowning experience. In "Daily Assaults," Beatrice Archer Watson writes of painful racism experienced by a mother and her daughter. In a touching story, M. Joan Baragar shares her experience as a school guidance counsellor who learns from children. The drawing "me and my shadow" by Heather Spears depicts a child at play. Sylvia Legris of Saskatoon writes sharply crafted poetry about food and body image, reminding us of our relationship to our body, and the dangerous prevalence of eating disorders in North America. Almost all of us know a young girl or a woman who has been wounded by Western society's emphasis on 'thinner is better'.

In "The Label," Iris A. Robinson examines her relationship with a psychiatrist. In a conscious desire to sort through personal problems, some people look to psychiatrists, psychologists, social workers or other counsellors for help. From "The Label" we learn that about some of the dangers of giving another person "power over" our lives. On a lighter note, Susan Zettell of Ottawa plays women's hockey and finds it enhances her self-image and her confidence. We know that movement and exercise are important for health. Hockey is an interesting and growing choice. Art by Veronica G. Green of rural Manitoba, poetry by Carol Rose and my story, "The Tin Box," complete this section.

Section Seven, "Singing Our Songs," begins with a comprehensive paper by Victoria Moon Joyce about women singing for empowerment, courage, healing, self-expression and fun. Joyce's paper is followed by her original song, "We Are Whole and We Are Holy", as well as original songs by Karen Howe, Trish Gould, Nancy Reinhold, Deborah Romeyn, Esther Kathryn (Klassen), Deborah Gabinet and Barbara Yussack. Barbara also shares with us her Sacred Circle Dance "Goddess Trinity," bringing dance into our circle of offerings.

Women have been focusing on healing from violence and abuse, creating safe places, defining boundaries and limits and encouraging more women to take part in leadership and decision-making processes. Many women have also been defining their spirituality.

Not surprisingly, Section Eight, "Women and Spirituality," includes art and poetry, and life-writing. Poets Di Brandt, Mary Toombs, Robyn Maharaj and Carmelita McGrath, and journalist/counsellor Karen Toole-Mitchell are among the contributors. Carol Rose writes a substantive piece entitled "Healing Toward Spiritual Wholeness." Judy Bancroft of Edmonton describes how the Motherpath Cards, created by Carol and illustrated by Lu-Ann Lynde, helped her to cope with a move away from her home city and friends. A drawing of "Leah" from the Motherpath deck is included.

In the ninth section, "Working For Change" we begin with the poem "finding words" by Keith Louise Fulton. Then we remember the fourteen young women, engineering students, who were tragically killed in Montreal on December 6th, 1989. Penni Mitchell, in "First Mourn, Then Work For Change" acknowledges them and the work of women in the gun control legislation passed by the

Canadian Parliament in 1996. Donna F. Johnson writes about the creation of the Women's Monument in Ottawa and shares with us a photograph of the monument. Keith Louise Fulton speaks at the dedication of the Women's Grove Memorial on the grounds of the Manitoba Legislative Building, telling us about the response of Manitobans to this tragedy. Two drawings accompany Fulton's speech. Member of the Manitoba Legislative Assembly Marianne Cerilli calls us to be globally aware. "The world is our neighbourhood," she says. "Tears and Stones," an artistically provocative piece by award-winning Anne Szumigalski of Saskatoon, and a photograph by Sandra Somerville taken at the Spider Women Retreat in 1995 conclude this section.

In Section Ten, "Afterword," "A Guide to Well-Being: The Personal is Political" provides a comprehensive wellness guide which takes the individual, her family, her neighbourhood and the world into account. "Women's Wisdom", the concluding piece, moves us into the next century with a vision of the future. End notes, and biographies of the editors and the contributors, bring the book to its completion.

Many strands are woven together in this book. May we be inspired to heal, to express our creativity and to find the wisdom to bring world peace and health to the planet. Author Susun Weed offers us this image of the wise woman:

I see the wise woman.
She carries a blanket of compassion. She wears a robe of
wisdom. Around her throat flutters a veil of shifting shapes.
From her shoulders, a mantle of power flows. A story band
encircles her forehead. She stitches a quilt; she spins fibres
into yarn; she knits; she sews; she weaves. She ties the threads
of our lives together. She forms a web of spiraling threads.[1]

Tracing the Healing Process

Joanne Arnott

Stage One: Something's Wrong

The first thing that must happen to move onto a healing path is often the most difficult. We get so busy adapting to the situations of our lives, to coping and surviving, that it often takes some sort of dramatic wake-up call to motivate us to move to this first stage, becoming aware and admitting to ourselves that *something's wrong*. I myself remained at this stage for a very long time, that is, until my life circumstances became safe enough and stable enough for me to move forward.

A poem illustrative of this first stage:

flatland summer

she sat there eating spiders
lamely off the walls
of inner tensions   pushing sliding
pulling taut and hang-
gliding through air
crunchy spiders
having nothing else to do
when the weeds
grow high around the porch
and the wind flies in
from the old road pushing
at the house
solidly still   solidly still   the
elemental walls they
are outside and in   they can be
still and hot   they can be
cool and dim   cool and dim
and the echoes of the silence
running soft and low within
her empty head
crowded head
eyes of fullness[1]

This is a portrait, very prairie, of an earlier time of my life, around puberty. Although there are a lot of words, really all I've said here is "something's wrong."

Stage Two: Transition

There is a time of transition which co-exists with, then follows, the recognition of uneasiness. The examples that I use to illustrate this stage, "Enter the Hard Place" and "Change Herself," are both strongly body based, and look at the discomfort of sitting with the discomfort, zeroing in on different aspects of the healing process. The conscious aspects of my healing process, moving from accidental fluctuations/improvements in the quality of my life to having a sense of being on my path, drew great energy from the decision to have a baby, with midwives, as woman-centred a birth as I could manage.

Change Herself

first my single woman's
scrawny form, taking on
roundness among the angles,
my single woman's mind explores
the meaning in being more—

where my borders are,
and the centre of balance,
pulled by unrelenting change,
secrets pulled from covert muscle,
secrets leap with energy and blood
through opened channels, flush about
my being, tumble out of disturbed flesh
and materialize in dreams—

labour intensifies the process.
labour, the real shakedown—
birth
is terrifying—
for i cannot say no to the infant,
but to say yes

is to lay the mind open
to the whole of my unabsorbed life
stashed away in my body.[2]

Rather than a snapshot, a still life, or a mood piece, there is some dynamism described here, both in the language itself and in the interwoven processes of pregnancy/birth and healing. It is this opportunity of *fulfillment* or re-embodiment that is sacrificed for women who, through necessity, choice or under duress, experience birthing in a highly drugged state.

Stage Three: Remembering

Here we come to the most famous stage of all, "remembering." Specific situations from the past, often complete with details and a wash of emotion, spring out at us and demand to be spoken, written, recorded, or otherwise shared and told. It is here that the term "expression" becomes so vital: situations that pressed in on us deeply, but we were unable to digest at the time, come to the fore and demand to be integrated with the fullness of our senses of self, life, reality, community and so on. This is history/herstory asking to be reclaimed, orphaned memories begging or demanding to be rejoined with the acceptable family of memories never, for whatever reasons, discarded.

the lot of them

i can remember
the lot of them
standing around the hole
in the floor
concerned
looking down
my father hoisting
the naked pale
body of my sister
up

out of the bare earth
out of the root cellar
into the house

i can remember
the lot of them

i can remember
moving stiffly away
tight
rigid with anger[3]

The language I found myself using in telling this story, in particular
the use of the word "lot," led me to several layers of recognition.
When I played with changing the numerical term, to "the bunch of
them" for example, I realized that the word "lot" also carried with it
a sociological comment, this is our "lot" as children, mixed race, female, poor people, or whatever. Further, I'd had my Catholic training early on, and the admonition to not remember, not grieve or rage,
to not *look back* in any way, is encapsulated in the story of Lot's Wife,
who is turned into a pillar of salt for doing so.

Stage Four: Digesting

What if

What if the snow
had drifted over us, locked in
by nature

unaided by the straw bales
the green pump
the slop pail

a small hill for the snowmobiles
for farmboys chasing down rabbits
nobody watching[4]

This stage is about reincorporating the new-found memories into
one's overall perspective: there is a definite sense of looking back, as
opposed to re-experiencing or re-entering the past in a present and
painful way. "What if" clearly expresses that this state of abandonment did not, in the end, prevail. A more lighthearted piece might
have been called, "Whew!" or "Close call!"

Stage Five: Reclaiming/Celebrating

The poems I include in this section are quite different from one another. "Healing Circle" is a homecoming poem, recording my return (for the first time) to the First Nations community. "Prairie Goddess" records a pleasant memory inspired by youthful female sexuality and power such as that historically embodied in the Sumerian Goddess Inanna.

Prairie Goddess

Walking through tall grass
stopping by ditches
for kisses

Halfway across the field
I throw myself
over his bones

His hands in my pants
I stumble over
my happiness

He is so surprised
and pleased
as I fall

Young girl ricocheting
between earth
and heaven

Inanna in the tall grass
O my wondrous vulva
O my shepherd

Ambivalence toward my own experience is flagged here in the use of the word "fall" (e.g. "fallen woman"). Nevertheless, it is clear that the girl in my poems "flatland summer" and "the lot of them" had some good times, too.

Healing Circle

Joanne Arnott

With unbelievable tenderness, you
wipe the tears from my face, the sweat
from my brow

you encircle me with the blanket
that has encircled many others
before this time

red candle burning, smudge fire
smoking for hours, drum
and feather

crystal making the slow
round of our hearts falling open
together

after I lay down the tears
carried for so long, and mourned
the brokenness

still, you waited

holding my two hands and calling
in the healing presence
of Mother Earth, of Creator

encircling me with your warm bodies
to remind me of the truth
that I am not alone

preceding my words with your words
my sorrow following yours, your words
coming after me

dark room of long quiet
slow voices and warm
gentle hearts

you extended to me the same
love the same time the same
presence

as to each one here

beginning the circle
and ending the circle calling in
those who need us now

history is very long, the world
both fierce and tremendous,
one person alone

is so much easier and stronger
when she joins within the circle
of her people

in the presence of Great Spirit

and recognizes, home[1]

Put It In Writing:
Outgrowing the Pain
by Creating Change

Keith Louise Fulton

Over the years some theories about women's lives and women's writing have become passion and conviction for me. I remember gratefully the Women's Studies students who refused to consider the course I had planned without talking about healing with each topic. I have continued to think about healing in relation to feminist research and literature written by women, particularly when I consider the academy's attempts to fracture the bond between activism and knowledge. Particularly when I consider the imperative in education to remember what you are taught and to forget what you know. Particularly when I consider how mystified we still are by what is "natural" and what is learned in ourselves and our society. So much is "made," and ours to remake!

Philosopher Marilyn Frye observes that acculturation, social learning, is not on the surface of ourselves in layers we can peel away to get to what is "natural" within: "We are animals. Learning is physical, bodily."[1] Just as the wind, rain and sun shape the tree, our environment molds our musculature, structures our skeletons, forms our nervous systems. As she says, once we are adults, the gender we have learned may well be biological. While we can work to identify and change our habits, effective social change will depend on our ability to nurture our growth. Change patriarchy by outgrowing it. We can create ourselves differently — slowly, as we build gardens; patiently, as we tend relationships with difficult children; joyfully, as we touch faces. What we have survived will not be replaced by our growth, but it will be rebuilt as a smaller part of us.

Perhaps because so many women feel exhausted, we sometimes think of healing as resting, sleeping. But that is only part of healing — the other, the greater part, is active. If I want to heal from the pain in my life, I must do some things differently, not just more slowly. But what could I do differently? How can I open up the cycle I am caught in?

I have learned over the years to keep my balance by writing things down. Lists. Fragments. Thoughts. Memories. Just bits. The words on paper are like the outriggers on an ocean canoe, stabilizing my craft, keeping me afloat. I put them out there, and I could pull them in. I could devise patterns for them, try out arrangements and consider the connections among them. I could feel pleased by what I have made. Even terrible words could carry back to me the comfort of knowing something true.

The pain of living as a woman is not necessary and inevitable, nor is it personal and individual. It is social and re-enacted daily by our institutions, our customs and our habits. These institutions have taught me to think of pain as private tragedy instead of as social injustice, for then I will be alone with it. As long as I see myself as a single victim, I will not notice the pain of others nor join forces with them. The remedy for pain is healing; the remedy for the oppression of women is a liberation movement.

I am healing by creating my own liberation — in my daily choices as well as in writing and political action. Since the present moment is when I repeat the cycles from the past, the present is where I can create change and escape that repetition. Sonia Johnson has written that patriarchy induces women to think of ourselves in either the past or the future — which keeps us out of the present, where our power is. I have loved her for that thought, and for writing it down.[2]

Consider the prospect: hundreds — no, thousands and tens of thousands of women writing ourselves on paper. Rooting ourselves in the writings of others. All those messages of where we have been or what we can imagine! Natalie Goldberg offers excellent exercises in writing to flex our writing bodies.[3] I love to use her timed writing beginning with "I remember…" and "I used to think…" By playing with the words I create myself out of my past, making a presence in my present. The stories we have learned we have also lived. By writing, we can create authority for ourselves within these stories.

Our accounts have been missing in the history books as well as the storybooks. They still are missing in most of them. And the patterns of history that we have learned are the patterns drawn from what was left after most women, working people, and non-white people were excluded from authority and significance. These patterns were not only inadequate, they were also those that would cover over and justify the exclusions. So repeating those patterns won't help me liberate myself or heal my pain. But learning to recognize those patterns — ahh, that's another story!

In London, England, on October 13, 1655, Elizabeth was fourteen and preparing to marry without a dowry. Young as she was, she knew that "'Tis a mighty thing to wed a man and have nothing."[4] At her mother's insistence, she began to keep a diary; while Elizabeth does record what is "of great import," she also develops her own style, "which does prove to have much satisfaction in it."[5]

Leaving traces of ourselves to be found later by other women contributes to balancing the accounts of human experience. For hundreds of years, the foremost diarist in English literature has been Samuel Pepys. But now we learn that Samuel was taught to keep a diary by his wife Elizabeth. Her papers have come to light 330 years after she wrote them. The pages, edited by Dale Spender, tell us about her marrying that December in 1655, and how she sustained herself by confronting her conditions in writing. Not only did she have to steal paper and hide her diary, but she suffered almost immediately from the "burning piss" and was often hungry and alone. She finally ran from his jealous violence when he discovered dishes from a meal her mother had brought her. After several years apart, during which time she earned a subsistence by doing translations from French, she returned to the marriage on the conditions of a contract she negotiated with Samuel. She insisted on a minimum income and the right to her diaries. She also decided to teach Samuel the pleasures of keeping a diary, reasoning that if he was occupied with his own writing, he might not begrudge her hers. She also hoped to learn about his affairs (financial and otherwise) and so to improve her bargaining position. Though his diaries have become famous for their transparent accounts of a man-about-town in seventeenth-century London, they are not, according to Elizabeth, proper diaries where he can learn from his own accounts.

She does learn from writing about her experiences, and we learn too. There is a pleasure in the company of her voice — for us and, obviously, for her as well. Her records of wash day and her attempt to save money by giving Samuel pigeons for supper instead of partridges are both terrible and funny. Writing can be part of the healing process, not in a cathartic sense of getting it all out and done with, but as a creative resource to the failed protections of denial. The numbing of pain and memory through denial only works for a little while, and then we are left in the same dangers but now confused and ignorant. Creative writing can balance our memory work on the line of our words. Outriggers on the canoe of consciousness, writings stabilize us as we remember our own presence. We become mindful of ourselves.

Of course, that writing sometimes takes us to expressions that may shock, depress, or frighten us, because through writing we can reach for a full expression of ourselves as complete human beings. Imagine that! Women as complete human beings — capable of rage, passion, hatred, anger and vengeance as well as of longing, compassion, wisdom and justice. The urgency of our words speaks to the conditions that would deny or limit our presence, to the misogyny that makes women small, false, insignificant, wrong.

Once we have written, we can decide what to do with the words, who we want to see them, if we want to share them, where we want to put them. Sometimes, a woman has no safe place to keep her writing. She could hide them under the mattress as Elizabeth did, or leave them with a friend, or destroy them. But the problem of finding a safe place to leave her writing should alert her to the larger and more important discovery that if she has no safe place for her writing, she has no safe place for herself either — no place for her mind, her view of her experiences, her consciousness, and finally no place for even her body to be present in the world. Because her body cannot be present if she must put her mind somewhere else.

In her recent *Notebooks on Poetry and Politics*, Adrienne Rich maintains, "You must write, and read, as if your life depended on it."[6] Because it does. Writing creates a space for the self, acknowledging our own authority, verbal control and will to speak. In 1964 Rich acknowledges that "what I know I know through making poems"; in 1993 she writes that she "knew — had long known — how poetry can break open locked chambers of possibility, restore numbed zones to feeling, recharge desire."[7]

When I used to talk about writing, I was thinking primarily about poetry as we recognize it in the genre. Now, increasingly, I think of writing as poetic (whether in the form of a novel, story, play or journal) whenever the writer is engaging with liberation and the power of language in our society. Poetry is personal experience and knowledge in public language. To write poetry is to make a claim on that public language to include your truths too. Women have long been taught that to write poetry is to make a claim on that public language. Women have long been taught to minimize our claims for anything, so when we claim language we are often afraid. In "North American Time," Rich admits that "Everything we write/will be used against us/or against those we love./ These are the terms,/take them or leave them." In that poem she confronts "what is meant to break my heart and reduce me to silence" and speaks again.[8] As Audre Lorde writes, "My silences had not protected me. Your silence will not protect you."[9]

Healing involves new growth — it's as simple as that. And new growth is what creativity is.

The Well

Keith Louise Fulton

My thoughts come to me
in code
short messages
sent where they charge by the letter
and money is scarce
the contents urge
resistance
brief warnings
whole poems are needed to protect them

in the dry land
arid
I plant with care
what I will need to get up in the morning

it rains even less now than I remember

always the struggle to make soil
before the garden turns to dust
and blows away

tears help wash away the salt
but I put my hope
in the well of anger
I have in reserve

so deep and sweet the waters there
so not-to-be-wasted these waters
I've tasted and raise slowly
to the surface

trying not to splatter or spill
I route this water along channels the tears
had made, sometimes building
aqueducts for the lines lost
when I did not have the sense to cry

The Primary Fibres of Our Transitions

Irene E. Karpiak

Nearly 15 years ago, I began my exploration of personal crisis, development, and change, and soon after, I became fascinated with this important life theme. I had recently begun a new job in a university, and was recognizing the need to learn more about this new work I was doing. I was enrolled in my first course, one that was to become the beginning of a long journey through a doctoral program. The subject of this course was adult development, an examination of how adults change and grow throughout life. Just prior, I had undergone a crisis, a life-changing event; and I had emerged from it with some profoundly changed views of myself and the world around me. This course on adult development inspired me to reflect once more on this crisis event, and now to come to understand its significance. Examining my own experience within the context of adult development theory, I began to appreciate crises for their power to transform us — to start us down paths that we might never have predicted nor even envisioned.

Since that time, after more than a decade, I have passed through other personal transitions, most of them less momentous than the earlier one, less precipitated by external events, and now more often the consequence of my own inner desires and strivings. From these experiences, as well as my own research, I have learned that whether they originate from without, or from within, transitions constitute the growth points in our life. They connect us with our own developmental potential. As we travel our developmental journey, and as we support that journey in others, we benefit ourselves and those around us. In the remaining sections I will share with readers my understanding of adult development, and of the interconnections of development, life changes, and transitions. Finally, I will explore the part of creativity and healing in each of these.

Our Attitude to Change is Not to Change
Both to undergo and to initiate change is, for most of us, very difficult. We are a culture of comfort, not of change.[1] In our society we prefer a model of stability to one of growth. We would rather not have anything happen in our world that disturbs our order. We would

rather live our life on a sofa. Likewise, our models of human behaviour are models of predictability and equilibrium. We study successful aging for its signs of adaptation, satisfaction, and stability, not for its signs of growth, wisdom, and integration. And when events and stresses do occur, we yearn for the comfort and security of the past. We are not inclined to be curious about what information or message the stress might carry about the state of our life; rather, we try to "manage" the stress, and to minimize it through strategies like exercise, diet, shopping, or socializing. Our aim is to recreate stability, and bring us back to the place where we were before. Still, events do occur uninvited, as do urgings from within. At those times, we glimpse the prospect that ours is a world of change, of constant motion, and movement. Yet, we continue to resist that notion. All said, we prefer a world of stability, sameness, and security...our sofa.

But recent advances in evolutionary theory and the new sciences paint a picture of life unlike the one we hold so dear. Prigogine and Stengers in Chemistry[2,] Jantsch in Biology[3], and Fritjof Capra in Physics[4,] describe a world in flux, a world on edge, hovering, both pushed from within and driven from without. These scientists describe a world that is stable...but only for a short time. While the surface might appear to be stable, the subsurface is teeming with life, bubbling with energy and motion. This is the nature of all living systems. All living systems — plants, people, groups, organizations, societies — pass through periods of calm, then turbulence, sometimes chaos, even transformation; and then they stabilize, only to encounter another turbulence, possibly chaos, perhaps another transformation. In sum, stability, change and transformation are the nature of all of life.

Evolutionary researchers have gone even further. Prigogine and Stengers[5] have detailed in simple chemical systems the processes of transformation by which these systems move toward a more complex form of their own structure. The most dramatic change occurs when a system is subjected to extreme stress. It can disintegrate, but, alternatively and amazingly, it can also spontaneously and unpredictably transform to a new and more complex form of itself. It can become more of what it was. The second way that these simple chemical systems change is a less dramatic means of transformation. Initially, one part of the system ventures out; and in time it "enslaves" the rest of the system to follow suit, finally completely integrating the old with the new.

With each of these change processes — the sudden, dramatic, or the gradual, persistent — a transformation, a new order can be reached. Every living system in the universe is capable of this sort of transformative change. Transformative change is the means by which our universe continues to evolve.

These ideas associated with the new sciences are compelling by virtue of their possible implications for human development. In this regard, Capra suggests that in humans this transformation expresses itself in our psychological development towards higher stages of consciousness.[6] It would appear, then, that the new sciences bear out in observable, physical terms, what the prophets, mystics and philosophers have professed for centuries — that change, crises, and even chaos can lead to transformation and to a new view of self and of the world around us. Still, while it may be in our physical natures to change and transform, strong forces all around act to deter it. As with other systems of our universe, our social world wants to heal any sign of change, as though it were a wound. Therefore, when we step outside of our social world, that world, in order to maintain its stable state, wants to encompass us back into itself. And so the forces compelling us to stay the same, to fit in, to take our place, present formidable challenges. Any woman who has determined to move beyond the boundaries of her family, culture, or social group, to return to school or move into the workforce, knows full well the strength of these social forces. Couple this with our distrust of change, our belief that we should keep our place and hold on to what we have, and our uncertainty of what lies beyond, and we begin to appreciate why taking the chance to change can truly be a heroine's journey.[7]

Our Journey in a Larger Story

Evolutionary theory tells us even more. Not only is our world one of change, dynamism, and movement, the direction of this movement is toward greater wholeness and complexity. Evolutionary theorists have attributed this tendency to all social, cultural, biological, and psychological systems. In humans this tendency is manifested as psychological development or growth of complexity. Psychological stage theorists, among them Loevinger,[8] Kohlberg,[9] and Wilber,[10] have detailed the stages of development by which this unfolding occurs. Complexity refers to the presence of many parts of ourselves and to the connectedness of each to the other. Developmental changes are readily apparent in the growth of complexity that we observe among children as they grow older. Only recently have we begun to pay attention to the continuing developmental potential in adults, as they journey through the stages of adulthood.

The journey of adult development, according to developmental theorists, means embracing a larger story — a larger view of ourselves and the world. To develop is to enlarge our perspective. We go deeper into ourselves, we move wider beyond ourselves, and we encompass both.[11] We become more inclusive in our view, that is, we include more of what has been left out, and we bring our parts together. Our story becomes more complex, includes more factors, reveals more insight, and has deeper meaning. We emerge wiser and more whole. It is as if we are moving ourselves into a new dwelling, a larger one. We take our contents, add new items, and then rearrange them all in a new, more spacious dwelling. Our clearest sense of our own development can be gained from rewinding the tape of our life and observing the growth in complexity that is revealed in our view of ourselves and the world.

Why, despite the fear of change, do we continue to move beyond ourselves, beyond our present state, sometimes even beyond our sense of who we think we are? We could also ask, why is it important to develop? Is it not just as good to be at whatever state of development we happen to be and to be content with that? After all, there are probably plenty of people who don't develop, and they appear to be fine. The benefit to us of our further development is that it permits us to become increasingly conscious of who we are, and to gain wider options for our behaviours and responses to people and events around us. Further, says Csikszentmihalyi, by unfolding our human potential and bringing our various parts into closer harmony, we are enabled to contribute more to the harmony of our world.[12] That is to say, as we develop we become more unique and varied, and therefore, more able to offer what is unique and diverse to the world around us.

Coming Undone Through Life Transitions

If we imagine development as our movement to a more spacious dwelling, then transitions are the vehicles that carry us from one dwelling to the next. And these transitions are most often precipitated by change. One certain thing about our life is the inevitability of change. We have all undergone change; we have become mothers or grandmothers, received a promotion or been denied one, moved to a new neighbourhood or part of the world, experienced an illness in ourselves or in another, returned to school or dropped out, faced menopause or divorce, been chosen or not chosen. Whatever the occurrence, our change becomes a transition when we vacate our comfort zone, our sofa. We experience events that are not totally congruent with what we had previously known. Our previous coping habits and ways no longer work. Transitions, by definition, are challenging because they necessitate the abandonment of one set of assumptions, and the development of a new set, in order for us to cope with our altered life space, roles, or relationships. We have to embrace new attitudes, beliefs, skills, as we encounter novel events in our lives. Occasionally these lead to some transformation of our sense of self and the world.[13]

Some transitions are so dramatic that our whole world is shattered. When Molly's husband of 24 years announces a divorce, she feels "like someone had dipped me in cement".[14] Most of us know those times when things come apart; we are cast adrift. Life is chaos. What was true before looks more like a lie now; what we valued then holds little worth now. Our assumptions about life start to become clear to us, and now we see how false they are. Usually, this sort of transition is precipitated by a trigger event — a loss, a death, an illness. This crisis represents the beginning of one sort of transition. Transitions can also be slower, less dramatic, perhaps precipitated by a gradual awakening, a new way of looking at things, a new experience of ourselves. The film *Educating Rita* offers us the clearest instance of this sort of gradual change initiated from within.[15] The film illustrates the process: Rita, a hairdresser, makes a change in one part of her life by going back to school as an evening, part-time, adult learner. She expects that only a small part of her life will be touched; she does not envision that the act of returning to school will alter every facet of her existence. But, in time, it does. Our own transitions might be initiated by taking a course, a new interest, a new job, a new role, or a new place to live. We notice ourselves feeling differently and behaving differently. This sort of change is less immediately apparent to ourselves and others, and less startling, but over time its effects can be as encompassing and transformative as those that accompany the first, crisis-oriented transition.

Special transitions of this second, gradual sort occur around midlife for both women and men. At sometime around age 40, as Neugarten observed, we become aware that we no longer count our years by how long we have lived, but by how long we have left.[16] We have glimpsed that we will not be here forever, that we are mortal, that our healthy, productive years are limited. We have reached, said Jung, the noon of life, the point at which the sun, having completed its ascent, now begins its descent.[17] A reckoning is about to begin. We begin to look back. What have we lost? What have we gained? What do we want to change? What childhood memories now present themselves for resolution? What part of ourselves, submerged under societal and cultural demands, still yearn to be expressed? During this period, many men note that their earlier need for advancement and power becomes eclipsed by the need for closeness and intimacy. In women, our inclination to nurture, to relate, and to care for others in our inner, familial world may reverse into a desire and need to express, produce, and influence others in our wider social sphere. A woman's decision to return to school at mid-life is perhaps the clearest manifestation of this internal change. These perceptions, feelings, and tensions present us with a series of decision points, crossroads of uncertainty; they also provide the impetus for further growth.

Healing and Creativity in Our Transitions and Development

Creativity and healing are not only central concepts in the chapters of this book, they are also essential and complementary features of our development and transitions. Creativity and healing parallel the two phenomena that, according to evolutionary theory, constitute the major processes of development: differentiation and integration. Differentiation has to do with moving out and beyond; it produces variation and diversity — a "manyness." Integration is the process of bringing our parts together; it produces a new "oneness."[18] These two actions, of moving outward and beyond, and then coming together, constitute the rhythms and processes of development. Creativity, in my view, can be said to correspond to the first — reaching out and beyond our present boundaries, and producing the "manyness," whereas healing corresponds to the second — drawing our parts together, finding the larger story, and producing a new "oneness." Thus, both creativity and healing combine as complementary processes of our development.

Turning first to creativity, I am reminded of Prigogine's remark that we have not inherited a world ready-made, but a world that is being created by us, right here, on the spot.[19] In our moment-by-moment actions we are actually directing the ongoing creation of our world. In this light, creativity has to do not only with artistic talent or particular gifts but also with the aspect of novelty, or rather how *we* respond artistically to novel situations. Lindeman, a social worker and adult educator, put it eloquently: "[W]henever it becomes possible to add a new quality to experience, we stand in the presence of creation."[20] Here we are being challenged to approach new situations, not from the rut or trench of our typical, automatic, tried-and-true responses, but, rather, from a vantage point that beckons us to be experimental, curious, and risk-taking. Creativity prompts us to deal with a novel situation in a way that is free from constraints of what should be, or what has been. Thus, creativity means reaching beyond, and being part of the constant renewal of the universe by the reactions that we, through our efforts, bring forth.

Novel events present themselves constantly in our lives — we encounter an intruder, we find ourselves in the midst of conflict, we hear about a career opportunity. Now we face a crossroads; we are on the brink of choice. Several doors are open and we venture through one. A part of us has moved, one foot has gone through. The rest is still waiting. As an example, we might decide to move to another country, take a new job, begin a new relationship. But we have not, through the process itself, or through that event, become transformed. Only a part of us has been changed, our location, our space, or relational world. We have accomplished the first part of our transition. The rest is yet to come. And this next process is the one of embracing, containing, encompassing, and healing.

Healing, I believe, is the complementary process of creativity in our transitions. Healing does not imply doing away with a wound or making it go away. When we nurse an injury, we do not expect to negate it, but rather, through healing, to allow our body to absorb it. Jean Houston observed that healing is a process of incorporating a situation, experience, or event into our larger story, or finding a larger story, or larger context that encompasses that experience or event.[21] Healing is essential whether we have experienced events as woundings and betrayals, or as gifts and opportunities. In other words, both seemingly positive or negative events carry a demand to be worked through, integrated, made whole. We experience a coming together, things become clear, consolidated, and we understand the pattern behind what has happened; we find a larger context into which the experience can be integrated, like finding a larger house in which that "unusual" piece can now be accommodated.

In my own life and through my research of life transitions, I have observed that as long as an event, such as a loss or a betrayal by a loved one, is separated out as something that should not have occurred, it continues to foster pain, anger, and resentment. Even years later it is still there, occupying space, time and energy. It is still not part of our "oneness." It has not yet been worked through. "Working through" is not to suggest that what happened was "OK," or that it needed to happen, or should have happened, or that it should be overlooked. Rather, working through in the service of healing means that what happened, *happened*. And that it now needs to be processed as an event, albeit a painful one. The wounding needs to be brought to the surface of our awareness, and then acknowledged, felt (even deeply), and named. And then the event needs to be integrated and brought into our larger story. Or, alternatively, a new story needs to be brought forth that can now encompass that experience. Arriving at this new "oneness" is nothing short of a confirmation that there has been development.

In summary, as I have tried to illustrate, both healing and creativity are essential aspects of development. While creativity and differentiation have to do with the act of venturing out and experiencing diversity and "manyness," healing and integration entail finding a larger dwelling, and a new "oneness."

As an adult educator, I have witnessed those times in life when there is the need to make a change, to move beyond our present dwelling, to begin to open ourselves to a possible future larger story. I have felt in myself this push from within, and have detected it in others, especially adult learners. I have similarly observed the forces that would bring it back into its harness and contain this urge to grow. Below is a summary of the major points concerning adult development and transitions that have served as helpful guides to me.

My Helpful Guides Through Change, Growth, Development
1. Change is difficult. We resist it. And for good reason. We believe that we are OK where we are, or at least the best we can ever be. We do not envision the possibility of moving to further levels of our development. We believe we *already are* at our furthest level.

2. Change can come upon us from without or within. Whatever its source, each is a call to growth. Further, each is a call to respond creatively to a new experience, that is, not to go on automatic pilot,

but to call upon something new from within our own depths.

3. We need appropriate supports when we undergo change. We need those who can understand us, to mirror and reflect back to us who we are and what we want. We need others to help us see the relationship between this situation and ourselves, not only to what we are now, but to what we are *becoming*.

4. Healing, that is, integration, is a necessary step to accomplishing any developmental transition. Without it, the events we encounter stick outside us like a thumb tack, not a part of us, yet poking us all the while.

5. A change in one small part of our life can, in time, bring about a transformation in our whole self, that is, a small event or chance occurrence can lead to a deep-order change in how we view ourselves and the world around us.

6. We can be puppets in the face of change; but we can also be dancers. Creativity offers us the possibilities of moving beyond simply adapting to our circumstances and the demands of others, to transforming ourselves (and perhaps them as well).

As I close this chapter, I hope that I have been able to communicate to readers the immeasurable importance of validating our own efforts to develop, and of supporting and nurturing others in their own strivings. We embark on our development through our creative efforts to define what is unique and novel within ourselves — our "manyness." We integrate our new-found resources into a fuller sense of ourselves — our "oneness." The tapestry of our life will reveal the pattern that these passages of creativity and healing have produced. The underside, especially, though messier, will illustrate how these fibres have actually been woven together. As we develop over our lifetime, our tapestry will bring forth an ever more detailed, unique, richly textured, and bountiful pattern.

"Head and Heart Line Connection" by Judy Springer

Desperately Seeking Self

Joie Zeglinski

Women healing, changing, creating, howling, singing, giggling, dancing, drawing, potting, grieving, weaving and celebrating. I cautiously dipped a pink toe into the web. Spider Woman smiled. I dipped another. She smiled again. I dove into the centre. She welcomed me home.

After the Spider Women Retreat at Gull Harbour, I returned to Ottawa, to my home, my medical practice and to "life in my head." Sparked by the encouragement of women at the Retreat to develop my reawakened creativity, I wove my way, eager and afraid, to California, for an expressive arts therapy program for therapists.[1] For three shape-shifting weeks my responsibilities were put to rest while I attended to my misplaced spirit, seeking my Self.

I arrived in San Francisco conflicted; ambivalent thoughts and feelings struggled like angry children. My dilemma: I appreciated the art of medicine, the miracle of the body, the power of drugs and vaccines to cure or relieve, but increasingly, I was aware of my disdain for technology, medical practice, my training and, ultimately, myself as a physician. I felt I was not enough. I could not give enough. I did not know enough. I experienced myself thirsting, and my tools as small puddles in a desert of pain and need. There was never enough time to learn, to help, to study, to live. I felt I could not be in the moment or I'd miss the next. I was forever racing the clock, chronically late, exhausted and stressed. Feeling impotent and depleted, I fantasized leaving medicine to paint, travel, have children, do therapy, dance, meditate and/or vegetate. I even fantasized illness as an escape. That got my attention! The list of possibilities seemed exciting, frightening and endless, yet I felt trapped. Clearly, no parts were giving up without a struggle. Letting go felt like death. Compromise was not in the picture.

On the first day of the expressive arts therapy course, my art revealed symbols of sun and moon distinctly cut off from each other. The sun was the masculine side: linear, heavy, medical model, father, serious, the Head. Responsible to "should" and "have to," concerned about money and logic. The moon was the feminine; mystery, spontaneity, Belly, mother, magic and healing. I longed for moon (Belly) in my life; somewhere, somehow, I had lost sight of her.

This conflict between sun (Head) and moon (Belly) seemed impossible to resolve, yet to remain obtuse was costly; losing internal colour and passion, dreading imperfection, experiencing acne, left-sided body aches and right brain neglect. Would I have to choose or could I contain both? If so, how could I manage to learn, practice and be all that seemed demanded of me? Would I ever be enough, know enough (and by whose standards)? What did I want? Who was I? Stitched tightly together, like a puppet in my own hands, I came desperately seeking Self.

As I asked the inner questions through art, sound and movement, my anxiety surfaced. How could I trust a process I did not know, trust the learning in a lump of clay, a dance, a sound? How could I trust myself to let it happen? If it did happen, would I know what it was, would I understand it? My body was quick to trust, my head to mistrust. Paradoxically, within days, I experienced my head wanting to rush the process, perhaps to expedite a psychic surgery of sorts; perhaps to quickly appease and disarm the enemy (body), thereby maintaining the balance of power (mind over body). I also sensed that to hurry the "not knowing" was to force a return to "knowing," to homeostasis.

In movement, I experienced the parts of myself kinesthetically, the feminine as Belly, rocking in her hips, gyrating fertility, creativity, sexuality. Contained within Belly's clay womb was the image of a sad and frightened child I named Waif. Waif was busily wiping the wet away and keeping "them" together (the walls, my parents, parts of myself, parts of my life). Waif seemed fragile, terrified of drowning in flow (menstrual, sexual, emotional, creative). She seemed in need of nurturing; ancient methods of feeding sprang to mind (grain ground by tribal women). In my teens, Waif had witnessed women's lives as sacrament to the status quo of inequality, loss of self, and abuse. She had witnessed women's anger and reclamation of justice. Being a woman seemed to be about injury and rage. I wanted none of that, and so I pitched the baby, Waif, then Belly, out with the bath. Head then took over in the movement, and in my life, dancing vertiginously, resonating with anxiety, winning medals and degrees, as panacea to Waif and Belly.

At age six, life had become serious. Schooling was strict in a religious, foreign tongue. It seemed I was to repeat my father's legacy as a displaced person. Being the smallest, feeling the dumbest (anglophone in a francophone school), Head stepped up to the task.

Good enough was never enough. Addicted to perfection, my standards were exhausting.

During the expressive arts program, in a dramatic enactment of Head, Waif and Belly, assisted by the helping hands of others, I was able to begin the process of moving from Head alone, into the knowing of Waif and Belly. The relief was visceral. A window opened into Self. Head and I felt lighter. My emotional river flowed. Buoyed by the strength and support of the other women, Waif floated and Belly celebrated.

Not easily dismissed, Head persisted in drawing my attention through movement and work with clay. I pondered what needs were still unmet, what messages were yet to be learned. Images came of an open-mouthed bird, a hunger for knowledge, security, containment, for acceptance and love from my father, and now from myself. Validating these needs through art and imagery, I discovered a sense of safety, strength and nurturance. I trusted in the process and embraced my intuition and feminine nature.

With Head, Waif and Belly in tow, I ventured repeatedly into corners of my shadow; a green slime monster with a punching eye, a bad little girl with a little curl and a mean bite. I saw dishonesty. I felt fears of being consumed, fused, or abandoned. There were fears, too, of violence, insecurity, inadequacy, being hateful, prejudiced, narcissistic, entitled. Frightened, perplexed and curious, from a safe distance I tiptoed in art and movement, drawing on my warrior and wise woman for guidance, strength, protection and wisdom. I feared loss of control, insanity and violence if my shadow took rein (childhood tantrums surfaced in my memory). Toward the middle and final stages of the course, my dreams, art and imagery began to show a taming of the shadow. For example, in a dream, I halted a shark with a ping-pong paddle. One particular drawing held the shadow in a golden light. I felt relieved and tearful. Witnessing internal boundaries gave me the sense of freedom to better know the contents I feared. A loving self was the container and the key to further healing.

The remainder of the course flowed rapidly. I found myself trusting my feelings and experiences. I felt malleable, flexible, happy and very much alive. I gave myself permission to follow "not knowing" and felt clearer about my direction. I knew I had to continue caring for and about my Self if I was to continue helping others. I now knew this in my body, mind and spirit. I imaged my medicine in healing symbols of clay, paints, herbs, a baby (my creativity), a golden cord (connected to the source), symbols of mysteries, and singing planets.

Months have passed since the course ended. My learning continues to unfold. Though my head still seeks the upper hand, I am quicker to notice. My reminders are: hanging stars, a belly goddess shaped from clay, a creativity doll knotted from rags, an art journal, a writing journal, and people who help by loving, guiding and containing. My boundaries are clearer. I feel less need for dramatic change and I feel less depleted by my work, more open to letting go, letting be and trusting in the unknown. My small puddle is now a pond, an oasis. My internal space has expanded; my container has grown. I care more about myself and others.

Chapter Two

Spiders in Our Lives

Spiders in My Life

Cassie Williams Aitchison

Spiders have been a part of my life ever since I can remember. In Denver, Colorado, my family cohabited an older house with black widow spiders. We respected them and treated them carefully. One female used to live in the cupboard above the sink, where we kept our small juice glasses. If she wasn't to be seen, I could take out a glass; if she was, I called Mum. At age seven, I saw a large female black widow hanging from our basement ceiling. We children had been told to report sightings of these spiders to our mother, who happened to be in the bathtub on the second floor at the time. Mum told me to get a jar, pour in some alcohol and then place a thin piece of cardboard above the spider with the jar below. The spider fell into the jar, which I proudly took to Show and Tell at school. To this day, I hate to kill spiders.

When I was in grade six, we lived a year in Tucson, Arizona. In the pleasant autumn weather, we used to eat outside on our back patio, which had a vine-covered trellis. A large female orb weaver had her wheel-shaped web there. She used to be our evening entertainment as we watched her, catching insects and repairing her web. She also laid an egg cocoon which we observed with interest, although I don't remember any spiderlings emerging.

While at university, I found myself drawn more and more to

zoological studies, which I pursued part-time after my children were born. The animals in which I specialized were the wandering spiders which do not build webs. Throughout my children's school years I continued these studies, working on spiders under snow, culminating in a doctoral thesis at the University of Manitoba.

Spiders can live in a variety of habitats: under stones, in caves, in leaves on the ground, in grass, bushes and trees, in holes in the ground and even under water![1,2] They have even been collected at 22,000 feet (6700m) in the Himalayas of Nepal.[3] These animals are extremely adaptable, taking up residence wherever there is potential food.

In many stories regarding spiders, it is the silk and the web that receive attention. Spider silk is a wonder of nature. It is produced from a number of spinnerets at the end of the spider's abdomen and, depending on which sort of spinneret produces a thread, may have several different configurations and functions.

The properties of the silk are extraordinary. Spider silk is made of proteins, has a high tensile strength and is very elastic; it is stronger and more elastic than nylon.[2,5] When wet, the silk undergoes supercontracting so that the web won't sag. The silk may be sticky for long periods.[4] People use spider silk for its unique properties. Due to its acidity, silk does not allow bacteria or viruses to grow on it.[2] Probably as a result, Europeans have used spider webs, especially those of funnel weavers, to staunch wounds.[6,7] In the South Seas the strong webs of the large orb weaver Nephila are collected, matted and twisted to make bags and fish nets.[6]

Silk is used during all stages of a spider's life in one of many ways. Dependent on the type of spider, i.e. its family or genus, silk is used to make draglines, aeronaut lines for ballooning, webs and snares, silk tunnels and retreats, sperm webs and egg cocoons.[1,2,6,7] Draglines are used by most spiders, fastened at intervals to serve as safety lines, or to retrace a path; this is the common way that a wandering spider uses silk. A variation of the dragline is the aeronaut line used for ballooning by spiderlings or some adults of small species. The spider climbs to the top of a projection, such as a stalk of grass, extends its abdomen upwards and lets out fine gossamer threads of silk which are picked up by updrafts of air.[6,7] The gossamer and spiderlings can travel considerable distances and have even been collected at 15,000 feet (4572 m) in nets on low-flying aircraft. This is a major dispersal method used by young spiderlings.

Most people equate spiders with the classic wheel-shaped orb web. This web contains up to 0.5 mg of silk and is built in 20 to 30 minutes. The orb web is almost vertical, with frame threads for the radial lines from a central hub and a sticky, catching spiral thread. It may have up to 1500 connecting points, mostly between the radii and the spiral. Some species of orb weavers rest in the hub of the web.[2] Other orb webs may also have stabilmenta, which are visible vertical areas with zigzag bands between neighbouring radii, possibly acting as camouflage (when a spider remains at the hub of the web), as a moulting platform or as protection against the heat of the sun.[1,2] Whether a spider stays in the periphery of the web, with a leg touching a signal thread, or within the hub, the orb weaver is able to sense from vibrations of the signal thread or radii when and where a prey is trapped. Then the spider can rush to the prey and wrap it with silk, prior to injecting it with venom and feeding on it. In courtship, the male will pluck a thread rhythmically at the periphery of the web to indicate that he is courting and is not prey.[2]

Other spider families produce different sorts of webs, such as the funnel webs seen in grass or in the corners of windows. There are also variations of the orb web, such as a fan-shaped web. Irregular webs, or cobwebs, and sheet webs, one being the bowl and doiley type (Fig. 1), may be constructed. Several spiders make special snares, such as the bolas spider Mastophora. This spider hangs from a supporting trapeze line and throws a single thread with a big drop of glue on its end (the "bolas") to entangle nearby insects.(Fig. 2)[2,4] The Australian ogre-faced spider Dinopys makes a rectangular web with a few parallel hackled threads, which are supported by silk lines held by its front legs, and hangs upside down just above the ground. The web is then spread and thrown at passing insects.[6] The spitting spider Scytodes squirts gummy threads from its fangs onto an insect prey, fastening it down (Fig. 3).[7]

A number of spiders make silk retreats, within a folded leaf, under a stone or within a tunnel. This retreat may be used for moulting, mating, laying eggs and hibernation. For those spiders in tunnels, there is sometimes a silken trap door as well, often camouflaged.[6] A most interesting silken home is that of the European aquatic spider, Argyoneta aquatica. This species lives in a "diving bell", a bell-shaped web located under water amongst aquatic plants, and which is filled with air that has been brushed off its hairy abdomen. This species hunts for aquatic insects and feeds in its "diving bell".[1,6]

Adult spiders have a specialized silk function. The males

construct a minute (about 3mm) sperm web of interlacing silk, onto which they deposit a drop of sperm from the genital opening in their abdomen. Then the sperm is absorbed by the palp, an expanded suction bulb in front of the mouth parts.[1,7] This palp then serves as the intromittent organ of the animal. After mating, females deposit their eggs onto a saucer of silk, which is then covered with more silk to form a cocoon.[7] The resulting cocoon may be spherical, hemispherical, flattened, pear-shaped or stalked; some are even suspended on a silk thread. They may be white, pink, green, blue or yellow.[1,6,7] Wandering wolf spider females attach the egg sac to their spinnerets (Fig. 4); after hatching, the young crawl onto their mother's abdomen to be carried about by her for about a week. The female nursery web spider Dolomedes (commonly called the dock spider) carries her huge egg cocoon in her jaws (Fig. 5).[7] Near hatching time, she ties leaves together and suspends the cocoon in them. This nursery web is guarded until about one week after hatching.[6] It is sometimes camouflaged with mud or debris and is covered with tough papery silk.[6,7]

Spider venom has been used in homeopathy, where minute amounts of a substance can bring about cures over time. A homeopathic preparation of the venom from the black widow, *Latrodectus mactans*, is used to treat angina pectoralis. Some preparations of venom of some orb weavers of the genus Araneus are also employed to treat ailments of the nervous system.[8]

When my children moved from home, I began studying something completely different, a body therapy called Ortho-Bionomy. Ortho-Bionomy was developed by osteopath Dr. Arthur Lincoln Pauls. I have also studied other disciplines developed by osteopaths, i.e. CranioSacral Therapy, Zero Balancing and Visceral Manipulation. Although this type of work is very gentle, its effects can be deceptively powerful (like a spider's venom).

Spiders are associated with healing in some native traditions. Recently I went on a vision quest, modelled upon native tradition. I spent three days alone, fasting beside a river. During an initial sweat of three hours, a friend and I offered many prayers to others and to the environment. My connection with nature was greatly enhanced and I heard messages from the Upper World (the spirit world) and the Lower World (the animal world). Coming from a rather dysfunctional family, I have always found it easier to relate to most animals than to people. Now I realize that I have communicated telepathically with animals since childhood. I assumed that every-one could do that. The main message from the Upper World was to help others understand the sensitivities and innermost things of life, whether it be sensitivity to their bodies, to others, or to the environment. From the Lower World, which includes trees, I received many messages, not surprisingly a number of which came from spiders. One handsome male funnel web spider, Agelenopsis, said that he was happy that there were some humans who appreciated and understood his type. The gist of the other messages was that I can weave and spin "a new fabric of consciousness" and that I can go to the smallest of places.

After many requests, I am now feeling a strong need to teach a type of energetic body therapy that is my own unique blend of therapies. Relying heavily on intuition and the extrasensory energies, it allows others to become more aware of their extrasensory abilities and of their surroundings. This teaching may create "a new fabric of consciousness." Going to the smallest of places with the energy ex-tending from one's hands is appropriate for consciousness raising and for healing.[7]

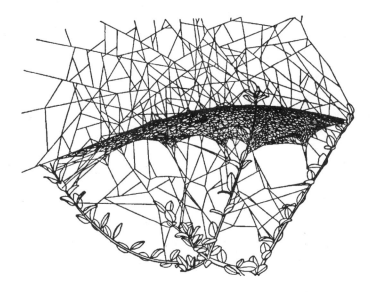

Fig. 1

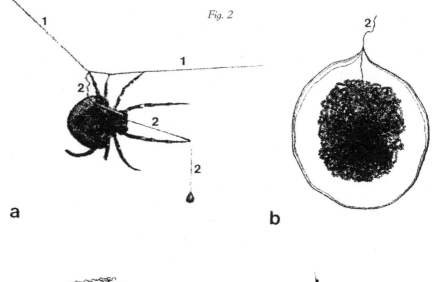

Fig. 2

a

b

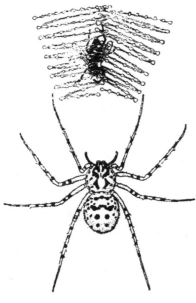

Fig. 3

Fig. 4

Fig. 5

White Spider

Libby Scheier

scaling the far wall

a white spider

        tiny albino eyeball
with outstretched veins

      the hand of my grandmother
      delicate and deliberate

pale flame

I had an out-of-body experience before it was trendy. It was 10 years ago, at my grandfather's funeral, a perfect place for transcending the physical. A group of 20 or 30 of us approached the family plot. I saw my name on a gravestone and the jolt went through me from head to feet. I looked again and saw it was my grandmother's name. Anna. Almost mine, Arla. I'm named after her.

My spirit rose slowly in the air, about 30 feet, and I looked down at myself and my relatives. My grandmother made contact with me. She didn't have anything to say, she just let me feel her presence. She felt like rotting potatoes in Rumania. A strong Jewish peasant hiding in a basement from raping and murdering Germans. Holding my father's mouth so he wouldn't cry out and give her away. The other four kids crouching around her. Her husband gone already, two years before, to North America, preparing their new life. Seven years later the rest of the family came here and grew up poor. She was known as a tough, immoveable woman. Everyone was afraid of her. But her children were loyal to her, more loyal than to husbands and wives or anyone.

Do you want to come back, grandmother, just for a while, and say hello to everyone? No, I've had enough of all that. Now I am a witch among witches and do what I want.[1]

The Onset of Day (A Work in Progress)

Libby Scheier

Queen's Quay at Little Norway Park, Toronto, August 1994, 5 a.m.

Saturday

A large white spider hopefully descends
from the upstairs balcony
its single thread mighty and weak
as my heart

A black sky tinges blue,
the air
uncleaned by night
hangs in a block over the city

The spider dances up and down its thread magically
edging sideways in air, racing

diagonally

across air, I
shift
and see in the grey-yellowing light

a web!

nearly complete
magnificent and intricate
symmetrical spectacular
completely centred
its navel a dark point in air I'd accepted as a speck
on my reading glasses
wrongly, so wrongly
and now I see it is the god-eye of the web and
I can get up and look at the web the spider
doesn't freak

like birds do at humans it keeps its focus
to its work art magic it keeps moving moving
and I think
so
so you take no notice of me
you there weaving your
near-invisible genius tapestry genius
of a billion spiders of everyspider you
there don't give a shit
about me, well,
just watch this, with one
swat of my hand I can
destroy
all your work
everything
and kill you too if I want but
it would be more fun to let
you live
in awe of my power
defeated
acknowledging me

I don't do it.

The thing in my forehead quietens, shame flushes
my heart red

(shhhhh, there, there, I won't hurt you)

The spider's system is opaque to me
in the yellow light whitening now
daybreak threatening

My pen threads over the page, dancing
in this poem and when I look up the
ever-moving spider is completely still, its body
covering the god-eye of the web, it
sits on its throne awaiting food and I sit
on my plastic balcony chair

Will our planet leave a trace in the universe?

Sunday

The spider is busy working when I get up at 5 a.m. the sky still dark
just starting to blue
it's repairing its web and scurries
as though the vampiric trap must be complete before the light of day
and

lo

as day breaks it settles into its god-crypt at the trap's dead centre
and waits, its task easier than Dracula
who must roam
it sits still as stone and I get my flashlight
to look at the web to give my admiration to the spider
who doesn't care and as I flash around
I see two more webs a white and a black spider sitting in each and
after I flash on the black one it leaves its web and tucks itself
under the rim of the white plastic box of green philodendron
wired to the balcony railing and
I wonder if it has a fear-of-humans gene lacking in white spiders
(wanting still to be a player in the spider's hermetic drama)
I train my light on the black spider's web, but can't find
its perfect circumference and the web is damaged beyond repair
it seems
or disintegrated by age
and is deserted now by the spider who
wasn't afraid of me after all but is resting under
the white flower box until it is ready to
start again and
I'll be here when you do

Something draws my attention back to the first spider, an insect
has hit its net and is gone
as the white-lightning spider dashes across, sucks that bug whole
into its body
and is back at the god-eye before any
future victims can take note that this spot is dangerous

here, at the spider's back it looks like the bug got swallowed into the
spider's body in a single chomp of stomach jaws
though I remember reading I think that they suck
the blood of their victims discarding the cadaver and now
I make a mental note to look up spider
in my *Britannica*
and put some order to
the poetic chaos, beauty, and terror of my pre-dawn turquoise-painted
wrought-iron balcony overlooking Norway Park
and Lake Ontario hidden by August trees
in full leaf set against the widest sky in Toronto
down here by the lake a sky
this morning scudded by purple cumulus clouds on grey
stunning in the slowly changing light
everything wet and new and quiet

Late morning

I return from computer to balcony
where I write in longhand
and my white spider is working hard
along the web's bottom where
I see if I stand in the right slant of light
a chunk has been knocked out of the web
how?
a too-soft breeze is an unlikely assailant
so I look with sad suspicion at my two cats,
fond of torturing small birds at length
preferably in my view
desirous of my approval
unlike the godly spider who is above all that
and who now works feverishly tying
silk end to silk end but
can't repair the damage and maneuvers slowly up
the balcony pole away out of sight
leaving its crippled web behind
between white flower box and metal pole
the trace of a great and common work of art
work of play work of work stuff of living

and I won't know if the next white spider I see
is the same one, I've lost a friend

How ridiculous I am

My cats
sit and watch me watch the damaged and abandoned web
so foolish in my pursuit of unrequited spider love
when I've only to turn around
and be with those
who love me

Spider webs photographed by Lillian Allen

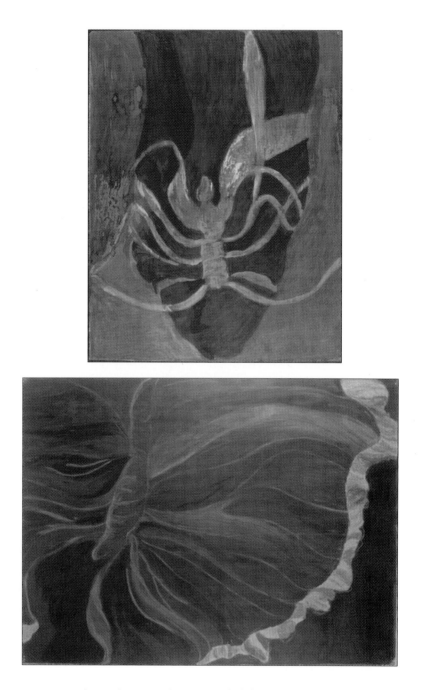

"White Spider" (top) and "Mourning Cloak" by Mary Louise Chown

"Waiting Women I" by Rae Harris

"Big Pink Woman" by Sophia Rosenberg

"Birthing Scene" by Janet Kigusiug

"Mother and Child" by Janet Kigusiug

"Sedna — Sea Goddess" by Germaine Arnaktauyok

"House of Tea" by Esther Warkov

"cat & bone" by Esther Warkov

"The Warrior & the Woman Warrior IV" by Aliana Au

"My Mother's Silver Bridal Head Piece" by Aliana Au

"Ukrainian Matriarchal Earth Trinity" by Maureen Stefaniuk

"The Moon" by Val T. Vint

"Rubedo/Sacrifice" by Trudy Golley

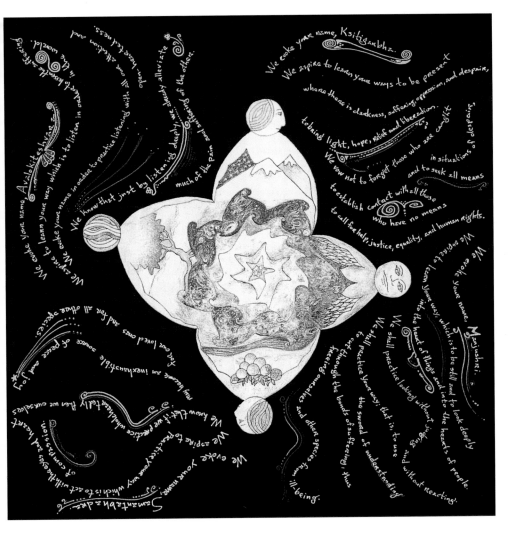

We evoke your name, Ksitigarbha.

We aspire to learn your ways to be present, where there is darkness, suffering, oppression, and despair, to bring light, hope, relief and liberation. We vow not to forget those who are caught in situations of despair, and to seek all means to establish contact with all those who have no means to call for help, justice, equality, and human rights.

We evoke your name, Avalokiteshvara. We We evoke your name, Avalokiteshvara. We aspire to learn your way which is to listen in order to practice listening with all our attention and open-heartedness. We know that just by listening deeply we already alleviate a great deal of pain and suffering of the other.

We evoke your name, Manjushri. We aspire to learn your way, which is to be still and to look deeply into the heart of things and into the hearts of people. We shall practice your way, that is to use the sword of understanding to cut through the bonds of suffering, thus freeing other species from ill-being.

We evoke your name, Samantabhadra. We aspire to practice your way which is to act with the eyes of compassion and heart of love, that we practice wholeheartedly that we ourselves may become an inexhaustible source of peace and joy for our loved ones and for all other species.

"Mandala" by Gloria Norgang

79

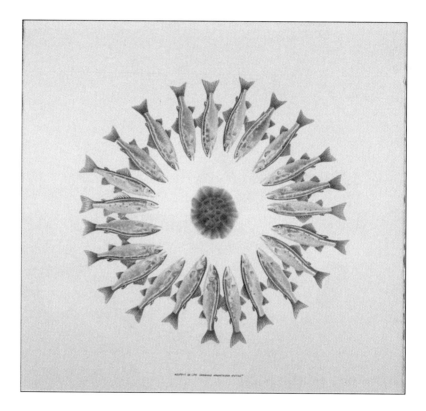

"Respect for Life" by Germaine Arnaktauyok

Chapter Three

Through the Dark

Pain

Lilita Klavins

It is only when we begin to look at the pain, hold it in front of us, turn it around, pull and stretch the edges, get to know the shape and feel of it, that we can hope for healing.

For years I walked through life pretending pain wasn't there, that my memories which weren't right were aberrations, invalid blips on some cosmic graph that would disappear spontaneously.

Pain had become a white noise, a dripping tap, the sound of a fan. Background. Nothing big enough to attract attention.

One day, a memory I thought was dead came at me as sudden as thunder. There was no denying it. The abuse from my "other life" had been with me as a shadow, a dark haze that coloured who I had become.

I began to write again, returning to a love I had neglected while playing so hard at "real life." Friends and family said I was dwelling on the unchangeable. Fixated. They were wrong.

Going back to the dark place, touching, unfolding it, is the first step in recognizing and appreciating the present.

Dark

Isabel Wendell

She heaved herself up from the bed. Wobbling a little, she looked down on the cocoon from which she had crawled. Shivering, she grabbed the corner of the duvet, pulling it smooth, covering her place.

She had wanted to rest, to float in the dark, but the dark had washed over and through her. The black had become darker and darker, gently pulling her down until something had snatched her back, forcing air into her, hurting her, making her feel.

Stumbling at first, on legs not yet used to moving, she stood in front of the wire rack. She swayed and stretched. And she knew. As if in slow motion, she removed the shiny disc from its case and placed it in the player.

The smoky blues massaged her body into fluid motion. Husky, hurting tones caressed her fingertips and brushed her eyelids. Alone in the soft velvet dark of the moonlit living room her voice rose from behind her ribs, shaped her mouth and flowed from her pain. Salty liquid healing ran down her face, seeping into her undershirt.

The final cadence nudged a solid presence into the room. She knew he was there. Slowly she opened her eyes to his shadowy form. Her breath caught in a lump at the back of her throat. Dark. He was dark. Her heart pounded out a rhythm of its own, desperately trying to save her. "Fear," she thought. "They call it fear." She couldn't escape. She would not crawl back into that numb space, the safe unfeeling place.

"It was not my fault. My fault," she whispered to the shadow, "was fear. I couldn't help you. I was, I am, afraid."

She sobbed. Her eyes squeezed tight. Her body shook with sobbing, shook with pain, shook with fear, until spent, she crumpled to the floor. There she lay, curling back into herself, pulling in tight, sinking, sinking... No! She would not go back.

She gathered up her body, unfurling from the base of her spine until she sat strong in the centre of the room. Still hugging her knees, she cautiously opened her eyes. Reaching back and lifting her feet, she spun slowly, her gaze timidly searching every corner. Up she rose to the very tips of her toes, her arms reaching out in wide circles. She turned through her living room, spinning circles. The warm light of laughter spilled from her to fill the room. He was gone. The dark was gone.

stay close

Cecile Brisebois Guillemot

cold air freezes the river
pulls my skin
so tight
it might shatter

a maze of ice traps
twigs and leaves
in shades of grey
ice dark and deep

the air is thick
filled with resistance
hard to walk through

as long as I get out
before the air freezes
I won't get trapped

wind grabs my breath
frosts my lashes
shadows my vision

you stand before me
peer into my eyes
your warm breath
melts ice crystals

you stay close
walk with me
slowly

back to shore
to shelter
you stay until
I stop shivering

fall asleep

daddy's girl

Lilita Klavins

at first you remembered
so much
a little three-year-old, chanting
> "I remember when daddy was here
> and he was so mad
> do you remember?"

my heart stuck in my throat
like a poisoned apple
I choked back my answer
hoped my silence would keep
your childhood light
and you stopped asking

one summer holiday
you suddenly seemed older
surprised, I heard myself
whisper
> "you know dad and I used to fight
> a lot
> and he would get angry
> do you remember?"

my words hung suspended
and you, wise for your years
held a blanket of forgetfulness close
your white knuckled fingers locked tight
you looked up at me
and quickly changed the subject

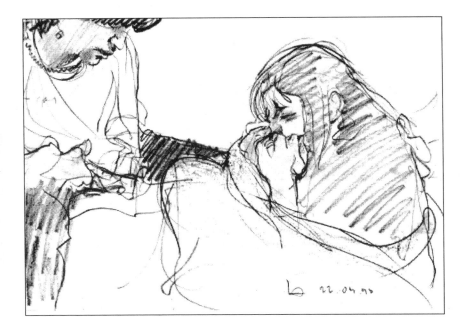

"tears" by Heather Spears

firewalk

Lilita Klavins

she floats
through liquid fire
holds a knife
cold as the moon
its sharp tip
burns her palm
sears smoking flesh
smoulders
as she pulls
at her memories
separates them layer by layer
splits the core

she remembers

Carol Rose

she remembers the camps
remembers him coming
behind her sister's knees
under her armpits
between her thighs
her breasts
her mouth
she remembers him saying
"my sweet little virgin
stay always
my sweet little virgin"
she remembers his eyes
obsidian dark
ablaze with desire
her sister's flesh
charred in the night

in the mousetrap
(for Kathy)

Lilita Klavins

she's on watch again
smokes one cigarette
after another
the one arm not in a sling
gives her baby half a hug
she puffs out a plan
built in smoke
the house lights burn
all night
fade into morning
she sits at the table
her ashtray overflowing
eyes moon-circled & red
in her mind she packs
her babies cats & memories
imagines a plan
her "some day" plan

she lifts a drawing
from the table
stares
at its lines & pictures
she found it in the basement
locked in the mousetrap
where he knew she'd look
the page reveals
a graphic portrait
of his dreams her nightmares
she studies
the black & white heads
so deliberately x'd out
runs her palm across the marks
tries to erase
everything

her pulsing fingers make
the figures
shake & dance
the black x's flash
images
of a tabloid
headline
now the severed heads
she contemplates
look too much
like her own

From Damage to Power

Donna F. Johnson

"The power of feminism is the power of the victim who has recognized a way to use her damage. There's a great line in an Adrienne Rich poem about knowing that her wound came from the same place as her power. When you get in touch with your damage, recognize and care for it, you also discover the source of your power."[1]

I read this quote to a group of twelve women who are face to face with their damage and overwhelmed by it. We have just done an exercise on physical abuse. The women are asked to write on pieces of coloured paper the types of physical abuse that they have endured in their relationship, one incident per paper. Each woman has ten pieces of paper; most use all ten, some ask for more. They appear to be writing dispassionately. Abused women often speak and write dispassionately. Most have had to distance themselves from their pain in order to survive. We do this exercise in order to get beneath the numbness.

The women are then asked in turn to put the papers up on a wall, and to speak aloud what they have written. The papers are placed on a continuum, from threats of physical abuse to murder.

The first woman gets up and places her papers on the wall. "He destroyed everything in the house." "Spat on me." "Pulled my hair out in chunks." "Twisted my arm." "Fat Lips." "Poked at repeatedly." "Black eyes." "Held down." "Choked until I nearly passed out." "Thrown down the stairs while pregnant."

The second woman gets up and places her papers on the wall. "Slapped." "Black eyes." "Left me alone when I was just home from hospital after a serious operation." "Broke my arm." "Spat on me." "Hurt pets to get back at me." "Held me down on the floor and mashed food into my face and hair." "Tried to push me out of a speeding car." "Made to walk five miles on a highway, in the middle of the night, when I was pregnant." "Raped."

The third woman gets up. "Split my lip open." "Many black eyes." "Beat me until I had bruises over my entire body." "Slapped because I wouldn't have sex." "Broken fingers." "Held a gun at my head."

"Hurled objects at me." "Drove recklessly when he was angry." "Ripped my clothes off me." "Forced me to have sex after an operation."

The fourth woman gets up. The air in the room is becoming tighter. "Raped." "Punched in the face." "Hurt pets." "Punched in the stomach while pregnant." "Threatened to kill me." "Fat lip." "Choked me." "Held our newborn son upside down by one leg and strutted around the house like that."

It goes on and on. The women have their heads bent. Some are crying quietly, some cry openly. One woman is very angry and leaves the room to walk in the hall. Another is nauseous. She lies down on the floor in a fetal position and rocks herself gently. There are still eight women to go. I don't know how we're going to get through this.

The fifth woman gets up, then the sixth, seventh, eighth, until all who can have placed their abuse on the wall, outside themselves. The wall is covered now.

The room is silent.

I look at the faces of these women. They are fine faces. They are strong, capable, dignified women. This is an "average" group, ranging in age from 20 to 60. I look at the writing on the wall. What makes these abuses more horrible is that each assault has been committed by men who profess to love these women. This puts the assaults psychologically in a very different category from the torture and brutalization of war or of criminal activity.

The women begin to speak. One says she's light-headed, like she's in shock. Another says she's relieved, in a way, to see it all up there (there are over 100 incidents documented). It confirms that she didn't imagine the abuse. Women who live with abuse are frequently told by their abuser that the assault didn't happen, or it wasn't that bad, or that they were the cause of it.

One woman asks, "How do they get away with this?" What is the answer? None of these assaults have been prosecuted.

The Burden of Proof
The legal system relies on proof that is beyond a reasonable doubt. How is a woman to "prove" that her husband has held her down and ground food into her face and hair? (And if she could, is it a criminal offence to grind food into your wife's face and hair?) How is she to prove that he threatened to kill her and her family and that

he ripped her clothes? How is she to prove that he held a gun to her head, tried to throw her out of a speeding car, held her infant upside down by one leg? How is she to prove the slaps and pokes and restraining? How, indeed, is she to prove the rapes?

If the political will existed, the abuse of women could be drastically reduced. Police officers would be thoroughly trained in issues of violence against women. Women would be believed. Police would recognize that women are often too afraid to speak. Men who are abusive or threatening would be arrested and charged at once.

Police would stop asking women if they want charges laid, as most continue to do, despite directives from the Attorney General for police to lay the charge. The death of 66-year-old Thelma Fokuhl, of Carleton Place, may have been avoided, because the police, who had attended at that house on several occasions, would have recognized her bruises as signs of abuse, and they would have taken the man who lived with her in for questioning before she died from the beating.

Women Withdrawing Charges

Women who approach the Crown and ask that charges against their partner be dropped would not be charged with public mischief, as they are now, for it would be known that threats and fear of reprisal often make women recant. The criminal justice system would be big enough to contain women's reality, not bound, as it is now, by static codes and procedures.

In July, 1992, an Ontario woman was brutally stabbed by a man who had physically and mentally tortured and terrorized her for years. When she disagreed with him, he would punish her by submerging her in cold water until she "cooperated." This was the history. Police, Crown and defence counsel had this history before them.

This man threatened to kill the woman if she took the stand against him. Terrified, the woman asked the Crown to withdraw the charge, stating she had caused the injury to herself. The Crown suspected she was being threatened, but, as the law exists now, there was nothing he could do. The woman, of course, denied she was being threatened. This was the Crown attorney's dilemma: if it forced her to testify and she changed the story, it would have to charge her with public mischief, and the charge of aggravated assault against the abuser would be dropped.

In October, 1992 the accused was fined $450 on a reduced assault charge. What is the message this man takes away from the court? A male judge gives him a scolding. A male lawyer shakes his hand and congratulates him. He has not been held accountable, and his behaviour and world-view have been reinforced.

I spoke to the Toronto-area Crown who prosecuted this case; he too was frustrated at the limitations of the system. The victim in this case had given a comprehensive statement to police at the time of the assault. A week before the trial, her arm broken from the latest beating, she recanted. I ask why the court doesn't consider the context of this woman's life, the psychology of the abused woman, the reality of brainwashing, the pattern of abused women recanting. Why can't they proceed from the first statement and from the medical records of frequent life-threatening injuries? But the rules of evidence render this impossible; the victim must take the stand and be tested on her evidence and her credibility. That is the rule.

The defence counsel, of course, must collude in this hypocrisy. He has the evidence before him. He has the history. He knows the criminal record of the accused. He knows why victims sometimes recant, for he has also defended battered women. Yet his aim is to obtain acquittal or a minimal sentence, regardless of the evidence. The conviction on the lesser charge is a victory for him. When I question the ethics of this type of representation, I am told that this is his job, our justice system is adversarial. And, somehow, I am expected to be satisfied with this answer.

But I am not satisfied. I am not satisfied with a criminal justice system that operates outside the context of history and of women's lives. I am not satisfied with a justice system that is not ethically informed. I speak to other Crown attorneys about this case; they say what is needed is "more resources for victims." As if a few counselling sessions with this woman would have reversed the effects of forty years of abuse. When I suggest that perhaps the legal system needs changing to accommodate the complexities of woman abuse and of women's lives, they laugh and say, "You'll never get this system to change."

"...And their message stupidly unchanging, stupidly forever the same. Their feat, after years of etymological reflection on the word, to have raised stupidity to a virtue. To stupefy: to deprive of feeling; to benumb, deaden; to stun with amazement. Stupor: insensibility, apathy, torpor of mind. Stupid: dulled in the faculties, indifferent, destitute of thought or feeling... The message: that the message never changes. A message that turns people to stone."[2]

When I protest that what is going on in our courts in regard to crimes against women is immoral, I am told to stop expecting justice from the legal system. Somehow one is considered naive to expect either justice or change. "Justice has nothing to do with what goes on in this building", a local Crown attorney told me flatly in the Ottawa Courthouse in December, 1992. This seems to be a well-known fact among our legal professionals. This is where the discussion ends. I believe this is precisely where the discussion should start.

Law and the Power of Reflection
In March, 1990, Pamela Behrendt of Ottawa applied, as part of a petition for divorce, for an order for interim exclusive possession of the matrimonial home. Her husband's behaviour was becoming increasingly bizarre, the home environment unsafe emotionally for her and her teenage daughters. The application was denied by Justice Louise Charron, because of contradictory evidence, that is, the husband was believed and the woman was not. On June 11th, some three months later, Pamela's husband murdered her with a chainsaw in their Sunnyside Avenue home.
    Imagine the possibilities for reflection and action at this moment. Imagine the power if Justice Charron had come forward to her Justice colleagues and said, "My God, look what has happened, see what is at stake here, it is women's lives, it is children's lives, nothing less. What is the message for us here as presiders in the courtroom?"
    Imagine the power of reflection and action if the defence lawyer in the case had stood up in that courtroom and said, "Your Honour, I cannot in conscience proceed on this lesser charge. I see what is happening here; it is legally correct but morally wrong. It would be an utter travesty of justice to exonerate this man with a petty fine."
    Instead, the legal system is quick to avoid accountability, quick to silence any movement towards reflection. At a Kingston panel on the law and violence against women, I speak to lawyers about the Pamela Behrendt case because I think it has much to teach us. The point is hurriedly dismissed. "That killing would have happened anyway. There is no protection for women in cases where men are

obsessed. The law only stops reasonable men." The case did not warrant 60 seconds of discussion by the lawyers present.

And so, in this way, the creative and transformative power of reflection and judgement is carefully avoided. And the status quo is maintained.

If political will existed, penalties for woman abuse would be severe. Incarceration would be automatic. Men who abuse and harass and make their partners live in fear would not be given a choice about entering into a peace bond. Infractions of orders to keep the peace or stay away would automatically result in arrest. These orders are rarely enforced. There's always a technicality. Or police will choose to issue the abuser yet another warning.

"How do they get away with it?" I am repeatedly asked. The same way whites get away with human rights violations in South Africa. It's a question of power. It's a question of political will. We, all of us, are guilty of a failure to exercise our powers of reflection and judgement and to create a legal process that is moral, contextualized and accountable to history.

As I sit before the wall of coloured papers, I experience viscerally the torture and brutalization of women. And it is not just these women, but women everywhere, in every country on this globe, in every city and town, every barrio and favela. And the words of Bronwen Wallace and Adrienne Rich come to me: *When you get in touch with your damage, you also discover the source of your power.*[3] And I know that it is essential that we go into our pain, for there we will find our anger. And it is our anger that will fuel our demands for change. The criminal justice system will not incorporate women's reality, in any substantial way, until women insist that it change. It is women who must have the political will. We will find that will in our damage.

being free

Denise Osted

the day she learned to speak
they gagged her
bought a ball & chain
kept her small feet
bound

when she chewed
through the gag
they got another
they clipped her wings
when she learned to fly

she found safety
in submission

she tried to obey
tried so hard
this infant/woman/child
she followed the rules
& swallowed her spirit

in the end
she just couldn't do it
broke the chain   untied the gag
so much easier
being free

back in death valley, again
(for Matthew)

Di Brandt

this sewing up of skin
this cavalier abandonment of bodies
the previous dead
littered across the sand
here and here and here

so many i have killed
so many wished dead
lost and buried
weeping in moonlight
my tears silver coins over their graves
sprouting wildflowers amid circles
of little coloured stones

in your hands i become
infinitesimal, the size of a rat
or small cat, its fur wet from the rain
you have taken me here
your touch searing my scarred
earth skin, old taste of ashes
in my mouth
here in death valley
with its green hot flashes
of radiation, danger!

in my dreams you become
mother, father, lover
my squashed cells resurrecting
one by one, dry bones
filling with blood, breath—
tar baby, bog woman
come back to life
fingernails, hair intact
heart cracking open

this excavation, this hauling up
abandonment
this dangerous sewing up
of skin.

"untitled (& if she wakes)" by Diana Thorneycroft

Waiting for the Dance

Irene Heaman

he comes into my room   bends over me   sits on the bed plays with his toy
this toy-like thing   calls me   "come see this
toy"   I sit in the closet   I don't want to go   I am happy
playing in the closet   on the floor with my hangers   metal hangers   but he
calls me   he is big and he tells me to come
I am curious   he has a toy

a big body comes over me   his knee is on my chest   he is heavy
he puts his arm on me   holds me down by the throat   on the bed
his knee is on me   heavy   heavy   heavy   black

I, Karen, waiting for the tide to turn in my life, wander the house, picking up articles of clothing, kicking at toys the cats have scattered. I'm aimless as autumn leaves, lifting and falling in the occasional gust of unpredictable breeze.

One part of my life has ended; the other has not yet begun.

Maybe this feeling of limbo is not from the marriage ending but from trying to exist and having nothing inside me to rest on. No bottom, no platform, no peace or place of knowing.

❖　❖　❖　❖

Karen knocks on the door of the therapist's house and is taken up by the therapist in an embrace that is sensual but non-sexual, personal in a totally non-personal way. There are others in the room, but Karen is carried in a wordless, musicless dance.

"There is no God," thinks Karen, "but there may be a dance."

❖　❖　❖　❖

I'm a child sealed inside a wall of silence, holding forever that wall of reproach between me and everyone else.

I'm a child watching. I watch people in the malls, in the cafeterias; an outer shell, invisible to others. I watch, seeing not only the others, but imagining myself to be who they are. No wonder it is so hard to make decisions and choices, always from someplace outside of myself.

Sometimes now I feel the child; I wake up feeling her small body, her arms and legs. I am the child and my large adult body means nothing, is foreign, belongs to somebody else. I rejoice and the adult who lives in my head longs to mother the child, longs to carry the pain away in my love.

I remember to praise, to say thanks for the sunshine, for the pain, for the cats, and even for the hopelessness, because then maybe I'll understand. I remember to say thanks for the good things, and there are some, and when I do, I come out of the well, out of the darkness, until later, when the pain hits me again, spiralling in on me, pressing downward against me until I can't breathe. I can't breathe, the wall rotates behind me, grids on the ceiling swirl. I can't breathe or cry out "Mom," "Dad."

❖   ❖   ❖   ❖

I wander with the pillow in my hand. I have taken it from my tormentor. I have come to the end of myself. But there is another self, dancing in the corner. I cannot dance, but she comes and takes me by my wooden hands and she leads me in a dance. She, with disjointed arms and body, leads me into the dance. Around, around, in the room, my feet unlock. I can move. I hear music. In time, in a long time, I connect with the dance.

❖   ❖   ❖   ❖

I slide down a bottomless tunnel with no stops along the way. Events or people jut out from the sides, but nothing breaks my fall. At first, there is a platform I have made from resolutions, beliefs and decisions, a platform suspended on chains. The platform dissolves and I am left falling, falling into blackness, a blackness with no bottom. I can not keep from falling. The sides speed past me.

I disappear, until someone touches me and I am back again, ready to fight for my life.

❖   ❖   ❖   ❖

I was probably two and the man came into my room. I was put away in my room every day for a sleep, and told not to get off my bed. I was left for hours in that green dismal room with the water patches on the ceiling and, if I was lucky, the curtains puffing out gently in the wind.

I played on the floor of the closet with wire hangers and he banged into my room. He was someone I knew, sort of, and he was unwanted. He loomed over me. I felt guilty, off my bed and playing with hangers. Then he sat on the bed and he told me to come to him, to come to see this interesting toy that he had. I think that he was young, because this thing that he had, this stick-like wobbling thing, was a novelty to him. And I who had few toys came warily but with interest, interest changing to dismay and fear, NO NO NO NO NO a call for MOMMY I WANT MY MOTHER and darkness and pain and fear, a still sad overriding fear.

❖　❖　❖　❖

I lay on my bed that day, needing and waiting and wanting mother, my mother, or someone, to come, please come, but no one came. Much later, the daylight fading and the heavy dusk shrouding the room, tired of waiting, soul sick from needing and waiting, my child slipped away from her body that hurt. The soul slipped away from the pain and the waiting and the crying, soft crying for which no one came. In grief and in pain, the child slipped away.

Finally, the woman comes to the door. "Karen, Karen," she wants me, and I run, my small body pumping with the energy I could not summon before. I slam the bedroom door against her, hard. She will be angry; I am off my bed and playing with hangers. And the abuser has said, "Don't tell your mother."

I don't know what she did or they did (my father was probably brought into it) but I believe they set me up at the table and they made me eat, food lodging in my throat, food stuck in the tears in my throat.

And I fall down the well constantly, my hands jutting out to catch something along the sides, but I keep falling. There is no bottom; I keep falling into the blackness, the pit of despair.

I wake up from my sleep — slam — something has hit me. I am awake and silly with fear. I go downtown to buy groceries and I am hit with the pain again. I return home. And I, Karen, wander the streets at night when the lights of the other houses are all out. I long to hit windows, to smash them, to feel and to bleed.

Days later the child and her sister are posed for a photo by their mother, against a background of trees, squinting against the sun. This mother, this powerful, demanding mother says, "Smile, look up into the camera," and the child, drawing deeply into herself can't do one more thing for this mother, but she asks, and the child, reaching deep into her darkness, pulls herself up, and picking up a flower, holds it out to her mother.

Soul sick baby soul you give give to those who have not seen you, who have hurt you, pick flowers, pick flowers, throw them wildly into mother's lap. After she has filled all her jars and her bowls and she can't use one more single flower, give her flowers, sweet dandelion flowers, lapfuls and fistfuls of flowers.

i have survived

Arlo Raven

i am the one
who has survived
with both wings flying
the light feathered one
the dark feathered one
both wings flying

i am the one who rages
who was lost & is found again
the flying high one
the circling searching one
the one who visions, i am

the visioning one
i create the future from
the dead bones of the past
wild-eyed, bones & ragged cloth
i let my hair fly around me
i let my hair fly around me
i am the one[1]

That Little Girl and the Moon

Val T. Vint

All that sleepy little girl had to
do was tip up her chin and look up through
the window to see the Moon and get herself tangled
in the branches of the trees outside.

The Moon looked after that little
girl often in the night and the little girl loved
the Moon.

The Moon sang to the little girl
lullabies, in the cry of the whip-poor-will and the
call of the loon.

She shushed her and soothed
her and gently kissed her when she cried. The
little girl went to the Moon and snuggled deeply
in her warm embrace.

The Moon told her stories and
calmed the little girl's soul. The Moon washed
the stained memories from that little girl's skin
and gave her a place to hide.

She hid that little girl from
      – her father,
      – her uncle
      – her mother's lover.

That little girl is scared again.
She cries and the Moon feels her pain. Her cries
awaken the memories hidden within my skin.

My skin knows the secrets that little
girl told to the Moon. I want to wash my skin and
like that little girl, I want my skin to forget
                              the pain,
                              the shame.

I understand now why the Moon speaks
to me. She has been by me always, giving me strength
and soothing my soul. She sang to me lullabies, in
the cry of the whip-poor-will and the call of the loon.

She shushed me and soothed me and
kissed away my tears. She washed the memories from
my skin and gave me a place to hide.
She hid me from
> – my father,
> – my uncle,
> – my mother's lover.

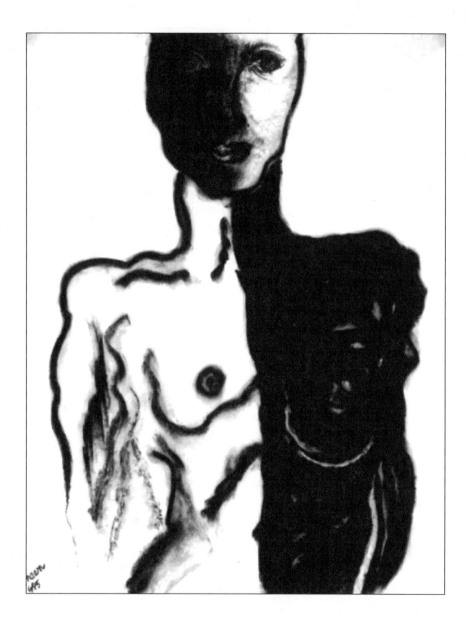

"Woman" by Veronica G. Green

From a series of paintings in response to the women I know who have developed cancer.

Chapter Four

Art and Therapy

Dried Flowers

Judy Bancroft

When I first became ill with an auto-immune disease, scleroderma, my hands were seriously affected. They became curled and painfully swollen. I was weak, not only physically, but emotionally and psychologically as well.

I don't remember how I actually got started, but I began to make wreaths out of dried flowers. When I was a teenager I had a part-time job in a flower shop, so perhaps the seeds for this creative undertaking were planted then.

This craft activity proved very healing for me, in two ways. I felt that I could still "do something" with my hands, and I was affirmed and delighted with the lovely pieces that came together in the creative process.

The wreath-making took me into new, uncharted territory, and that helped me discover new aspects of myself. One moment especially stands out for me. I was making a wreath of dried sweet peas and baby's breath for my husband's mother. I really wanted to gift her with this wreath, as a sign of my affection for her, and for all her generosity to us, her family. I remember the wreath forming itself under my wounded hands. I remember that I felt a sensation of real joy in my body, especially in my womb. I also felt that I was being shown the joy that comes from being able to express myself creatively. This was, for me, a healing and a creative moment intertwined.

A Rich and Nourishing Place

Sophia Rosenberg

My paintings (including the two in this book) were done as part of a personal healing process that started about eight years ago. My friend, Janet Oakes, and I began painting together once a week on Tuesday afternoons. We developed the ritual of having tea and talking about our lives, and then painting. After working for several hours, we'd stop and look at the paintings together. We'd talk about how it felt to paint, what we learned while doing it, what we saw when we looked at the painting, and what new information came from the painting in relation to the events of our lives.

This process has been an enormous support for both of us. As well as strengthening and healing many aspects of our lives, it has helped us to emerge and develop as artists.

The act of witnessing and of being witnessed is a powerful healing force. The companionship of entering into dialogue with myself, side by side with Janet, as she does the same, has been a comfort in the solitude of the healing journey.

The paintings are like snapshots taken on the journey, reminders of an inner landscape. The landscape has grown more distinct and vital over the years. It is a rich and nourishing place, and I find I spend more and more time there. In some sense, all of my paintings are self portraits, even when they are abstract or when they include pictures of places, or of other people. They are a response to an inner question: "Who am I?" The result is continual dialogue, an unfolding of both the work and myself.

The Art of Therapy:
Using an Artist's Tools

Lynne Mitchell-Pedersen and Susan Curtis

Introduction

The following narratives describe the passage of a poet, Susan Curtis, from a constricted place in her life to a vibrant claiming of her own ground. Lynne Mitchell-Pedersen is a therapist who walks with Susan through her difficulties. Each relates her view of a powerful and positive joining together to accomplish Susan's goals. Susan speaks first, which is appropriate.

Susan Curtis

I will begin by addressing the theme of this anthology: healers and artists. I should state at the outset that neither Lynne nor I identify her role as that of healer. Her term is "accompanist." I borrow mine from Miriam Greenspan: "trustworthy companion."[1] To describe someone as a healer is to immediately disempower the "healee," and place the power in the hands of the "healer." As Lynne observes, only the self "heals" the self. No one can do it for you. While Lynne applies the term "healing" to what we do, I do not. I find the term sentimental, and overused to the point of triteness. For me, what we do is more like deconstruction and reconstruction, de- and reconfiguring. This particular story is about terminology, language, tools, methods, as much as it is about effectiveness in sorting out the psyche of Susan Curtis.

It's difficult to track the development of the methods we use without giving some background on what happened before. I had been depressed for a couple of years. I can best describe it now as a kind of self-imposed halt to "normal" living, a period of reassessment. I crashed, as sometimes people do in middle age. The chief manifestations of this crash were intense ongoing anxiety and a cessation of writing. My "poet" seized up and wouldn't/couldn't work. Indeed, there were periods when I couldn't even write a letter. I boxed myself in somehow with a strange ethic of not taking up space, of stepping aside. This led to a creative paralysis and intense anxiety, caused in part, I think, by the manacled poet.

Since I am a poet and express myself through this medium, the loss of the "poet" was devastating. This state of affairs made me feel useless in the world. I turned to visual art, taking drawing and painting classes with varying degrees of satisfaction. At least that "hand" could still work. I began to think about returning to university in Fine Arts. Yet, when not in class, I did not draw or paint spontaneously. Again, creative paralysis.

I spent a few sessions with Lynne talking, but found I couldn't "get in." I wasn't sure how much I had been influenced in what to say by people around me. I told Lynne I would like to "let the body talk" without being prejudiced by verbal speech.

Lynne recommended a body worker and I moved on to that mode. At first, I found this method extremely interesting and useful. Imagery is, of course, a basic tool of the artist, the poet. I informed the body worker of what I wanted to do — no talking, just imagery. Unfortunately, the body worker decided to override my wishes and instructions, assuming, I suppose, that I didn't know what I was doing or what I really needed. She tried to manipulate me into a standard counselling process, as if I didn't know what was best for me. I stopped seeing this person. This betrayal confirmed many of my suspicions about the "healing" industry. It was patronizing, insulting, manipulative and self-serving. This event also introduced me to "counselling" as dialectic, as an argument, the so-called "challenge" method, which is patriarchal *in extremis*.

My depression deepened and I was working on my own, trying to do spontaneous drawings and keeping a diary. Neither of these techniques worked. I couldn't seem to produce the "correct" expressions, and I couldn't "read" it back. I was trying to squeeze someone else's idea about how to express myself into my "tools." It smacked too much of conformity, too little of authentic creativity. I felt I was being asked to impose some sort of "healing" content on my art. This set up another dialectic. My "poet" rebelled and would have nothing to do with this prostitution. Whatever truth is to be expressed must always arise with the poem, and not be imposed on it. "NO," said the poet and shut down altogether.

I began to work with another counsellor. Sadly, this person utilized the "challenge" method, thus entrenching and exacerbating the already dialectical nature of my so-called "healing" experience. Because her techniques were adversarial — what I can only describe as an endless stream of stupid counsellor tricks — I found myself constantly at odds with, baffled and damaged by, the methodology itself. I wasted time and energy in argument with her approach, and with myself for trying to conform to it, while simultaneously knowing perfectly well what appallingly bad methodology it was. This went on for about four months. It boiled down to something like this: this counsellor did not recognize or make any attempt to utilize my tools. Where I assumed metaphor, she assumed literal. I didn't understand her language, she didn't understand mine. Stalemate. I came out of it feeling patronized, disrespected, not listened to, misread, manipulated and bullied: at war with myself because I was at war with the methodology.

I got out of there, did some ritual work to "clean" away that experience, to chase away all the self-doubt — and by self-doubt I mean doubt about my own understanding of myself and my ability to sort through the rubble of my own psyche. I tried again to write down my thoughts. I began to collect diaries. I then returned to a self-model I had formulated some twenty years earlier: a model of conflicting beliefs — that is, an unresolved dialectical double belief system. I drew a chart of these beliefs, peppering each system with mythical characters and personifications chosen or invented to represent attitudes, reflexes, functions and influences. I began, in short, to use my own tools.

My own tools are, essentially, metaphor and intellect. Under metaphor I would place imagery, story, dream, theatre, ritual, tarot cards, all the literary and artistic devices I have always used to explain myself. It comes, I suppose, from assuming the world itself to be a sort of metaphor. The intellect is the analyzer, the interpreter, if you will, and the strategist. In the previous "counselling" encounters these tools were bypassed, ignored, literalized, belittled. When I said something was a metaphor, acknowledging I was using literary devices, I was "hiding, denying, avoiding, lying" (the usual litany of pejoratives). When I would coolly analyze, I would be accused of intellectualizing" (why is this wrong?). This counsellor more than once pointed out my intelligence in such a way as to make me suspicious of it. Because I was not using the "correct" tool (emotionality), my own tools were denigrated and insulted. Emotionality is not my tool. How could I respect and work with my own instruments, when it was constantly made clear they were the wrong ones?

It was by chance really that I lucked back into seeing Lynne. I had gone to see her for a marriage counselling session, but my husband couldn't make it. I hadn't talked to anyone for weeks. There we were. Lynne said to me, "If you don't mind my asking, where is your poet?"

Good question. Nobody else had asked it. I didn't know where my poet was. Somehow I knew it was connected to the third chakra which I had been trying to clear for months. My poet felt bound and pressured. (I ought to be writing about my feelings, etc.). I began to talk about a force field, the pressure, the not reading chakra, and somewhere in all this things went yellow, something came off my chakra and I said it didn't matter anymore what I did or didn't write about. Somewhere in the doing and the telling and the sensing, the poet went free and something went Aha! My shoulders went down, the top half of my body untensed, and the energy began to move down toward the second chakra. Lynne noticed the untensing in her fourth chakra and felt the breathing and the sudden change. What happened?

This was the first freeing thing that had occurred in a year of "work." What was it? The poet got free to write or not write, and "I don't care" released me from the shackles of worrying if I was "doing it right." I could use metaphor until my head fell off and no one would imply or tell me I was "lying, hiding, denying, avoiding, intellectualizing." The tools of the poet became my tools again, became legitimate.

The question "Where is your poet?" was a simple interested interrogative instead of a pointed and calculated "challenge." In the instant of that question, how it was posed, what had been dialectic became dialogue. This may seem a small thing, but for me it was enormous. It freed me from the ridiculous constraints of being set against myself. Without that externally invented and applied compartmentalizing of my psychic innards I trusted myself again. "Where is your poet?" Nobody had wanted to consult the poet, she always said the wrong thing like "this is a metaphor." The poet's tools, those wonderful literary devices, became the tools of the work we do.

Dialectic becomes dialogue. We hadn't exactly thought about it, but, in fact, this transformation provided the basis for fundamental rules in sorting through things. Nothing must be lost, banished, thrown out, excised or exorcised. What is not wanted in its present form is to be transformed, composted, recycled. Even the most negative influences can be mined for gifts. The effect of this approach is to make every life experience valuable.

We utilize my chart of the double belief system using colour, especially to represent chakra energies, moods, connections and emotional content, and correcting, replacing images and terms that are either inaccurate or that have altered. At this writing, we are still working heavily in the patriarchal (acquired) belief area, and have not yet moved into the innate belief area, but the inner dialectic between the belief systems is beginning to dissolve; the either/or belief underlying the separation between the systems is breaking down into bridges, water systems and colour bands. Simultaneously, I have been filling up cheap scribblers which I pass on directly to Lynne. I can't say it creates a dialogue with myself because I don't read them, but Lynne uses them as a basis for suggestions regarding direction or questions to consider, and I think it provides her with a fairly good picture of my state of mind, whatever that might be at any given time. The work is far from done, but I feel like it is getting done. I didn't feel like that before.

Here are some suggestions which I offer to therapists from my own rather dubious experience of the industry: listen to your client. Suss out her tools. DO NOT IMPOSE YOUR OWN. Do not insult her and waste her time and energy by trying to end-run, outsmart, trick and manipulate her. In other words, THROW OUT YOUR BAG OF COUNSEL-LOR TRICKS. Learn to listen. If she says "no" to something, then "no" it is. Respect that and don't trespass. This is not a chess game. Enter her idiom, don't try to force her into yours. And don't try to force emotions through manipulation, bullying and taunting. Either they will arise authentically or they will not. In my case, all the bullying and taunting merely pushed my emotional content and sorting out of same further away. A person's emotions do not have to conform to your expectations. Don't push! You probably believe that you are "challenging" her to "face her feelings." You are not. You are insulting her and trying to shove her through an industrial sausage machine. You are depersonalizing her experience. You are ensuring that whatever her feelings are, she will be damned if she shares them with you. How can she trust you if you are constantly insulting and tricking her? You do not know better than she does. Your methodology may not be the best and only way. If you have to use words like "trust," "respect," "safety," then you are not creating those conditions. A smart client will sense trust, respect and safety if you have created them, and will not be bamboozled into thinking they are there just because you use the terms. If you have to say it, you haven't done it. Do not assume she doesn't trust you because she's scared you are going to make her "confront her fears" or "face her feelings." That is pop-psych nonsense. She doesn't trust you because you are untrustworthy, and she knows you don't respect her because you patronize and trick her and because you don't listen. Period.

My stated goals were to be writing poetry again, and to get rid of anxiety. When I began working with Lynne I was in a state of constant anxiety. After a couple of months of working in this new mode I woke up one morning to realize I had not had an anxiety attack of any significance for weeks. And I was writing, not just in my scribblers, but presentations and papers for university courses. The odd bit of poetic language would pop up here and there in the diaries. At this writing I am not yet creating reams of poetry, and I still get the odd anxiety attack. The work isn't finished. But completion is well on the way. Finally.

Lynne Mitchell-Pedersen
The Client/Counsellor Relationship

Susan is indeed an artist. I do not see myself as a healer. Susan is her own healer. She has all the resources she needs with which to recover her state of well-being. Rather, our relationship is akin to that of a singer and a sensitive piano accompanist. In this relationship, the singer claims the territory she knows, while the accompanist claims what she knows. The role of accompanist is essential but it is not the role of leader. The accompanist does not impose an agenda on the singer. This is a duet where Susan is the singer; Susan knows the words and the music. The roles are balanced and complementary.

An accompanist brings particular skills to her art. She does not compete with the singer. She works with the singer. An accompanist sets structure and context within which the song can most appropriately be heard. She knows when to play more loudly and when to soften so that the singer has the support of the music but is not drowned out by it. An accompanist is responsible for pacing and timing. But the song belongs always to the singer. The singer and the accompanist together work for the most meaningful expression of feeling. Both attend to the singer's body tension and breathing. The accompanist knows not to vie for control. A quote from Susan's diary underlines the importance of leaving a control where it belongs:

"When the therapist gets an agenda, the work is no longer about the client; it is about the therapist."

Process

Susan created, with pen and paper, a metaphorical map to give us material with which to work. She did this at home in a short space of time using the tools she brings as a poet. What was remarkable was that she was able, so swiftly, to identify all the essential symbols needed to work through to her well-being. We have not yet discovered that anything has been forgotten or ignored. In making the map, she called upon her essential understanding of metaphor, her linguistic gifts, her self-awareness, including awareness of her particular historical influences such as her upbringing as a Catholic. Her Wiccan background, knowledge of goddesses from several traditions, of the arts and science, and general erudition informed this map.

The map initially revealed primary parts of self that were at the beginning in opposition to each other. *(SC: What I have described as dialectic).* On the right hand stood Swordgirl, whose belief system was that produced from having been raised in a patriarchal culture. Swordgirl represented Susan's rational mind, balance, awareness. *(And my bullshit detector. A word about the creation of Swordgirl. Some months earlier I had been looking for a symbol to represent these capabilities and reflexes. I chose the Page of Swords from the Tarot. This got shortened to Swordgirl).*

On the left floated Pandora *(I chose Pandora to symbolize the desire and curiosity to "open the box" of the hidden and the unknown.)* In their process, the two initially antagonistic parts were able, gradually, to send out and receive messages of compassion and understanding to each other, supporting a sense of unity of belief. It was important that Susan and I communicated clearly with one another that these "characters" were not seen as literal but as metaphorical. They did not exist as separate entities; we took care not to reify them. *(Note this sentence. It is essential to the success of our method.)* They variously represented a role, a mood, a pattern, an experience *(And a belief.)* Once we were clear on what these characters meant to each of us, we were able to relax and to use their names as a means of giving ourselves a working language. Susan was able, at that point, to write in her diary (which she brought each session for me to read), "Well, dear selves, with your energy, I can manage," without worrying that I would literalize what was intended as metaphor.

The map serves both as guide to work still needing to be done and as record of changes and growth resulting from the therapeutic interaction. Our working process gradually took on a general pattern. At the beginning of a session, I check out where Susan's energies lie at that moment. Sometimes current issues take priority and the map is left aside. Generally, current issues trigger dynamics described in the symbolic map so that we are able to move readily between past and present with the map as focal point for both. I watch Susan's body for signs of tension, and to note shallow or deep breathing. Shallow breathing often indicates that we are moving close to a point of tension. Deep breathing at that point often provides the energy to break through impasse. Susan experiences such breakthrough moments as a bodily feeling of release at ever deepening chakra points. Interestingly, I often experience body tensions similar to hers. I use my awareness of my own body tension to suggest the need for deep breathing, which sets the course for an opening moment. I understand this interaction to mean that we are in deep rapport. *(This is one of the most interesting and important aspects of this relationship. Our energies, chakric bodies, always seem to be in sync. Lynne's "body" reads mine and resonates with it. Lynne is not afraid to get involved. This level of trust works both ways: I trust her, and she trusts me. What a concept!)*

When I feel stuck I say so, and we work together to find a route through the "stuck" point. Susan interprets this style as respectful of her capabilities. I frequently pick up possible directions by asking such questions as, "What are the gifts? What communication needs to happen here? Who needs to be brought in (from the map)?" Susan describes our process as a magical approach, a reference to her Wiccan background, where energy is directed toward a goal, and then allowed to do its work.

Principles

Several principles guided our work.[2] First, nothing from the system must be lost. Energy formerly used to maintain limiting patterns may be used to transform or redirect in a way positive for the current self-system. Nothing must be negated or exorcised. We came to regard the process as similar to composting, old garbage transformed into humus essential for new growth. If Susan does not feel ready to deal with some aspects of a phenomenon, that phenomenon can be symbolically contained to wait for her to be ready. For example, a character called the Black Bishop, representing the arrogance of patriarchy and male sexual dominance, needed to be put behind bars for a number of months until other parts felt strong enough to deal with him *(Also so that a picture could be developed, as in a darkroom.)* Second, the old patterns must be honoured as having been essential for survival of the self for the age when they were developed. *(Ergo the Page of Swords, which represents youth.)* Third, while old patterns might be currently limiting, they hold gifts that can be used in creating new patterns. Every dark part has its wisdom which must be used, not lost. We named such wisdom "the gifts" of the old system. Gifts became a vehicle for transforming previously limiting patterns into new ones helpful for the current system. Finally, the self as a whole is to be honoured for its wisdom in having maintained itself through confusing and debilitating early life messages and experiences.

The Therapeutic Approach

When therapists see human beings as integrated and whole, we can gain entry to the person through several domains: the body, the emotions, or the mind, including both the rational and imaginative capacities of the mind.[3] One separates these domains only for the purposes of discussion: in visualization, for example, one is entering via imagination. We immediately engage feelings, however, including old, deep sub-conscious emotions,[4] as well as tensions within the body. One takes the first step through a particular window but one gets access to all domains almost instantaneously. The human spirit seems to underlie all three domains, so I do not make it a separate category. What is important here for the therapist is that if one chooses the window that reflects a client's way of perceiving and experiencing the world, the client feels understood and the work progresses easily. If the therapist tries to force a client to work through the windows which are the preferred entry routes of the therapist, then the client will feel misunderstood and bluntly maneuvered. Susan's preferred mode of entry into therapeutic work is via her mind which includes both her intellect and her highly developed imagination. The woman is, after all, a poet!

When she had previously been accused of intellectualizing, and thereby "denying her feelings," she felt that the strongest, most valued part of herself — her mind — was being devalued. The message that it is better to work via emotionality than through the mind added to her feelings of low self-worth and deepened her depression. A quote from her diary describing this experience reveals her anguish:

"I feel crowded, judged, shoved by it (the "healing" process); I feel as if I'll get eaten by it and I'll come out the other side not myself with no access to my authentic self, concerns, feelings. I worry about being steamrolled and shaped by someone else's point of view or expectations." When we worked with the intellect, we had immediate access to the emotions as well as to the body responses.

The message for counsellors is to find the window that opens to the voice of the singer, not to push to use the window that fits for the accompanist. Susan lives in her mind first. She described in her diary how she experienced our work together: "We enter into an energy field together. We have no pre-set agenda. Our process trusts that what the self requires, it will speak and do. The process is similar to that of nature. Nature knows what to do." *(This process of nature is the same as magic. It is the magical approach.)*

The Work

Susan came to therapy because she was depressed and could not write poetry; she could not write anything at all. Since she makes her living as a writer, she was in crisis. Her depression and her writing crises were adding to marital strain. It is not necessary to describe the private details of Susan's early life traumas. Suffice it that they were significant. Our approach would have been valid whatever her "presenting problems" might have been.

How, then, did Susan and I use her gifts and her way of experiencing the world to help her move toward well-being? I shall describe the process of a one-hour counselling session to reveal how a shift occurred for Susan that represented another step on her journey toward full reclaiming of herself. To make sense of the work of one session and to reveal the continuity and connection between ensuing sessions, I shall first review briefly the outcome of the previous session's work. I shall describe in detail the process of the session under focus and then indicate how it laid the groundwork for the session to come.

Susan's journey might well have been titled, "Susan's Reclaiming of Herself," because that was part of what was wrong for Susan. She had "lost her poet," and was unable to act from a sense of herself. Her actions had become guided by reflections from the mirrors others held up for her. She had lost trust in her capacity to act on the basis of knowing what was right for herself. Hence, it was important for me, as therapist, not to undermine any futher her sense of self through implying that she did not know what was right for her.

The previous session had focused on the conflict Susan had experienced from having been raised in the patriarchal tradition of the Catholic Church. She had acknowledged the anger she carried about the struggles women undergo resulting from the roles and rules of patriarchy. That session honoured two principles. First, our axiom of never discarding anything dictated that the energy provided from her anger could be used to transform what had previously been experienced as negative into something positive. Second, we searched for the gifts in the old patterns. We were able to identify the gifts that "Catholic girl" brought to the self: knowledge of suffering, awareness of the elegance of theology and of ritual (*And how to transform suffering into something useful and redemptive.*) Catholic girl's gifts were useful indeed. Identifying and naming the gifts set the stage for the session of focus here, where Susan knew she needed to deal further with her ambivalence about her religious upbringing.

We both reasoned that Susan should hold a dialogue between Swordgirl and the Virgin Mary, who had been drawn in a central place within the right-hand side of the map, and who would be aware of the gifts carried by Catholic girl. Mary is, of course, the ultimate product of patriarchy's constriction of the female divine. In spite of this diminution, Mary endures and brings gifts that can be used: motherliness, compassion, a sense of justice.

Susan's pain was, like Mary's, a product of patriarchy. To use the ultimate symbol of the same issue laid the groundwork for Susan to transform her own pain into something useful for herself. Using inner visualization, Susan held a dialogue between Swordgirl and Mary, with Susan playing both parts. By naming and honouring the gifts Mary brought, Swordgirl worked a tremendous emotional and physical transformation. Swordgirl's appearance, in Susan's inner eye, began to change. What had been a black and white dress of armour became papery and was surrounded by a blue colour similar to the colour of the blue energy that surrounds Mary. Swordgirl began to shed this papery cover, much as a snake sheds its skin. Swordgirl's exterior shifted from being a rigid, tightly held stance to a more fluid, open, more penetrable stance. For the first time, Swordgirl was able to receive a gift from Mary, the gift of Mary's compassion. Instead of judging herself harshly, (her self-judgement had been harsh indeed), Swordgirl was able to feel compassion for herself.

The outcome was a surprise! (*I never expected "Swordgirl" to shed* her "skin" and share energy with Mary. They became two blue energy fields sharing back and forth, in some kind of communion. But that is nature knowing what to do and when to do it. Something trusted something.) Nothing was lost. Swordgirl, who has been on guard against loss of self, did not have to give up anything of herself. She shed her skin (Voluntarily and without any prompting or manipulation.) but the energy that had previously been used to guard had been transformed into a softer kind of energy that could glow throughout the system, the energy of compassion.

Swordgirl had been on the alert at all times. What had she been guarding? She was the bullshit detector. Susan had previously been hearing that she was wrong, not doing things right, using her mind instead of her emotions. She had known that there was something very wrong with previous suggestions that she might be a multiple, and with what she described as the "savage machinery of healing" approach to therapy. However, she had been exhausted, vulnerable and desperate to feel better. She had experienced momentary relief at having a name for her troubles. At the same time, her "bullshit detector" was aware that something was very wrong with the whole thing. Swordgirl wanted to take, not abdicate, responsibility for what was wrong. (Oh thank heaven for that "guardian" reflex, that trusty bullshit detector. Tired though I was, I yanked myself out of there and cleaned the shit off. Instead of telling the "Swordgirl" reflex to go away, I thanked myself for it and gave it total power to make decisions.)

Swordgirl feared that being dismantled meant chaos would ensue (And it damn near did. Always listen to yourself.) Something vital to the self would have been lost. Had I, as therapist, set out with the agenda of breaking down Susan's rigidity, Swordgirl would have had to make her armour even thicker. Her fears of annihilation would have increased. (This is not about Swordgirl's survival as Swordgirl, since no such personality exists as such, but survival of the integrity and authenticity of the self, of which "Swordgirl" is a symbol.) Swordgirl made her own decision about what she was ready to do.

Following this event, a sense of relaxation and peacefulness prevailed within Susan and between Susan and me. Susan's body visibly relaxed. Together we did some deep breathing and Susan reported feelings of her second chakra opening up. She noted a sense of greater space within her physical body. She began to envision what might yet develop in her life as her body tensions diminished.

Interestingly, Susan's map has many checks and balances in it.

For example, high on the left-hand side, overlooking the whole map, sits a vulture which, from earliest mythology, symbolizes that nothing must be lost, but must be composted. The vulture had appeared to Susan during a visualization with a previous therapist. The vulture had its wings spread. This image became the basis for a later ritual where Susan was finally able to declare her right to take up her own wingspread space.

This session, then, set the stage for the next, where Susan transformed another part of herself. Three sessions' work took Susan to the place where she could begin to address how her old patterns were limiting her. Susan began to reclaim her poet, her right to space, to speak from her own sense of what is right for herself. Susan's improved well-being has ramifications for her marriage, her spiritual life and her art.

Summary

Susan has summarized clearly the implications for counsellors arising from our experience. To work from a client's frame of reference is the real message. *(And with the client's own tools.)* Working with Susan has been a deeply meaningful experience for me. Susan has moved from a sense that her poet was silenced to a sense of owning her poet-self. She feels entitled to take her rightful place in her marriage, her family and in the world. She reports that her anxiety levels dropped enormously within our first month of working together. She reports a sense of comfort with her own space. The singer will soon be singing beautifully, a cappella.

Susan Again

In the few days since I wrote these pages, I have looked at Lynne's "take" on our process, and have a few comments to make: creating story the way we do reminds me of how the simple literary device of deliberately isolating and personifying — inventing symbolic representations — creates a wonderful (if artificially "compartmentalized") panorama of the self. It reminds me too of how insisting again and again on the metaphorical nature of this creation had previously risked for me those pejorative labels — and how not insisting used to get me smiles and gold stars. And again I am reminded of another term that can be applied to this joint effort between Lynne and myself: lucid dreaming. I can quite easily enter a slightly altered state for visualization which simultaneously opens the energy field around the chakra system and the imagination. A bit like Swordgirl taking off her skin and becoming energy.

I also came across a splendid article in *Common Boundary* magazine (July/August, 1995) by psychotherapist and author Miriam Greenspan. In it she criticizes contemporary therapeutic ethics and practices, in particular the rigid language and ethics of "boundaries." She states, "The healing potential of psychotherapy has less to do with pseudo-objective distance than it does with safe connection. It is not about detached neutrality; it is about passionate but trustworthy engagement."[5] In proposing a "connection model," she suggests that "safe connection is about *trustworthy companionship*.... And trustworthy companionship starts with an absolute and unshakable respect for the integrity of the person called patient or client."[6] (My italics.) She states further that, "This respect includes some very specific skills, including the skill of "active listening." This is not about listening for the preordained categories that fit our theories of the patient, but rather listening with an ability to surrender one's theoretical understanding into the living presence and self-knowledge of the other person."[7] (Yes! Yes!) She goes on to point out that there is a habit in traditional therapy "of interpreting patients' complaints about the therapy or the therapist as matters of transference, resistance or pathology. If patients do not have the right to question their therapists' work without the risk of being labeled or pathologized, then therapy comes to resemble the closed and well-bounded systems we call cults."[8] And, "There is no one-size-fits-all rule of safety in psychotherapy."[9] (Nor, I might add, is there a one-size-fits-all therapy, not to mention language of therapy.)

Strong words. But Greenspan puts her finger exactly on my own feelings coming through the past system. Resistance, transference, pathology — precisely what was suggested of me if I disagreed or didn't come up with the "right" answers. Without meaning to, I am sure, the last two therapists left me feeling abused. How did they manage that if they meant well? Greenspan concludes that from her point of view, "It is safer to see the therapist as accountable than to see the client as pathological. It is safer to value empathy for the client than to regard it with suspicion as something that makes one lose one's objectivity. The connection model is safer than the distance model. Healing happens when someone feels seen, heard, held and empowered, not when one is interpreted, held at a distance and pathologized."[10] (Yes, yes and yes!)

I would characterize my relationship with Lynne in this work as "trustworthy companionship." An excellent term. Are you listening, healing industry?

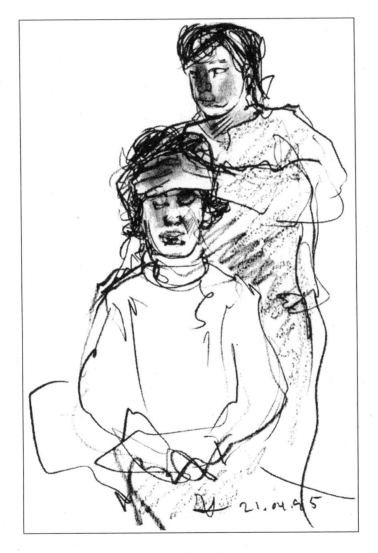

"Caring Hands" by Heather Spears

body images

(for Joan Turner)

Carol Rose

you massage me into a dream
the sea & an old ship i'm
a fish slithering beneath
the ship's worn belly searching
for a rope to raise its anchor
i pull it up with my teeth
release it from the depths
you talk to me whisper something
Karen always says "jaws loose
like a moose" stroke my cheeks
dig into bones for hidden tears
you remind me to breathe i exhale
sighs so old & distant they sound
like someone else's cry in me
i open my mouth & pain comes out
in trembling waves you touch
my body lovingly caressing sinew
muscle tissue i uncoil softening
in the blue green light a sea hag
clings to the curve of the anchor
changing as she rises into a wolf
then a bear standing on hind legs
totems bringing health endurance
power i grow into myself taller
rounder exquisite in the wisdom
& caring of your hands[1]

Celebration

Gwen Satran

the land scarred her body   left her
weakened   now she wades in the sea
plays joyfully in the mediterranean
dances knee-deep in azure waves
her jeans rolled high   legs free
to splash in the bubbling foam
she loosens her hair   thick & wild
in the warm december air   her body
mind & spirit caressed by the sun

she walks confidently into the blue
mediterranean   where sea & sky
meet at sunset   she feels herself
healing   celebrates life

Art Changes Lives
An Interview with Joan Hibbert

Joan Turner

Joan Hibbert is a Winnipeg counsellor and artist.
She was interviewed in her home on October 13, 1995.

Joan Hibbert: In preparation for this interview I tried to think about when I have been most creative, that is, when I have expressed myself through my art work. Sometimes my drawings and paintings have helped me to cope with tough life experiences. I have also done some of my favourite work when life felt "good." Either way, I seem to experience a heightened sense of who I am, and how I am connected to others, when I am expressing myself creatively.

I think creativity is important to the living process. I think it is life. There is a button on my bulletin board that reads, "art changes lives." I believe that. I have experienced it and have witnessed it in the lives of others. I can't imagine life without art, whether that be music, writing, dancing, cooking, or the visual arts. I choose to express myself through the visual arts. It has also helped me keep in touch with my little three-year-old granddaughter, Lindsay. I mail her hand-drawn postcards, and my daughter, Vicki, says that when Lindsay gets the cards in the mail she puts them on the tree I painted on her bedroom wall.

JT: Can you tell us more about the tree?

JH: I wanted to give Lindsay something special. I thought, "What if I drew a tree on her wall that she could sit under?" I used the whole wall. When the tree was finished, I added a rabbit, a caterpillar, a ladybug, flowers, mushrooms, and an owl. I loved doing it. I'd never done anything like it before. I painted it on New Year's Day, the first anniversary of my husband's death. When Vicki saw the owl, she said, "Mom, the owl looks like Dad." I see now how my gift to Lindsay was also helping me to grieve.

JT: How did you feel after you finished?

JH: I felt absolutely marvellous. I have always seen the tree as a symbol of life and fullness. The little rabbit was a challenge for me. Words of advice from an old teacher ran through my mind. "When you draw a tree, be a tree." So I said to myself, "Okay, Joan. Be a rabbit." I wanted the rabbit to be sitting at the base of the tree, so there I was lying on my stomach, painting on the wall, all the while attempting to be a rabbit. What a hoot that was! To capture the soul of the rabbit became my goal, and I like to think I accomplished that. I love that little fellow. I enjoyed hearing that Lindsay took her sleeping bag and curled up under the tree. Now she takes my postcards and puts them on the tree.

I draw things I think Lindsay will enjoy and I write a short story about the picture on the back of the card. I try to relate the stories and drawings to members of our family. For example, I did a drawing of the bananas growing in my brother and sister-in-law's living room. Lindsay thought that was funny. I hope that when she does meet them, she will remember that story. Lindsay and her family live in Saskatoon, hundreds of kilometres from the rest of us.

The postcard idea came out of the Woman Healing for Change weekend retreat. Gloria Norgang, of Ottawa, gave me a block of blank water colour postcards. So, in a sense, she started it all when she introduced me to a very special way of communicating. Gloria and I took a mandala workshop at the retreat. We sat next to one another all afternoon and into the evening, drawing our mandalas. There was little conversation between us. As I look at my mandala (page 133), I find the colours fascinating. The central part is very gentle and almost jewel-like, and then the colours become much bolder and more vital as they flow out of the central part. These colours and shapes are connected, but to me they do not feel as contained as the inner colours do. I was inspired by a basket of moss and a root that Tami Reynolds brought to the workshop. I feel that these women and I connected in a special way. I sense that I am preserving that feeling of connectedness with my mandala. When I look at it, I remember with fondness what it is like to "be" in a room with people who celebrate the artist in one another. I am happy that Gloria's mandala is also in this book.[1]

I had a similar experience in a private art class. I spent three hours working on a pastel drawing of an onion, and I wept the whole time. That's it, on my living room wall. As I drew it, I experienced a feeling of "letting go," a peeling away of some of my defences. My teacher was very respectful of my needs. She gave me space, she did not intrude, she did not question my tears. I experienced healing through my art work. The drawing hung in my counselling room for a while and I was struck by how many women were moved by it. Ah, another connection.

JT: I, too, am moved by it. Have you done other types of paintings?

JH: Yes. When I was a lay member of the Ministry Team at Augustine United Church, I met and worked with fascinating people and I wanted to capture their character and their spirit. I knew I needed more training to be able to do that. They inspired me to take portraiture classes. I have done some portraits and I can show you one. I did this piece for Alvina Pankratz. Using pastel pencils, I drew this woman's face on a piece of muslin and Alvina stitched it to her quilt. There's a photo of it here in *Lifelines: A Quilted Portrayal of Life*.[2] The quilt depicts an elderly Mennonite woman sitting in a rocking chair stitching a quilt which drapes over her lap. This gives a three-dimensional look to Alvina's quilt. I have also done several other portraits on muslin. I like working on the raw material in this way.

JT: You mentioned a woman artist who has inspired you.

JH: Oh, yes. Myfanwy Pavelic, of Victoria, British Columbia.[3] I think she does exceptional work. My daughter, Liz, had the privilege of interviewing Myfanwy and she said she is a grand lady, world class. You may have seen Myfanwy's famous portraits of Katherine Hepburn and Pierre Trudeau. See the movement in her work. My work is still tight. I aspire to be like her. I hope that one day my portraits, like hers, will capture much more than a likeness.

JT: I regret I don't know her work. How sad it is that many of us don't know more about Canadian women artists who do fine work.

JH: There are many like her. I remember when Emily Carr was not recognized or celebrated for the wonderful artist she was. She was practically a neighbour of mine when I was a child. I would love to have known her.

JT: What influenced you to work as a lay minister and counsellor, rather than as an artist?

JH: I guess I never thought of art as a vocation. I thought of it as a way of expressing myself, rather than employing myself. I remember believing that you had to be educated in art in order to call yourself an artist. I don't believe that today. There are many people who didn't go the formal education route and who are very fine artists. I grew up in a creative home environment but no one in my family chose a career in the arts. I don't recall anyone suggesting that I do so.

Listening, as a way to support people, has always been a part of my life. My work at Augustine helped me decide to get formal training in counselling. So, after my fiftieth birthday, I began taking related courses at the University of Manitoba.

JT: At the Spider Women Retreat, did you experience any tension between the artists and the therapists? Any differences?

JH: I wonder what you mean by tension. It seems to me that artists express themselves through their work. In the therapeutic process, the therapist encourages others to express themselves in ways that will help them identify and begin to make personal changes. My experience with the therapeutic process is that if one introduces an art form, whether that be visualization, clay, drawing, drama or music, etc., it alters and enhances the process.

Lucille Meisner and I just did a retreat on body image and, as a follow-up, we met with the women last night. They spoke of important shifts. At the retreat they drew, worked with clay, visualized and talked. I see this as an illustration of how valuable expressive art can be in therapy, not as tension, but as a coming together or a union of two media. In significant ways, working with the art forms changed how the women felt about themselves. Perhaps those therapists who have not used art forms in their work will experience it as tension.

JT: It sounds like you believe that art facilitates the work of therapy.

JH: Yes, I do. Art can also be healing. I'll give you an example. Many years ago, a dear friend of mine who was in her early 40s died of cancer, leaving her husband and four children to mourn. One of the sons, who was nine years old at the time of her death, began "acting out." His father asked us to keep him with us for a while, which we did. I was working with clay at the time and I remember how this young lad scoffed at it — "stupid clay, what are you doing with that stuff?" I didn't attempt to answer him, instead I handed him some of the clay and told him I'd like to see what he would do with it. To begin with he pounded it with his fists, and then he began forming ghoulish-looking figures. They were death-like, covered with long cloaks. When I asked him what he wanted to do with them, he said he wanted to finish them. He painted them with a black glaze and I fired them in my kiln. During the week that this took we could see the change in him. He let his grief out, and with it, his tears. He became less and less angry. The clay seemed to give him a way to express his anger and his deep pain.

At that time I sculpted a likeness of his mother, which helped me to mourn my loss.

May I tell you how working with clay changed a part of my life? Years ago, my husband quit his job. We had four teenagers at the time and I was not working outside our home. Ironically, that same day I bought a kiln and a ton of clay. 40 boxes of clay! My family will tell you there was seldom room for food on the table, but there was always room for clay. One day I was rolling the clay out like you do pastry — I'll show you what came out of it — little Dickens characters, all poor. I called them "Joan's little people" and they sold like crazy. They became a source of income for us. Those little urchins helped us get through a difficult time.

JT: And they all represented poverty?

JH: Well, they seemed to. But, they were so cheerful. They all have funny little faces. I like to think of them as wholesome, like "Oliver." They were so simple and yet they were so popular. People related to them in some way. I know I did. After that I did Manitoba Miniatures, small paintings on wood, two inches square, or less. I painted a lot of scenes of the Interlake, a part of Manitoba with which I am familiar. They also helped put food on the table.

JT: When you were making your urchins and your little miniatures, did you think of yourself as an artist?

JH: An interesting question. Those were times that I needed to make money with my art. Think of myself as an artist? I don't know that I ever thought about it at the time. I remember being pleased that they were so popular and thinking that it was a bit of a miracle! My son,

James, the one who is now a potter, was also down in the basement working with me, so the two of us connected in a special way. Maybe what I did for him was to plant seeds. Alvina did that for me with her quilting. She inspired me to make the quilt I'm currently working on.

JT: I appreciate that you're showing me samples of your work.

JH: For the first time in years I am been surrounded by my work like this. It's a little like "show and tell," isn't it? There's an excitement to it because the next milestone in my life is that I will be 65 and I may be retiring.

I went to the Spider Women Retreat weekend at Hecla to stimulate my creative juices. It did help me. You are also doing that for me because you are giving me an opportunity to talk about my art.

JT: Is there something that you want to do now?

JH: Yes, I want to develop and improve my portrait work to better capture a person's spirit.

JT: In the way Myfanwy does?

JH: Yes. I believe she does that. As we speak, I am thinking how my work influences my art. I know that the subjects I choose to paint, draw, or sculpt, the medium I choose, and my interpretation of those subjects is enriched by all the women and men I work with.

JT: Do you have plans for your retirement?

JH: I like to think of it as "moving along" rather than retiring. I seem to move from one art form to another as I move from one phase of my life to another. So, in the next year or two, I may explore some exciting new medium. That's an appealing thought! After Steini died and the children moved out, I created a room for myself. So I have a studio in which to work.

When I "move along," one of my goals is to talk with people like Sigrid Dahle, the Winnipeg artist/curator who presented at the Spider Woman Retreat. She knows the artistic community well. In the future, I would like to be part of that community.

I am beginning to realize that not only did art change my life, but my life experiences changed my art. Quilting today, portraits yesterday, little people and miniatures when we were poor, creating a logo for the church when I worked there. I know that expressing myself through my art has enriched my life, helped me heal, brought me hours of pleasure and it has made a difference in the way I work with others.

JT: If we were encouraged to express ourselves through art, then our children, female and male, would more likely create art whole-heartedly and with confidence.

JH: I think our children benefit from knowing we value art, in all its forms. It is important that they be given the opportunity and the encouragement to express themselves creatively in whatever art form they enjoy. Art is a central part of the lives of two of my children. James is a full-time potter and my youngest daughter expresses herself through her paintings and jewelry. I would like to think that maybe the clay, paint, and paper that covered our kitchen table had something to do with that.

JT: Thank you, Joan. May your "moving along" years be filled with art and the full expression of your creativity.

"Mandala" by Joan Hibbert

Remembering and Healing

Carol Stewart

"The idea of physical immortality gives people an opportunity to unravel their death urge and free themselves from the tyranny of the deathist mentality. The ignorance of physical immortality leaves people in the prison of misery, self-destruction, fear, failure and insecurity that causes illness and pain, violence and war, power struggles, impotence and cruelty, human degradation and death itself. The philosophy of physical immortality unshackles the human imagination, gives access to enormous reserves of energy and creativity, creates a motive for patience and simplicity and is itself a test of love and intelligence."[1]

It is unlikely that we human beings could live or manifest much of anything very well without conscious or unconscious ideas guiding what we are doing. Ideas are the funnel that hold and shape the flow of our experience of the deeper energies, bringing Spirit and Soul into existence. Great ideas can awaken and heal by stimulating expansion and imagination, making room for more life force to enter our being. With healthy ideas about ourselves, we can open, breathe, be inspired by life, and give birth.

Ideas can also hurt and limit us by cutting us off from the rest of Creation. For example, the destruction of war is often generated out of a clash of cultural, political, or religious viewpoints. We tend to think that what we think is all there is and, therefore, that it is right.

Whatever we call our ideas — comprehension, understanding, knowledge, or wisdom — these alone will not heal our relationship to ourselves, to each other, or the planet, as long as we hold any of these levels of consciousness in a righteous manner. The mind is a great trickster, necessary to our awakening, yet very troublesome to deal with at times. Clear ideas are different from righteous ones.

I remember my own awakening in 1978. This vision gave me the theoretical underpinnings of my life and work. It was a great illumination about the impulse of life moving us into physicality, not out of it, as various philosophies about life on this planet had purported. Ideas about life on Earth being only a school, or an illusion, or punishment for sin, were views that devalued life here, disconnecting us from our bodies and from the planet. I saw how these ideas had disastrous consequences.

I was joyous with the fullness and clarity of my vision, and with its potential to be more nurturing to life on Earth. I could easily have assumed that my ideas were "right" and then started a religion! Yet, my Spirit was compassionate enough to let me know that as great and clear, good and beautiful as my illumination was, I was only looking at the universe through a pinhole.

This is not to discount the value of what I saw. My intent here is not to encourage cynicism or skepticism about the mind and its ideas, but rather to connect with the question, "Are your ideas about yourself, about reality, great enough, loving enough, to support the flow of life force from your depths into your everyday life, so that you can live all that is in you, and live it in a way that is healing and life serving?" That is what is important about ideas.

Ideas are to be taken lightly, not heavily. Ideas, even great ones, are points of light; they illuminate and serve things around them, for a time. To have ideas without clinging to them for a lifetime, to let go of assuming that any idea is reality, is quite a challenge. With love and humour, our ideas might seek to nurture, not dominate, life. Learning to be flexible with our perceptions is grace at any age. But it seems clear that we cannot live without ideas any more than we can live without romance or love. So what are your ideas? Whom and what do they serve?

What I want to talk about now is healing, big ideas about healing. Please keep your mind strong, yet open. I am here to stimulate you with my perspective, not to lecture you or pretend to tell you any truth about life or yourself. Feel what I say, and see what moves inside of you as a result. Positive or negative, honour these feelings within you. Maybe this will help to highlight or clarify ideas of your own. Let's see where our ideas lead.

I have been working with the Tarot symbols for over 20 years now, and what Soul learning it has been for me.[2] This work has kept me in sweet relationship with many other people I have worked with over the years. As a tool and a discipline for Self awakening and remembering, my exploration of the Tarot symbols has been a vehicle for an ever-expanding and deepening contemplation of the dance of individual and collective human process. Self-awakening and Soul-remembering may be what healing is all about.

Often, I have heard myself say to a client, "You know, if we finally get a sense of healing in this life, we still have our genetic and psychic memories to heal. We are not alone, but interconnected with all life, and none of us are home until all of us are home." This may be overwhelming to some who feel that they may never heal from what they have experienced in this life. Yet, one healing might encourage the other, so it may be of value to consider the necessity for both.

Some wounds may be carry-overs from the Soul patterns of lives past, or from the genetic stream of energy our body carries into existence when it is born. If we look at these patterns and at our rigidity or stuckness in them, we may discover how we identify with those patterns as well. A fresh perspective about our wounds, and about the Self/Soul-negating patterns they often generate, can serve to heal both this life and lives past.

More people in the world believe in reincarnation than don't. This is a concept which reflects and supports the presence of an eternal Self or Soul within each of us, moving through vast spaces of time. In the Tarot symbols, the Soul is represented in the suit of Cups. A Cup is a singular receptacle for the infinite possibilities that the Self, Spirit, or Life Force offers us. Spirit movement arises in the suit of Wands. With the interaction between the Spirit or Life Force and the Soul or Heart Force, Creation stirs itself into our dreams. Then, we must have ideas, reflected in the Sword suit, to support bringing what we dream into physical manifestation, represented by the suit of Pentacles.

If we believe that what we dream is "impossible," then everything stops for a time; nothing gets lived. That idea, itself, is a wound. It limits us.

It may be that dreams are our Soul essence; that each one of us, each individual Soul, is a part of Creation that yearns and needs to fulfill itself. Thus, what each of us carries is unique, irreplaceable. I have said countless times in affirmation of my clients: "We each are a piece without which the puzzle of collective existence would remain incomplete." Each one of us has ultimate value, a particular purpose, in that we are a part of some great Wholeness or Holiness that is seeking to realize or manifest itself. This is a long-term project! We are wounded, when we conclude (from what we are told or experience) that what we deeply are, cannot be lived. The need for healing is not a problem, but a fact, a part of existence that just is. All the dimensions in which healing can and should take place can be overwhelming or exciting, depending upon our psychological attitude or readiness.

Soul healing, a kind of remembering which serves to heal the collective, is the kind of healing I like to work with. I am not alone here. This is a great dream that many others are already working on, somewhat shyly, but also very consciously.

Our emotional and creative "lostness," chaos, and the stuck places that are born from woundings that our Soul has experienced, is reflected in the Tarot symbol called the 5 of Cups. There is an image of a person, all dark and heavy, bent over 3 Cups that have fallen over, their contents spilt upon the ground. There are 2 Cups behind, still full, apparently neither noticed nor attended to.[3] This symbol points to a need for healing and it raises a question. Do we heal by focusing on what was lost, or by turning around and making use of what is still standing?

For example, whether or not women have had a specific memory, many carry, within their psyche, the memory of the witch burnings as the archetype of the attack, by the partiarchy, upon women and their Earth wisdom. Many can relate to the terror of being dragged out of a hiding place and persecuted for what came, out of love, from within us. We feel vulnerable when we activate the mystery of being a woman, related to the Earth in the way that we are. So we tend to hold back what is best in us. There are centuries of horror to be released as we dive into layers of Soul history.

For men, there are the centuries of being encouraged, cajoled, or forced into war. While there may have been some glory attached to this at times, there never was glory in the individual man's encounter with the brutality and terror of war. The cost was his connection with the feminine soul within him. Men have felt little room to remember or express these assaults on their Soul.

Also, we forget that women suffered in fighting wars and that men were burned as witches. The enemy is not which gender suffered the most, nor who is at fault but, rather, the horror and reactivity we experience when we see fear winning over love, time and time again; or, when we experience the separation that is not individuality, but rather, disconnection.

We replay these scripts in small and large ways, over and over again. In psychological terms, it might be called "repetition compulsion"; the need to undo something, or master it, by doing it over and over again. It is like a record that gets stuck in the groove. This behaviour might seem strange but it is part of the reaction to authentic traumas to the Soul. Ironically, we become trapped by our captors; those who made us afraid, those whose eyes we looked into and found there was no one there. Disconnectedness is our enemy. In an attempt to heal, we are vulnerable to making that disconnectedness our lover. We cling to our wounds as if what we feel in relation to them is all that we are, angry, fearful, grief-ridden, powerless, etc. We forget or lose touch with what we were attempting to share in the first place. Then we perpetuate the trauma by living in a disconnectedness of our own.

What we fail to see are the two standing cups in the 5 of Cups card. The possibility always exists, if we let go of our fixation on disconnection, that we can be seen. When I have looked into the eyes of someone caught in such a memory or trauma, from the near or distant past, I say, "Well, look at you, you are still here! I see you."

We can live continuously under some threat of loss, or hurt, or death, that totally controls our lives way beyond the original wound. What we don't realize or remember is that deep truth that "nothing was lost." If someone didn't see us in the past, it doesn't mean we do not exist or cannot be seen. It only means "at that time," they did not see us. Someone, somewhere, at some time, however, will recognize us. From there we can be renewed and healed. It may be just a matter of timing, just a matter of remembering who we are and not only seeing ourselves in the loving eyes of another, but also, believing what we see. The 2 of Cups symbol in the Tarot celebrates this meeting, this healing, this triumph.[4]

In my sense of life, we do not die. Our Soul essence, eternal and indestructible, seeks life, wholeness and manifestation on Earth. Natural wisdom has always taught us that life cycles through birth, death and rebirth, and that this happens over and over again. We can recognize that we are still here, perhaps in a new form, maybe from a stream of many previous forms, but we are here now! We still carry the same soul longings, gifts, and talents. Each lifetime is a renewal of opportunity for us to manifest and share what is deep within; those gifts and viewpoints that are uniquely ours to give. Instead of focusing on renewal, if we focus on loss early in childhood (perhaps an echo from some past lifetime), we may remain lost.

If we believe we are doing the best we can, we can activate some compassion for the human condition. It will take us deeper into the dilemma of what it is to be a human being on the planet now. We might need to see that currently we may be very confused, wounding others with our own woundedness, and trapped in our addictions and compulsions. Yet, with courage and daring, we can reclaim and affirm our gifts again, and then we can see what happens this time. We may need to understand and accept that timing is of the essence.

So, what creativity, what Soul dream do we need to move us forward, to shift all of this?

I often visualize the Soul, before each birth, looking over this great tapestry of Creation which, slowly, we are collectively weaving into existence. What we see before us is the result of countless lifetimes of effort. From this pre-birth vantage point we see how we are doing with the project of Creation. There are still eons of weaving to be done. This tapestry of existence is a work of art. Yet, as we look, we can see mistakes we have made. There are "rips" and "tears" from wars in this fabric of our existence. These have to be repaired. Also, we can see "knots" of pain and confusion that need unraveling. There are the edges we don't want to see frayed, so attention must be paid to the edges of existence as well. What a wondrous and challenging effort to create beauty. It is what we are about.

Some brave Souls, looking over the project, might say, "Well, this time I may have a strong enough connection to the Life Force to help repair this rip, or perhaps to undo this knot." So the Soul leaps into the middle of a big mess by being born into a war-torn country or into an abusive family. Some of the strongest Souls take on the most difficult situations. These Souls stand the risk of profound disconnection, of losing themselves. We pray, with guides and with the support of others around us, that in our lifetime we may have a breakthrough that helps us to understand what we are doing. Then we will be able to throw ourselves, more consciously, into the task of repairing and reweaving.

This is particularly poignant at this time in our evolution, with so many secret and destructive behaviours being revealed. Consciousness improves the chance that we might be healed more directly. As the dark seems to be getting darker, support groups are forming. Souls are putting their heads and hearts together to comprehend and perhaps transform the knots of existence into the original beauty that can be there. People are working together to discover and create ways to do this. It is a very touching time.

It all comes back to perspective, that other "idea" about creation and healing, which simply may be a process of remembering a much bigger picture.

We do not die. What is deep and essential within us is never lost.

It loses its ground in a body, in time and space, for a while. This is what we struggle with in being human. At the end of life, we go back to the drawing board, only to return to take another step in the awe-inspiring project of bringing Spirit and Matter into union.

What steps are you taking? What is your life energy here to rectify and heal? Look at your wounds as your teachers. Remember who you are and of what you are a part. Keep faith with your heart's deepest dreams and visions. Let's look upon ourselves and each other as the pieces of Light and Life we each are. If we assumed this, if we focused on this, how different might our lives be? What different choices might we make?

Of the choices we must make in life, the most important and challenging one for me is to open, no matter what! I can fling myself and all my dreams into life. I can struggle with the consequences, and know that this is all that there is to do. I can do the best I know how and forgive the ignorance of others by accepting my own. And I can affirm, as often as possible, that under all the pain of those spilt cups, what we deeply are is love and joy intermixed. We are searching for communion and reunion, and we will never die.

A blessed friend sent me this very relevant poem by Rashani:

> There is a brokenness out of which comes the unbroken
> a shatteredness out of which blooms the unshatterable.
> There is a sorrow beyond all grief which leads to joy
> and a fragility out of whose depths emerges strength.
> There is a hollow space too vast for words
> through which we pass with each loss,
> out of whose darkness we are sanctioned into being.
> There is a cry deeper than all sound
> whose serrated edges cut the heart as we break open
> to the place inside which is unbreakable and whole,
> while learning to sing.[5]

May we all learn to sing our Soul's song. May we discover how to stand with our deepest dreams and, in so doing, heal ourselves and all life, over and over again. May we find ways to give ourselves room to breathe, to weave our dreams into existence, expanding our perspective whenever we can. May we find ourselves endlessly turning around and looking at each other, remembering who we deeply are and the Great Mystery of which we are a part.

Courage at 4:00 a.m.

Robyn Maharaj

I awaken nightly
to the hiss and whisper
of a low moan

I am comfortable
in the empty space around me
not prepared to try any longer
I have returned to my own soil

the wick from a tapered candle
dips and bows
with the grace of a falling leaf
turning my back on a flame
affected by breath and shadow

gardenia and sandlewood are scents
I carry like treasures
time in an ivory box
gathers momentum
a metal pocket watch
held to the flesh
warms under the pressure
of my palm
rescued
it is with this knowledge
that I will embrace
my grave

she brings me her dreams

Carol Rose

curious about imagery   she brings me her dreams
all neatly typed   bound in a floral diary
no room for surprise   i think to myself
so tightly wrapped   swaddled like the babies
in her birth scenes   blue & premature   falling
on their heads whenever anyone else tries to hold them
there's probably nothing i can do to help her
dreams are part of the process
they need time to unravel themselves
i want to say *you've just got to hold the tension*
live with the anxiety a little longer
sense this is unsatisfactory
offer an exercise to help her see her own inner world
wait for the healing to come on its own as it always does
when the dreamer stays tuned to the tellings inside
know she will leave here wondering why she came
pages from her journal tumbling to the floor[1]

Harnessing the Imagination

Carol Rose

I've often wondered about creativity, about that special state that I seemed to know about, even as a child, when I had to write a paper or prepare a project. I didn't know what to call it back then, or even how to access it. I just knew that if I went to bed and thought about what I had to do, relaxed, daydreamed, or even fell asleep for awhile, that later, I would wake with an idea waiting to be written. I didn't realize that this was a "technique"; in fact, I always felt a little embarrassed about the way I went about doing my assignments. It didn't seem to be "active" enough. It didn't feel like I was "doing" anything. It almost felt like something outside of myself was doing the work. I suppose I was what we would now call a spiritual child, or maybe all children (given the opportunity) are spiritual. In any case, whenever I had to do a creative project, I felt like some kind spirit had joined me and that, with the help of that spirit, I could think differently, see differently, know things in a way that was completely different from the way that I was learning at school. I felt as if I was "receiving" information, not acquiring it through my own efforts. Today, I would probably call this "grace" or "being in the hands of the Divine," though I certainly couldn't name it then. Because this was such an unusual way of doing things, when my parents asked me how I was doing on an assignment, or if they offered to come into my room to help me, I'd quickly jump up from my bed, a little embarrassed and afraid of what they'd think if they saw me just lying in bed and dreaming. This was not anything I felt I could talk to them about; it seemed so out of the ordinary. It also felt a little like cheating, because I wasn't really "doing anything" and still the ideas came to me, fully formed.

Years later, in a creative writing course, we were asked to talk about how we prepared ourselves for writing. The instructor mentioned that she often sat with a dictionary, opening it anywhere and just focusing on the words, focusing on their meaning, or on their placement on the page. *"A kind of meditation,"* she said, *"I suppose it's a way of turning off the ordinary mind and tuning in."* Suddenly, I understood my own childhood strategy, my own private way of tuning in. What a relief! Another person seemed to know about this process, too, and she could name it. She could identify it and talk about it as a legitimate way of preparing to write.

Nowadays I spend most of my time writing, and although I'm not as innocent as I was back then in my childhood, I still find myself dreaming or "quieting the mind," prior to the actual act of writing.

I now know that this is a very useful technique, a way of centring myself and focusing on the impressions that are stored inside my head and my heart. I've also discovered the usefulness and importance of "turning inward" in other facets of my life as well.

For the past 20 years, I have been studying with Jerusalem psychologist and wise woman, Colette Aboulker-Muscat. Madame Muscat, who comes from an illustrious Algerian family of healers and spiritual teachers, learned Jewish Kabbalistic teachings from her grandmothers. She also learned a great deal about neurology while apprenticing with her father, a well-known neurosurgeon. Her formal studies included psychology, physiology, anthropology and philosophy. In Paris, she worked with Robert Desoille, the well known French expert in waking dream therapy. Based on her broad educational background, and on her many years of personal experience, Colette has developed a system of healing which she calls "imagery." In North America this type of therapy is often called "visualization," though Colette prefers to call her work imagery, because she believes that ideas can come to us via any one of the senses, or even several of the senses at the same time. When one quiets the mind to external stimuli, one can begin to perceive with an inner eye, or an inner ear. One may then "see," "sense," "feel," "hear," or even "know" things, based exclusively on messages from the inside. This technique is often used in healing, and it is especially popular with cancer patients and their families. It can, however, benefit everyone. For just like in dreams, we can receive valuable information from our images, albeit in code. When we learn to attend to our images, to translate them and to understand their messages, then we may find that they help us solve a problem, or cast things in a new light, or even show us a new direction. We may be able to frame things in categories that we have never even thought of before. In short, imagery is a systematic meditative technique, not unlike my writing instructor's use of the dictionary, or my childhood strategy of going into bed to relax and reflect. It is a way of shutting down the outer "information gathering mind" in order to get in touch with what the inner self has to offer. Despite the similarities, however, imagery is a very conscious act. It not only quiets the mind, it directs it as well.

The people who come to study in Colette's little Jerusalem garden are people with a variety of life experiences and careers. They may have come there because they are artists suffering from creative block. Or, they may be scientists who have an intuition about their work, but who cannot get the results that they want using their usual processes. People with grief or trauma-related issues, or those suffering from various illnesses, also find their way to her garden behind the blue gate. Naturally, many of the people who study with her are counsellors and therapists, healers from both traditional western and eastern disciplines. What they all have in common is the conviction that we can and do know more about ourselves and about our abilities to heal and renew ourselves than we are generally aware of. They come to learn ways in which to access this information. It is not as though they expect Colette to play the part of a guru; rather, they come to discover what it is that they already know, about themselves, about their work, and about their own healing. Mostly, they come to learn the imagery techniques that Colette has developed in her 65 years of working with people.

What exactly is imagery, and how does it relate to the topic at hand? Perhaps the simplest answer is that imagery is what we humans do when we are called to act in the moment; called by a specific task, event, or situation. We begin with an intention ("I am going to write," for example) and then we sit (or in the case of my child/self, lie down) and focus our imagination, directing it toward what needs to be done. Perhaps we need to give a speech, or write a letter. Perhaps we need to decide what to pack or to wear or to buy. We may be afraid, or we may be looking forward to the choices we need to make. Regardless, we are busy previewing, seeing in advance what we expect will unfold for us in our waking lives. This information may come to us in pictures or in sensations, and it may be a totally unconscious act. As Colette has often said, "images are our first language," and they are speaking to us all the time. The goal of healing imagery is to "harness the imagination," to take this very human, very natural ability, and to direct it so that it can work for us, in the moment. Otherwise our imaginations will virtually run wild, and that would be a misuse of mental energy that could drain us, or drive us further into our fears. When we learn to harness our images, to direct them, they can become a great source of creativity and

healing power. Images can free the mind; release it from old defini-
tions and categories, old limitations and fears. The trick is to become
aware, to know that we are always using our imaginations, and to
learn ways in which to guide our images so that they can benefit our
lives and help us attend to what is essential for us now.

During the years that I have worked with Colette, I have learned
that change is possible, that healing is possible. I have come to
understand that as creatures created *in the image* of a Divine Creator,
we are creative, in fact, we are divine. We can and do affect our own
lives and our own well-being. Colette has often said that the model
for all change is found in the Biblical story of creation. In that story
the Creator has an intention — to create a new world. In order to
proceed with that intention, the Creator must first quiet everything
and bring it into a state of wholeness and harmony. It must remove
chaos and confusion and make space for the creative process to begin.
Once there is space, the Creator can see (as it were) because there is
light; because all distractions and divisions have been cleared away.
Then the Creator can begin to form an entirely new reality. It can
gather all of its energy, all of its power, and it can articulate its
intention, *"Let us make humans in our image."*[1] It is then that the Creator can breathe life into its new creation.

The two most essential elements in the creation story, *space and
light,* are vital components in Colette's therapy . Clients always begin
with an intention of their own choosing (in Hebrew, a *kavanah*) which
quiets the mind and allows it to focus on what the individual is
addressing at the moment. Then a simple breathing technique is
introduced, to clear away distracting or competing thoughts. As a
result of the change in breathing, beginning with an exhalation and
then an inhalation (reversing the habitual order of breathing), the
client is relaxed yet totally attentive. As in the creation story, a "clear-
ing away" must take place in order to remove chaos and confusion
from the mind, the seat of all creativity and healing. After a cleansing exercise, clients often sense a feeling of clarity or expansiveness.
It is then that the actual imagery exercise is offered. Although it is a
guided image, the client very quickly takes control of the work. For
after all, it is what the client sees, hears, senses, or knows that is of
paramount importance. It is the individual's own creative response
that is sought in the work of healing imagery. It is the individual's
personal *insight* (seeing from the inside) that is being invited into the
process. The overriding belief, in this system, is that each of us knows

what is best for us; each of us understands our own life and our own healing. Healing, for Colette, means "coming into wholeness," returning to a state of balance and unity with the Source of all life. It is this wholeness that healing imagery strives to achieve.

As I said at the beginning of this article, I've wondered about creativity, about that state that allows us to make something new, something expressive of who we are and how we understand ourselves and our world. I've wondered about our ability to heal and to renew ourselves daily. I use the word *wonder* not to mean "I am suspicious of" rather, I use it to imply a sense of *awe*. I am awestruck by our potential for newness, our ability to be receptive to new ways of looking at or discerning life. I wonder at our receptivity, our ability to be open to the Divine flow of energy and light. I wonder at the state of grace that we can place ourselves in.

I wonder and I rejoice at the simplicity of it all; a brief intention, a change of breath, an image and, suddenly, we are totally different than we were a moment before. We have changed how we understand ourselves in the moment and, consequently, we have changed how we view our past and how we perceive our future.

I think it would be helpful now, to describe the process, and to present an example of a cleansing exercise. The individual would begin by formulating a *kavanah*, an intention with a direction. She (or he) would sit quietly, in a place where there is the possibility for inner as well as outer peace. Generally, Colette suggests that imagery exercises be conducted three times a day; before breakfast, at twilight and again before bed. I suspect that this is related to the change in light ("seeing things in a new light," as it were). The individual then breathes out slowly three times, beginning with an exhalation. This helps one empty the self of all that is disturbing, toxic or no longer necessary; imagining these thoughts leaving the body on a thin film of grey smoke. A "cleansing" exercise (one that allows the individual to sense what is crowding the system and keeping it from making necessary change) is introduced. A classic example of this type of exercise is described below:

Imagine going down a path that leads to a meadow or forest. While walking through the green, peaceful landscape, see a small branch on the ground. Know that it is there for you to use, and pick it up. The small bough seems to glow in the sunlight. With this small golden branch, begin brushing your body gently, from top to toe. Sense how all that is unnecessary is falling away as you lightly brush your body with the branch. Hear the sound of dead cells falling to the ground, and know that all that is disturbing you, on the inside, is also falling away. When you are finished briskly brushing the body, return the bough to the ground and walk toward the sound of flowing water, coming from the right side of your path. See a lake, brook, river or waterfall, and cup your hands, taking some of the clear, cool water into your cupped hands. Splash the water on your face, neck or on any body part that seems to need it. Take a few sips, feeling the cool freshness invigorate and cleanse your entire body. You may enter the waters, if you wish, to refresh your entire body. When you have completed this cleansing, return the way that you came, passing the small branch left behind on the path, returning to this room, to the chair you are sitting in, knowing that you have renewed and refreshed yourself. Breathe out, and with open eyes, sense the effects of this cleansing on the interior as well as on the exterior body.

It is at this point that a specific exercise, directly related to the individual's intention (the individual's *kavanah*) is introduced. If the chosen work is related to healing, the therapist will use an exercise specifically designed for healing. If the goal is to enhance creativity, the work will be directed toward that end. In either case, the work is evocative, inviting the client to participate fully in her or his own renewal. An attentive therapist may have gathered clues about the client's images from the cleansing exercise, or from the discussion that preceded it. These may provide the therapist with the necessary language to formulate an appropriate exercise, one that is suited to the individual's personal goal.

I would like to offer two recent examples, based on the client's own imagery. In the first, the woman describes herself as being in a projectionist's booth. She is watching the same movie repeat itself over and over again. The story seems to be about a cowboy who is "saving everyone." The woman recognizes that she is the cowboy. I ask her if she wants to continue seeing this film. She says that she would like to change it. I then ask her who the projectionist is. She smiles and says that she is the projectionist. I remind her that projectionists often have more than one movie on hand, in case of an emergency. She imagines herself changing the reel and setting up an entirely different film. She says that she has been watching this one for far too long, and that she is looking forward to seeing the new movie.

A second client has been trying to get in touch with her creative self, the self that she feels she has put "on hold" while pursuing her academic career. After a general cleansing exercise, she tells me about a woman who she sees walking near her home. She has never met this woman, but has only observed her as she passes in front of her window. The woman is elderly, dressed in a heavy coat and boots. Something about this woman attracts her. She may even remind her of her own mother, she muses. I ask her to imagine the woman passing in front of her window. In the image, the older woman looks up at her. Her look is friendly and welcoming. I then suggest that she ask the woman if she can come out and join her under her coat. She imagines being under the coat. It is large and roomy, and she feels safe inside the coat. I ask her if she would like to put her feet inside the woman's boots, and she does. Immediately she is transformed into a little white mouse or a rabbit. Even though she is inside the woman's clothing, she feels that there is room for her; that the woman has made room for her. She is small and she feels that she is frightened, but protected. She actually feels her body tremble a little. Yet she knows that she can do whatever she wants to do under this coat. When the exercise is over, the client says that it reminds her of a previous exercise, where she created a protective circle in which to do her creative writing. The coat reminds her of that image, and reinforces it. She realizes that she does have the space (and the time) to do the type of writing that she wants to do.

These insights may not seem dramatic; however, they have brought about a change in perception. Both of these women have sensed something about themselves and their lives. Their images have provoked a light shock, *a surprise* and, as a result, they are able to proceed with their lives in a new way. They understand that they have choices.

Both healing and creativity are states of mind that I have referred to as similar to dream consciousness or alterations in perception. Depending on one's belief system, I could easily have included the word "magic" (if by magic we mean a change in the use and direction of energy). Both of these mental states soften external focus (much in the same way that we soften our eyes when looking at an oil painting) in order to sharpen internal awareness. They permit us to move out of ordinary consciousness, out of our habitual ways of looking at or doing things in our lives. They seek to align the self with the timeless Eternal Source, whether that power is called God, Divine Feminine, truth, angel, muse, or inner wise one. As described in the exercises, they require a "letting down," a release of the logical and linear ways in which we generally tend to operate. They encourage us to make new associations, to release the hold of the past on our current thinking. They remind us that we have the power to remember; to put our lives together in ever new and changing patterns. Although most of us do this quite naturally and quite often, we often do so unaware. The hope of this article is that we will recognize healing and creativity:

a) as similar states of mind

b) as legitimate alternatives to our usual mental processes

c) as useful techniques that we can direct, invoke, or "harness" at will, in order to access the power and the energy that we each have in guiding our own lives.

How I Healed Myself with Imagery

Adira Rose *

I used imagery to heal myself of a wart. Every night before bed I imagined that each of my fingers had something special attached to it. One finger had balm, one had light, one had a knife, one had a needle and thread, and one had an eye.

I used my eye to see what I was doing. I used my knife to cut off the wart. I used the balm to stop the hurting. I used the needle and thread to stitch up my skin, and I used the light to heal everything. In three weeks my wart was gone.

* 9 1/2 years old at the time of writing

TSS

Margo Reimer

my body is a desert   parched   seething
veils of sand erupt into rapids smashing on rock
razors slash my soft skin   i scream inside
my body knots into sheets soaked from thrashing
days blur into nights   the clock glows eerie green
my body is TOXIC
it tears away from lucidity
falls over cliffs into the dark
my skin is bludgeoned   torn from its bones
poison scalds my flesh
my body is in SHOCK
it empties into a crypt of dead faces   spinning
i ride a winged horse that flies through orchids
death's tangled green fingers brush my feet
curl around hooves   wings strain to rise until
God awakens from Her tomb   rushes me in spiral funnel
up through Toxic Shock Syndrome
rolls back the stone   like at Easter
enables my resurrection

Chapter Five

Relationships

Halinka

Anne Szumigalski

It is right, they say, to bury a stillborn child with a mirror on the pillow beside her. That way, at the resurrection, when she opens her eyes for the first time, she will see her face and recognize herself.

But that's not for you, little daughter, little flaccid creature. For you, there never was such a thing as a face. There were hands and fingers, curled feet with curled toes. There was a heart in your chest, red and whole as a candy, and a white iris growing in the place of your understanding.[1]

Olivia & after the rain

Gloe Cormie

My strong agile hand   spans
the width of Olivia's chest

❖

My friend   her mother   says breast
feeding is thought sensitive   her breasts
begin to swell and surge with milk when
she thinks her three-month-old is hungry
even if she is across town &
many miles away from her baby
her milk begins to flow

❖

How knowing the body is
Wiser than the mind
body and mind in a dance
the mind mostly the foolish thing
that puts a kibosh
on the body's wisdom

❖

My body no longer hides
from the rain   it feels like
forever i have been walking with
rain-soaked socks   inside a chilled body
a fiery heart

❖

a sparrow dislocated after the rain storm
too little to be on her own &
forced to fly   haltingly   she manages
to survive

❖

Olivia snuggles in her mother's arms
a rock garden   bursting   with bright flowers
fuschia   amethyst   cadmium yellow
petals tickling her plump cheeks

❖

the floral patterned dress
of the beautiful woman i imagined as my mother
spreads before me the   balm of my orphan
childhood dreams

❖

My strong agile hand   spans
the width of Olivia's chest &
embodies a rainbow

Writing My Way to Recovery

Anna Olson

My third child, Jennifer Lindy Olson, was born when I was 40 — some 19-and-a-half-years after my second child. Talk about a mid-life surprise! At least that's what I told people. But six months after she was born, I had a dream in which she shook her finger at me and said, "You forgot about me." Then I remembered that I always thought I would have three children: first a girl (Kristen), then a boy (Jeffrey), then later on another girl (*voilà* — Jennifer).

Jennifer was born with a particular combination of heart defects known as Tetralogy of Falot. In a routine examination two days after Jenny was born, a nurse heard a slight heart murmur through her stethoscope. A pediatric heart specialist later diagnosed Jenny's condition. At five months of age Jenny had surgery on the blood vessels near the heart to increase the flow of oxygenated blood and at two-and-a-half-years of age she had open heart surgery on the defects themselves. In spite of the heroic efforts of the doctors and nurses, Jenny died eight hours after the second surgery was over.

I have written a lot about my troubled pregnancy and my travails as a single mother of a child with a heart defect. I've written about the love, the happy times, the struggles. But here, I will talk about Jenny's death and how I used writing to help me recover from a blow that shocked me to the core.

The death of a child is one of the worst traumas a person can endure because a child's death goes against the natural order. A child is supposed to grow up, become a responsible adult and eventually bury his or her parents. It's horribly painful for parents to bury their children, even if the parents are in their 80s and the "child" is 50.

And no matter how a child dies, somehow the parent feels guilty. To be a successful parent means one must keep one's child alive. Therefore, if the child dies, the parent must be guilty of neglect. At least that's what the emotional self says, even when the parent has done everything possible to keep the child alive.

I learned a lot about recovery from The Compassionate Friends, a self-help group for bereaved parents. That group, the help of personal friends, and my writing saved my sanity and helped me to keep functioning.

For years journalling helped me cope with life, even when no crisis was present, so it was natural for me to turn to my notebook immediately after Jenny's death. The morning after her death, I couldn't sleep, I could hardly walk. I tried to write the words "Jennifer has died" in my journal. At first pen and paper didn't want to connect. The paper didn't want to see the truth and the pen didn't want to write it. Gradually, the words took shape on the page and reality came pouring out. This was the start of my recovery, facing the truth of my loss.

I also turned to one of my favourite books, *Writing the Natural Way* by Gabriele Rico, which teaches ways of listening to the right side of the brain (the emotional, intuitive side) in preparation for writing. An example is "clustering," one of Rico's central writing techniques.[1] You put a "seed word" or phrase in a circle and add words and phrases in circles around it until you feel the urge to write. Here is an example in which I clustered on the word "survivors":

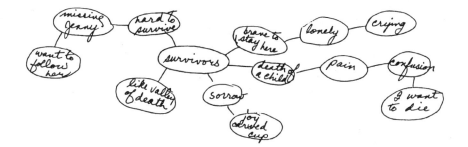

This is the prose poem that resulted:

The Survivor

We who are left behind
    In the shadow of the valley of death
We know about sorrow from the bones out.

We who choose to stay behind
    And not follow our loved ones through the portal of death
We are the brave ones.

We who survive abandonment
    By children who left unwillingly
Struggle through the lonely night, into the empty day.

We who drink this cup of sorrow
    Need to remember the joy
That carved the cup so deep.

Another one of the techniques Rico teaches is called "modeling."[2] This means taking someone else's poem and clustering on the first line, but with your own ideas. Then you write a poem in the style of the original one, but with your own content. I did this, modeling on "Portrait VIII" by e.e. cummings:[3]

Jenny Benny's
gone now
    who used to
    toddle garble and
        drool
Learning so fast to count   onetwothree
    Migosh
She was catchyourbreath beautiful
    and what I want to know is
Why are you so lucky to have her
Mister Death

Rico also teaches the value of metaphor and simile. These have the power "to surprise us, make us catch our breath, illuminate an aspect of the world that is totally at odds with the conventional way of seeing it."[4] A star can become a flower without a stem, the sun can be a big ball of fire playing hide-and-go-seek with the clouds. Rico encourages us to be like little children, letting our imaginations roam unchecked. Here are two pieces that emerged from that exercise when I clustered on "Jennifer was like…" and "Jennifer's death was like…":

> My Jennifer was like an angel. She touched this earth briefly to open our hearts and teach us to love. With her big blue eyes and soft golden curls, she even looked like an angel. But it was her smile and gentle manner that won people over. Maybe her heart defect affected us too, drawing more concern and compassion than if she had been healthy. She could have stayed longer, but for some reason, she chose to resume her angel duties on the other side.

> After Jenny's death
> Depression nipped at my heels
> Like a small Pekinese.

Another favourite book that helped me recover through writing was *The Power of Your Other Hand: A Course in Channeling the Inner Wisdom of the Right Brain* by Lucia Capacchione. She came to her insights the hard way — through illness and mental suffering. In the course of her recovery, she learned the value of dialoguing between the right and left hands. (The right brain is connected to the left side of the body and left brain to the right side.) Writing with her non-dominant hand seemed to access different parts of herself. It led her to find a frightened Vulnerable Child, a silly Playful Kid, an outrageous Woman in Red, an Inner Healer, and a serene Wise Woman.[5]

At first I was skeptical about writing with the non-dominant hand, but as I worked my way through her book, I became convinced of its value. I have done dialoguing between the hands as well as left-hand journal writing ever since. Here is a dialogue between my intellectual right hand and emotional left hand that surfaced when I recalled how I felt when it was time to leave the hospital the day that Jenny died:

The Longest Walk

It's time to go now. It's over. We have to go home.

But I don't want to leave Jenny.

She has died. The doctor says so. We have to leave her here and go home.

But she's my little girl. She doesn't look dead. Maybe she's just sleeping. She still looks pink and healthy.

She is dead. The monitor says her heart stopped beating. They took out the tubes and turned off the machines. They let us hold her to say good-bye and now we must leave.

But I can't. She's my baby. I have to look after her.

It's time to go. Say good-bye to the medical people, turn around and put one foot after the other down the hall.

I can't. My legs aren't working very well and I don't want to leave Jenny.

I know, this is the hardest thing you've ever done in your life, walking away and leaving your child. But we have to hold ourself together. Now move your left foot, then your right. I'll help you and the others will help us. Some day we'll understand about death, but right now, we have to just keep walking.

An exercise I devised myself is one I call "the repeating question." The creative side of the brain seems to like being asked the same question over and over again. Left brain, or logical thinking, says, "You asked that question already. I gave the answer, so let's move on." But right side doesn't seem to mind and it looks for another slant, another inspiration, another layer of feeling. After Jenny's death, I used this exercise to explore the grief I felt. I kept asking the question, "What does my grief feel like?" and tried to get between 10 and 20 answers. I combined some of the answers to make this prose poem:

What is Grief Like?

Grief is like a large bruise that does not heal.
Grief is like a bucket in my heart that keeps filling with tears day after day.
Grief means an empty crib that I should give away but I'm having trouble doing so.
Grief is like having my arm or leg amputated. I am still alive, but I'm in shock and I don't function very well.
Grief means I've lost my little girl. I search for her in my dreams at night but I can't find her anywhere.
Grief hurts.

In her second book on writing, *Pain and Possibility: Writing Your Way Through Personal Crisis*, Gabriele Rico devotes a full chapter to humour and recovery. She believes, like Bill Cosby, that "if you can find humour in anything, you can survive it."[6]

Humour was helpful to Rico when, as an adult, she attempted to recover from her mother's death. Rico's family had been caught in the strife of war-torn Germany in the Second World War. Three weeks before the war ended in 1945, Rico's mother was killed in a bombing raid. "[My mother's death] left our family vulnerable, confused, afraid, and in great pain," Rico writes in the preface to *Pain and Possibility*. "I pictured a long, jagged crack across my small heart. I felt fragile as glass, and I wondered if glass could ever heal."[7] Rico had repressed her grief for too long and now, as an adult, her health was suffering because of it. Through drawing and writing exercises — and the search for humour amidst the chaos of her pain — she fought her way back to wellness.

"Laughter is the other side of darkness," she writes, "Laughter is the sound of freedom. Our returning sense of humour tells us we have entered the spiral of healing."[8] I decided to take Rico's advice and try to laugh(!) about Jennifer's death. Here is what happened:

With eyes closed, I asked aloud, "Is it possible for me to laugh about Jennifer's death?" I promptly burst into tears at the idea. As the tears rolled down my cheeks, in my mind's eye I could see Jenny's spirit hovering over me and pulling on my left arm, trying to lift what seemed like a lead weight. I heard her say, "That's the idea, Mom. Lighten up!"

Was that for real? It felt real to me. I have had other experiences of communicating with her spirit as well as that one and I don't think I'm crazy (not certifiably so, anyway). So I take that interchange as her way of encouraging me to recover from her death and to let humour brighten any dark corners of my existence.

Through all this writing work I must have been recovering to some extent — at least that's what part of me saw. I attempted a dialogue with my Magical Child as per instructions from Lucia Capacchione in *The Power of Your Other Hand* and was surprised at what came out. Capacchione encourages the reader to get to know the various children within all of us. There's the Vulnerable Child, Playful Child, and Magical Child (among others), she says, waiting to be discovered.[9]

> Adult Anna (right hand): I am adult Anna. I understand about logic and gravity and rules and housework. Who are you and what do you understand?
>
> Magical Child (left hand): I am the Magical Child part of Anna. I understand about fairies and goblins and animals that talk and princes and magic apples. It's a fantasy world where thoughts take form.
>
> Adult Anna: I am more logical. You seem kind of flighty to me, not solid based, not realistic. Why should I listen to you?
>
> Magical Child: I tap into the mysteries of the world. You are tied to the material world. I see further. I see past form into essence. I am joyous and happy because I am part of the spirit world.
>
> Adult Anna: Well, I didn't know I had you inside me. Have you always been there? I haven't heard very much from you. I wouldn't want you to be in charge of our life though — you're too flighty, pie-in-the-sky, flippy dippy.
>
> Magical Child: You're right. You're needed to keep us grounded and functioning. I've been here all along but I've been buried by the pain. Now that you're healing, maybe you can listen to me more.

Losing my daughter Jenny was horribly painful, but I have found some comfort in writing about her death. Grief is a reality of life, unfortunately. The longer we live, the more people we tend to lose. But through writing (and art and song and dance), we can work through our grief and create a tribute to the people we love. It's a way of saying, "Thanks for being a part of my life; thanks for walking with me a while."

Jenny & Anna Olson

Letting Go

Marj Heinrichs

Thomas James Heinrichs was born in the same season in which he died — under the harvest moon. He was my first-born. The eldest of five. I gave birth to him on August 25, 1976, when the fields were ripe for harvest and the smell in the country air was of sweet alfalfa hay and golden grain.

Tom died in a motor vehicle accident on August 23, 1994, at the tender age of 17, two days before his 18th birthday.

He was killed by a combine at harvest. It was too soon. He was not yet a man — still a boy. Always my baby.

The combine had finished the harvest in one field and was moving to begin another. The combine did not reap what the farmer sowed in the next field. Instead of taking a crop of wheat, the combine took the lives of three young people. Tom, his cousin Rachel, and their friend Michael. Three teenagers killed instantly when their half-ton truck collided head on with the inadequately lit combine on a dark country road.

For some, it was a comfort that these three friends died together. It was my sense from the beginning that Tom went on his journey into the next world alone. I can only imagine his shock at realizing he was dead. He wanted to live. One of the last entries in his journal reads, "I have seen tomorrow and I don't want to die."

Although we are surrounded by family and friends, each one of us who loved Tom has had to take this journey of grief alone. Somehow, I, Tom's mom, had to let him go. I have never felt such pain. I have never felt more alive. I have never been so conscious of everything around me and everything in me. I felt pain in the depths of my being. I felt physical pain in my womb as the hours turned to days and I knew the spirit of my son was leaving.

Early in the morning of August 25, 1994 (it would have been Tom's 18th birthday) I wrote him a letter.

Darling Son on your birthday,

It is 1:30 a.m., August 25, 1994. Eighteen years ago today, I gave birth to you at this very hour. Two days ago you died, suddenly and tragically. In another day we will bury your body in the ground.

This pain I feel today, this pain of being separated from you, is not unlike the pain of childbirth.

You were a few days early, in a rush to be born, eager to begin your life's journey. I remember now, how I fought the contractions of my body as you fought to be released from the confines of my womb. I remember howling in pain and fright with each agonizing body-wrenching pain. I thought it would never end. For a time I could only feel pain and it seemed that I forgot there was a life inside of me, struggling to be free.

But then, oh my darling, darling first-born son, you were born. When they put you in my arms that first time, I experienced a love and a joy and a wonder unlike anything I had ever known.

There is sameness here, precious child. For nine months I nurtured you in my womb. For nearly 18 years I nurtured you in my home. You nursed at my breast and I loved you and taught you and then, slowly, but deliberately, I started to let you go. The pains of this separation started long before you died. It started when you began to walk and talk and care for yourself. I helped to teach you to be independent. You took your independence seriously and you played the part of eldest child so well.

But now, dear child, you are gone too soon. I really wasn't ready. I would never have been ready — the pain of separating mother and son has begun again. As you left the safety of my womb, you are leaving me once more and I am fighting the reality of your leaving with all my being. I am howling with pain and fright. The pain of separation wracks my body. I hurts so much and I fear this pain will never end.

But again, you are struggling to be free. I feel it. I know it.

My hope, my only comfort, is knowing you are somehow being born into a new life. I must remember that there is life at the end of this pain. Somehow, as I go through this agony, as I let go, I am freeing you.

And one day, the pain of this parting will end for me too, as I experience again the overwhelming joy and wonder of you as we are reunited in Glory.

Happy birthday, Tom.

I love you,

Mom.

Saying Good-bye
And so he was gone and we had to say good-bye. It is very strange to say good-bye to someone who is already gone.

I resented the fact that my friends had months to plan their daughters' weddings and we had only days to plan a funeral.

The planning was done as a family, by my husband, (Tom's dad), Tom's three sisters, his brother and me. Our large extended families and our friends helped where they could. The funeral, we decided, would be Friday afternoon. Tom would have hated to get up early to go to a funeral. We chose a coffin. We were pleased to all agree on the brown one with a flat top, cream coloured inside. Not white. Tom didn't look good in white. We chose his clothes. Grunge. Pants down on his hips, T-shirt tucked in just so, boxers, and a sweater. He loved sweaters. We put change in his pocket. Tom loved change in his pocket. And a guitar pick. He always had a guitar pick in his pocket. One earring and a nose ring. We needed to bury him looking like our Tom.

There is comfort in tradition. The traditional Mennonite funeral meal consists of raisin buns, cheese, and sugar cubes to dunk in coffee. We added brownies to the menu because chocolate is comfort food in our house.

How do you have a meaningful funeral service for one so young? We wanted this to be a time of remembering Tom, so we brought his stuff into the foyer of the church. We set up a table around which Tom and his friends had often gathered in the local rink. Each of the gang's faces had been etched into the wood and coloured with pencil crayon. There was graffiti on the table and it looked like a work of teenage art. On and around the table we put Tom's skateboard, guitars, ghetto blaster, sports paraphernalia, jacket and boots. Tom had written a song about "friends" and we made photocopies for everyone. The chorus said, "Good friends are good friends, notice that a lot. They're not here forever, don't forget. Hold onto the things in life before they dissipate to dust. My friends, my friends..."

What could better comfort than words from Tom? We chose guitar music instead of the traditional organ. The pallbearers, friends of Tom, were asked to dress for Tom, not for the funeral of an old person. Tom's friend and youth pastor spoke from his own broken heart about Tom's life. He told the young people that if they were to die, we would grieve for each of them as we were grieving for Tom. He told us God didn't take Tom, but received him when he came. He spoke of Tom's integrity and respect for people. He spoke of his faith and spirituality. He said, "We must remember. To celebrate Tom's life is to give hope and meaning to our lives. To laugh and to cry at the stories that celebrate may seem confusing at times, but it is also the way we know we are truly alive…allow Tom's life to challenge you to live with more authenticity."

I also spoke at the funeral, paying tribute to my son. I spoke of his life, of our love and our loss. "Grieve with us for a life taken too soon," I said.

Then it was time to bury the body of one we loved so well. It is the usual practice in our community to have a short service at the graveside and then go back to the church for lunch. The body is then lowered into the ground by the funeral directors and a backhoe comes to fill the grave. I couldn't bear the thought. We had to finish this ourselves. We asked Tom's friends to help us bury this beloved body. A few words were said. Marking pens were passed around and those who wished were invited to write a message to Tom on the coffin. I wrote, "This is my son, in whom I am well pleased. Good-bye, Tom. I love you. Mom."

There was a prayer, committing the body to the earth. The casket was lowered into the box in the ground. The lid was nailed down. Then we, the family of Tom, took shovels and began the work of filling the grave. After a time we backed away and let the friends of Tom do what they needed to do.

As a car stereo blared Tom's favourite music, including a song he sang and recorded with his band, the friends of Tom gathered around the grave. First they sat in a circle around the open grave. Someone lit a cigarette and passed it around. It was like communion, someone said. Then, taking turns, they picked up the shovels and began to fill the grave. Before long, the shovels were tossed aside and the friends of Tom took the earth in their hands and filled the grave. Someone tossed in a cigarette. Another threw in his hat. A locket. A key chain. A daisy. When we bury you, we bury a part of ourselves, Tom. You will always be a part of us.

Adjusting

As my son was being born into a new reality, so was I. So was my family. A world without Tom. It seems I knew instinctively, hours after he was gone, that we would need to get away. We were overwhelmed with people and their acts of kindness. We live in a small community and come from large families. Someone counted 300 people dropping in the first day and 200 the next. Over 1,000 people attended the funeral and it seemed each one vowed to bring us food. In the beginning we would gather with our remaining four children after everyone was gone at end of the day and have a time of family debriefing. These were precious moments, but soon we were too exhausted to carry on with the ritual. Day after day and week after week, the people came. We had to get away. In the midst of the difficult Christmas season, we decided to spend the insurance money on a family vacation in Hawaii early in January.

It was not a fun holiday. We all bemoaned the lack of privacy in two hotel rooms. The trip cost double what we expected, causing us considerable angst about money. My husband and I were overprotective and the children were quarrelsome. It seemed every nerve was on edge.

It wasn't all bad. The weather was perfect. There was comfort and healing in the warmth, the sun, the sand and the water. There was much to see and do. We found ourselves fascinated with sights and sounds that did not constantly remind us of our loss.

We kept to ourselves. We felt a freedom to laugh and tease in a way we were not comfortable with at home, for we felt the community mourning with us, and they expected us to look sad all the time.

It was only after we returned home that we realized the full benefit of the trip. All the quarreling, it seemed, had helped the children to establish a new "pecking order" without the oldest brother. The oldest sibling is now a girl; there is no middle child. Billy doesn't have a brother and the girls have only one. Roles changed and needed to be learned. I compare it to getting used to your body after losing an arm. It takes time and effort. We are beginning to learn a new "normal." We are beginning to heal.

Dad Died This Week

Deborah Gabinet

My Dad died this week. They said, "it was a mixed blessing." Now he is free and at peace. He didn't have much peace on earth, not really.

Dad's life was filled with duties, commitments, disappointments and broken dreams. Some people in our little village called him "Stoneface" for the hard persona they saw. At home, he could be a very strict and angry man. But those of us who knew him also knew a comic, an actor, a fiddler and a hard-working husband and father. Adorned in hat and tie, he was always a gentleman. At the annual variety concerts he performed with comedic flair. Offstage, he would wiggle his ears and his nose to the delight of the little kids. How he loved to get a laugh!

Dad's love was "tough love" and there were many times I hated him. But when my Dad became an old man, he became my friend. I saw the miracle of second childhood transform him from a tyrannical man to a charming and innocent youngster.

I began to understand that Dad wore his cold, distant, unapproachable Stoneface mask to cover up his frustrations and sadness. He had not wanted to farm, but he was the eldest son. He had not wanted to adopt children, but they told him he was sterile. He had not wanted to sell insurance, but they took out the railway. He wore his frustrations like a noose.

As time went on, he lost his job, his wife, his car and then his home. They said he was demented, took away his independence and placed him in a nursing home. I returned from far away and consoled him, perpetuating the myth that he was on some sort of a retirement holiday. He wanted to believe me but he felt so alone and afraid.

One day, I, Deborah, his little adopted daughter, now a grown woman, held up my bib and accepted him. He held up his bib and asked me to help him. We opened our hearts to each other. I was his "Angel," he said. We danced together in the light singing:

Oh we ain't got a barrel of money
Maybe we're ragged and funny
but we'll travel along singing' a song
Side by side.[1]

One day, not long after the singing, my Dad took a deep journey into a coma. I stayed by his side, singing softly, describing what was happening to him and all the while loving him. With the help of additional angels we guided my Dad through the door. He was at peace.

My Cotton Blue/Mauve Coat

Helen Levine

This morning it was close to zero. I could tell from how trembly I was when I got out of bed and the taste of the air in the bedroom. I suddenly thought of gloves and mitts and thermal underwear that have been out of sight for months.

A certain mood descends when autumn's crisp cold air hits me for the first time. It is a kind of combined weather and clothes consciousness rooted in the need to protect my rattling bones and fragile flesh against the coming blasts of winter.

And so the ritual begins. I take out my cotton blue/mauve coat with a hood that has hung in the hall cupboard for many years. I find my tam lying on the shelf, waiting patiently for a bit of attention. I feel jaunty with my white hair and purple tam. My hands dig into the well-worn coat pockets and sure enough, they're full of dingy Kleenex from last spring, and a pair of black wool gloves undoubtedly in need of a wash.

When I'm all dressed in this garb, I feel deliciously at home — old, familiar, sporty in a kind of faded, worn-down, been-round-a-long-time kind of way. The cozy feel, the musty smell. The unconditional comfortableness of it all pleases me enormously.

Why is it that people (including me sometimes) hunger for the new, the stylish, the different-from-last-year sort of clothes? Why is the new valued more than the old? As I ask the obvious, I suspect my own motives. Is it all just a transparent rationalization for shoring up the "old" which I have become?

There is a story of sorts buried in these meandering thoughts. It's about my daughters, Ruthie and Karen, how the three of us bought this same blue/mauve coat with a hood, many years back, wanting to be some kind of mother-daughter trio. I loved us strutting along together as look-alikes. For me, it was a way of connecting, of telling the world that we belong together, in a special and slightly kooky kind of "fashion."

Now I have to tell you that my kids threw away their blue/mauve coats long ago. For newer styles, more "with-it" clothes.

And me? I wander around, cozily and nostalgically, every fall, in that same old coat, the same old tam, with the same old feelings. I guess, along with being comfortable and familiar, these old garments keep me, in some special way, connected to my daughters.

I don't think Ruthie and Karen know that. But I do. I'll have to tell them.

Word for This

Elizabeth Carriere

My sister writes a note
to all of us.
It is the season of Christmas.
As the oldest she is guilty
for each of our moments
of despair. Why is this?
She lights candles to burn
away the dark. Cigarettes
to burn away her heart.
Walks through her garden in patient
ceremony. She is my sister.
We never speak of what joins us
Silence among all our words,
our letters voiceless.
But we shout
into the hearts of men.
We call into the air
above the children's heads.
Once, we sang until we cried,
and just before morning
the room we were in turned blue.
There must be words for this.[1]

i'm thinking about her again

Allyson Donnelly

i'm thinking about her again
my head reeling
her image in front of me
barely visible
lit by dim candles
both of us nude
spinning in the dark

i'm thinking about her again
her warm body touching mine
flesh against soft flesh
i feel her power entering me
& i surrender

i'm thinking about her again
though we're no longer spinning
together   separate in the dark
we find our own power
i'm lonely for the dance
my soul aching
as i think of her again

Reflections from the Middle of the Mattress

M. Joan Baragar

Six years ago, on our 27th wedding anniversary, my husband took me to our favourite restaurant for dinner. After dinner the "Maitre d' brought us a complimentary liqueur in honour of our long and happy marriage. Two months later the door closed on that marriage and all the hopes that had gone into it. The man who was my husband left the day before my 50th birthday. I remember saying goodbye. I don't remember hearing an answer.

Waiting in silence to see what my body and voice would do next was anticlimactic. Initially I had reacted with frantic disbelief, followed by pleading and anger. Twenty-seven years! After so long, how could this be a throwaway relationship? We had negotiated our way out of difficulties before. Wasn't that a normal part of marriage? This time, the deadline for negotiation had apparently passed, undeclared, until an irrefutable decision to walk had been made. Finally I asked myself: if the unthinkable had become the inevitable, was there any longer a point in resisting? Could this be the kind of cockeyed truce couples reached when they ran out of options?

I could find no sensible answers. But, oddly, the panic in me temporarily subsided. There was no parting hysterical outburst, very little feeling of any kind. There were sparse tears with the good woman friend who was with me when the door closed, and later, when I made a few phone calls to the chosen ones who would graciously keep me company as I entered "the first day of the rest of my life."

Some called that evening's event a 50th birthday party. Others called it a wake. The photograph album, as albums often do, records our wishful thinking: faces smiling, arms wrapped around each other to suggest that no one is missing. But what's really out of place in this picture is me, looking as if I'm at someone else's party. The shock, still an icicle, is buried deep inside. Had my birthday occurred after the thaw, I might have found the whole notion of celebration too painfully absurd. Yet, when I review these photographs, it's as if I can hear the beginning of a whispered song of hope, myself the singer: "Happy birthday to me…" In the midst of that unreal occasion, with the year turning on itself in the most murderous fashion, some remote part of me must have been choosing new life by deliberately making the claim, I AM.

It was after that birthday party, after the washing-up and the last goodbye that I began to reflect on one of the first lessons a significant separation teaches: eventually, all the well-wishers go home. I had to turn from the door and face myself. All by myself. In the empty stillness. With the lights off. If I screamed, who would hear? If I chose to do something horrible to myself, who would stop me?

Wild thoughts pursued me upstairs. On many other occasions I had stayed alone in the house, but this was different. I had the idiotic urge to check under the bed for monsters in men's clothing, a ridiculous camp song whirling around in my head:

> My mother said, "Always look under the bed
> before you blow the candle out
> to see if there's a man about."
> I always do — oh, yes, you bet—
> but I have never had the luck to find a man there yet.[1]

Surprise and relief—my wry sense of humour coming to the rescue. I stared at the double bed that, until this week, had been meant for two. And I took a flying leap onto the centre of the mattress! With a twisted grin, I reminded myself that I could now sleep anywhere on this territory, anywhere I chose. The HIS/HERS demarcation line existed no longer. This is MY bed!

It was a good thought, a funny and important fact in the midst of a terrifying time.

I'd like to say that I immediately took charge of my mattress and my life as a newly single woman. But I had to remember that great ideas are not in themselves great solutions. For instance, if this was really MY bed, why did it take so long for my body to believe it? No matter how hard I tried to retrain myself, I woke up, like the good little wife, in my familiar place, even when I started out in the middle or on the other side. Habit died hard. So, too, did the conviction that I was still married.

Contemplating all this when I awoke one morning, I began to learn lesson #2: recovery from anything has its own time frame. Perhaps I would be wise to recognize and respect mine. A therapist by profession, I began to counsel myself: be patient, grief is an individual self-defining thing, like a fingerprint. I liked that thought. It was comforting, maybe even wise. Surely I had the right to the "fingerprint." I began to say without apology, my healing will take as long as it takes.

Not everyone shared that attitude.

Some people decided I should be getting on with my life— regrooving myself — after only a few weeks. Others noticed that I wasn't as focused a listener as I had been. I was raw, sometimes in shreds, often distracted; they were not used to my putting such demands on a friendship. The query of one acquaintance got back to me: "How can this thing be so hard for a counsellor? Shouldn't she be an expert in handling changes?"

Lesson #3: suffering is no respecter of persons. It discovers the vulnerable spots in us all, no matter what our experience, profession, or expertise. And it knocks askew most of our certainties, for a while at least. No "should" can change that fact. A universal part of the grief process seems to be the emotional undertow that follows the shock of grief. It pulled me this way and that. Which feelings could I trust? At three a.m. I would be suddenly and completely awake, my consciousness hooked to some heavy anchor in my stomach. How black and turbulent the sea was then! If I managed any sleep after that, I opened my eyes to the hopeful possibilities of a new day, only to sink again under the dawning recollection of where and how I really was. By two in the afternoon, I'd had enough of the day. I, for whom 24 hours had never been enough! If I could share the evening meal with someone, life felt normal for a while. If I could not, then dinner hour was the hardest time of all. What was the use of eating a solitary meal? Once, I even set an extra place at the table for my husband before I realized what I was doing. I permitted little or no joy and forgot how to laugh at myself. The burst of optimism that followed my inner pep talks became the reaction I distrusted most. Such distortions extended to the familiar world around me. Streets I'd known all my life appeared strange. The city itself (my city) felt hostile. All territory, inner and outer, became shaky underfoot. I'm losing my grip, I thought. Will the person who knows what this craziness is all about please stand up?

An answer came from a woman friend who shared her own version of an experience I had thought was only mine:

"I remember morning after morning when, in the brief

moment between sleep and total consciousness, I would be aware of a great lump of fear in my belly before being awake enough to remember what it was all about. I remember the clownish way the world around me feigned normalcy, and how I participated, robot-like, in the illusion. The reality was I had days when my anxiety level was so high I felt I was going to spin right off the edge, and other days when depression hovered like a black bird around the periphery of my vision. There were moments when I felt clear and competent, and days when I would make three return trips home before getting to work in the morning, because I kept forgetting things. I moved between unpredictable outbursts of fierce anger and rare surges of reckless euphoria. However different your experience is from mine, I know you are hurting, and I am truly sorry."[2]

Here was a friend, a sister in sorrow. What relief came with tears as I read that letter! Marilyn was joined by others who knew about suffering, and were walking the walk with me. I began to value particularly the tough, caring women who taught me to look at the world as it now was, and to deal with it. One small group of friends bought me an attractive nightgown and sent it with a note that said, "Wear this for you."

Putting one foot in front of the other, I measured off the weeks and months, as if by doing the same thing every day in much the same way, I might restore order and sanity to my topsy-turvy world. Like so many people in my position, I hoped, wildly, that this was all a nightmare. Or, if I must call it reality, that at least I could find the key somewhere to put the wrong things right. As a female, of course, I had to be at fault: Woman with the Fatal Flaw. I have since decided that it was far too easy for me to assume all the guilt on the basis of my sex. Letting go of that assumption has been, in itself, a valuable lesson.

Still, I needed to explore what had gone wrong. What personal responsibilities must I realistically face, past, present and future? Finally, the futile scream in my head became a phone call to a professional.

It was validating to me and my vocation to claim an hour regularly with a skilled therapist who knew how to listen. I loved the luxury of being heard. And as someone "in the business," I was determined not to defer or to apologize. I let my needs and wants be known, moment by moment, (which was the only way I knew them myself). I suspect I was arrogant at times, but before long, I also realized how confused I felt. Once I'd said my pain out loud, I didn't know what else, if anything, to do with it.

"How old," my therapist asked, "do you feel right now?"

Shocked silence. "Ten," I whispered. "Almost."

My therapist and I began to work. I heard things I had said to others. I heard new, exciting and frightening things. I experienced healing silences. And I felt accepted by this man as a person in my own right. He said, "I believe you're the expert who has most of the pieces to this jigsaw puzzle. I will have some to add. Together, we'll make a picture."

And make a picture we did. The almost-ten-year-old was having trouble growing up enough to accept the failure of a marriage. Gradually, it became possible to see that the failure was not hers alone and that it did not need to contaminate the entire relationship. Somewhere down the road was the need to forgive herself and the man she had loved and lost. Nevertheless, at the time, she mainly felt a sense of failure. And she was not used to getting F's. In fact, for a long time, the fear of an "F" on life's report card had kept her little, and sometimes on the verge of shame. Now the fear began to transform itself into anger which, at last, she could safely express out loud.

She had to admit that pitching ice cubes was better therapy than climbing into the deep freeze! That would be worth reflection, after she caught her breath. Certainly, she was learning some unusual and satisfying ways of discharging her anger. Pitching ice cubes harmlessly into the sink was only one of them. She also improved her cardiovascular system by using a skipping rope exercise to jump up and down (in fantasy) on whatever, or whomever, was currently messing up her mind! In the privacy of her home, she filled the air with the positive resolve her anger fueled: "Me? A tragic heroine? Forget it!" This was different from the bleats and whispers that had formed the substance of previous self-talk. This time, she was beginning to believe and be strengthened by what she was saying— beginning, perhaps, to grow up.

The question was, would she "get there" in time? Still insisting on not rushing the recovery process, she found it difficult to attend to the practicalities, called survival skills, that were demanding her immediate attention. She could not, like Alice in Wonderland, find a potion marked "Drink Me" that would make her a Big Girl in a hurry. Neither did she dare to wallow in the helplessness that kept her too little to function. If only she could find a "fast-forward" button to move her quickly into the mainstream of independent daily living! Of course, she would need a "pause" button, some slow time, to recover emotionally. But at 50, the future presses in as "Time Left."

So if there is no magic, I reflected, and I don't know what to do next, I can act as if I do. Was this called faking it or simply acting in faith that more clues would follow? As far as I was concerned, this was a lesson in faith. I started by talking to the ten-year-old who still wanted to hide under the covers. I knew by now that she needed a firm hand, but she also needed the assurance that she could allow herself to grow up and survive alone.

It took all the faith I had.

As a woman who had not been employed full-time in the community since the birth of my children, I had to educate myself to comb the job market. At the same time, I was dealing with divorce proceedings, paying household bills, and trying to resuscitate an old car with which I felt a remarkable kinship. When I was finally fortunate enough to get work, I discovered it was backing me into corners in the sense that I seemed to have time for nothing else. Necessity can be a cruel taskmaster, but I had committed myself; I would not be a tragic heroine. So, who was I turning out to be instead? One day, I would feel like Alice in the weird world of Lewis Carroll.[3] The next, I would be "Spiderwoman" or someone else in the "super" pack, overcoming adversity without even breaking into a sweat.

I learned some more lessons: found out what was under the hood of a car; took a woodworking course and observed more closely the mechanical workings of the everyday world; did a little choral singing in the nooks and crannies of my unstructured time, and even practised dancing. None of this brought my ex-husband back or kept me from grieving my losses. I had to acknowledge at last that I was no longer a married woman. I had to ask my friends to be ruthless with me if they saw me turning into what I called a "hard old broad." And I had to begin practising the most difficult task of all — forgiveness — without the folly of forgetfulness.

When I reviewed my life at day's end, from the middle of my mattress, I had to admit that something was shifting in my body, mind and spirit. I had not found the "fast-forward" button. I had not found anyone under my bed to sweep me off my feet and away from reality. And I was not yet all grown up. (Does anyone ever want to be all grown up?) But I was in the process of becoming someone who could face impossible nightmares and continue to dream impossible dreams. Once in a while, a dream actually came true, which gave me the courage to pursue another one.

Friends and family, including my grown-up children, supported me with unconditional love, and now I could see them go home without being afraid of being alone. I continued to validate the fingerprint of my own recovery process, without claiming any monopoly on grief; there was plenty of company on this road. Recognizing the presence and validating the needs of others, and being able to reach beyond the boundaries of self-preoccupation, were authentic signposts of recovery. These signs came slowly, but they did come.

Gradually it dawned on me that, as a human being, I would always have moments of failure. I would also have moments of triumph, and the right to my joy and anger. Above all, I had the faith to choose life, again and again. I was able to write with some of my old curiosity and with acceptance of past, present and future:

> With those who help me spin my dreams
> I move
> embraced
> released
> to meet the music
> form the rhythms
> match the tempo of my life.
> And when I find myself alone
> the bittersweet of longings and new hopes
> (from somewhere deep inside)
> will keep me dancing still.

How close am I to finally coming of age? Having lived so long on the growing edge, I know that I'm well past ten!

ms.

Carol Rose

i've learned to live without you   to love
myself again   i toughen my heart   rock
myself awake   i've learned to separate your life
from mine   no yellow traces streak my egg-
white foam of womandreams   i move about
unscrambled   often in moonlight   shadows
of you shock my eyes   insanely open as you rise
from memory   i've learned that love dissolves in pillows
& only rage lifts my head from the bed I made & lie
in still   warmed by a blanket's arm

Yellow Roses

Helen Levine

I have much to say and write after our vacation in Georgia, my cataract surgery and the uncharacteristically quiet days after the operation. I woke up this morning with freefall ideas scurrying around in my head, something like the wildly multiplying brooms in Disney's *Fantasia*. Themes kept popping up, banging into each other and sprouting in all directions. "Could you calm down a bit," I wanted to tell them, as if they were hyperactive children who were out of control.

From the chaos in my head came this tale of yellow roses and the strange and unexpected connections that sometimes light up a life. The other day, at a neighbourhood florist's shop, I bought myself two yellow roses. I lovingly arranged them in my mother's ancient cut-glass vase and set them in front of the big living room window, where they could constantly catch my eye. I glowed together with the roses, and pondered why this was the first time I had bought such a wonderful gift for myself.

I am no stranger to periodic waves of self-indulgence. Not for me, any longer, the pedestal of sacrificial wife and mother. It was from my own gutsy mother that I learned the meaning of being "lady for a day," signifying that life for women should hold much more than drudgery, subordination and self-sacrifice. She taught me lessons of entitlement well; lessons that helped me survive a woman's existence in a male-dominated world.

I treated myself to two yellow roses because I'd been hurt and disappointed when no one in my family thought to bring me flowers after the cataract surgery. It has been no secret, over the years, that for me an important form of tender, loving care, especially associated with illness, has to do with plants or bouquets. How could they, I asked myself, rhetorically and resentfully, be so unaware of ME?

On the other side of the disappointment lay the wisdom of my 70 years, the reminder that we all give and take in different ways for different reasons, that no one is aware all of the time, and each of us has credit in the "bank" of caring that can often cover missed opportunities. I have to remember this painfully acquired wisdom around my infrequent illnesses because it is then that my intense reactions, so clearly rooted in childhood experience, turn raw and threatening.

In the midst of all the ambivalence, I also began beaming inwardly at my own brazenness. Imagine having the nerve to buy roses for myself, roses that I had hoped might come from others. Imagine feeling like a minor heroine for breaking all the unwritten rules about modesty and social niceties and "waiting to be given to."

That same evening, a box of flowers arrived at the house for me. I hesitated, checking the greeting card. I worried that the gift might be a guilt-ridden, post-facto, unenthusiastic offering from Gil or the kids. No joy for me in that.

Not so. The flowers turned out to be from Eva, my oldest friend, the friend who, on special occasions, wires me beautiful spring bouquets, even in the depths of winter. But this time, she had sent twelve glowing yellow roses, twelve glistening yellow roses that reached down into my heart in tender, special ways.

It felt like some kind of magic. Two old friends, still in sync. Strange that we both communed with yellow roses on the very same day. I felt "known" in that very special realm where women understand each other. Because of our shared history, she had tuned into my childhood connection between illness, nurturing and the meaning of flowers. And she had succeeded in lighting up my space, my spirit, my soul.

Now, more than a week later, the yellow buds have opened wide and begun to droop. I've watched them blossom and bloom, seen the minute, kaleidoscopic changes as the petals curl and curve and begin to grow discoloured at the edges. Some endure more sturdily than others, but they are all beginning to wilt, to lose their close-to-perfect beauty.

I watch my flowers begin to decay, as intensely as I watched them in their pristine beauty. They give me joy at both extremes of their existence as they spiral into changing shapes and states.

These yellow roses, the two in my mother's vase and the twelve in my Danish vase, will linger long in my memory. They will continue to remind me of moments that create the truly important riches in our lives.

Revisiting a Very Old Friendship

Helen Levine and Eva Kenyon

My friend and I know well the ups and downs and crises of one another's lives. How lovely when, with age, the pretenses slip away, the complexity of life is acknowledged, and we are so much more ourselves, warts and all. We would still prefer to have the world's approval and love but not (any longer) at the price of who we are and what really matters to us.[1]

We two old friends have decided to look back at the evolution of our relationship. The experience has created an amazing moment in our lives. We tell our story — or parts thereof — because we have some sense of the taboo and the silences that still surround the telling of women's real-life experiences. And partly, because finding, developing and keeping friendships has a great deal to do with the challenge of women and aging.

One area we have not written about is the mother-adult daughter connection, even though motherhood has been one of the most profound experiences of our lives. It was simply too large a topic to tackle. Yet mothering and grandmothering can be complex arenas for older women. We each have two daughters and two grandchildren. We cherish the connections and caring among us. But we also know our children have to work at their own lives in the same way we have had to work at ours. We are not interested in repeat mothering or regular caregiving with the next generation. We just want to enjoy and to be enjoyed.

We met at the School of Social Work at the University of Toronto in 1945. We have been friends for 46 years now, sometimes very close, sometimes far apart, but always drawn together in important ways.

We were in our early 20s when we met, full of vague, romantic ideals and passionate temperaments. A war refugee from Poland and a middle-class Canadian Jew, we meshed in our mutual need for personal closeness and social significance.

In 1945, the horrors of World War II and the Holocaust had created in young adults like ourselves a hunger to help make the world a better place. The idea of contributing to building a just and peaceful social order was in our bones. Though our ideals and priorities have changed over the years, the notion of social responsibility, in one form or another, was to become a driving force throughout our adult lives.

As we think now about women and aging via our own aging experience, we find much common ground and some strong differences between us. We have never lost the need and the drive to be actively involved in, rather than observers of, social issues. But we have taken profoundly different directions. At times there has been prickly tension and conflict between us. In the process, we have had to learn much more than we ever wanted to about living with each other's difference.

We want to highlight some elements that characterize this ancient bond between old friends. We want to explore some of the similarities and differences as they play out now in our lives.

Work

We both officially retired at age 64, Helen from the faculty at the Carleton University School of Social Work, Eva as director of the Family Therapy Training Centre at Oolagen (a children's mental health centre). Despite "retirement," work remains an important force in our lives.

So how or where do we two old friends, a feminist activist and a very professional social worker and family therapist, coincide around work? Rather than seeing retirement as a golden opportunity to dump work and take to our gardens and grandchildren, we both have maintained a vigorous interest in continuing to be seriously involved. Eva uses her administrative and program talents in doing contract work at senior levels. Helen continues to be actively involved in many ways in the women's movement.

Eva was the one who always knew work would be a central part of her life. She sought power, influence and recognition in her beloved field of social work. It was her energy, drive and determination that helped make it possible for her to actively pursue career and family without the classic guilt and turmoil of North American women. No disabling fear of maternal deprivation here, as she returned to work part-time soon after each of her daughters were born.

Helen, by contrast, was smitten with the myth and romance of motherhood. Paid work took second place for many years. She was ambitious about motherhood. She worked outside the home only at jobs she enjoyed, always part-time. It meant stops and starts, much fragmentation and many doubts about finding a niche in social work.

As a feminist, she has completely redefined women's work. She now thinks, speaks, and writes about the paid and unpaid work of women, about motherwork and women working at home. Convinced the personal is political, she and her husband have made drastic changes in the division of labour and responsibility in their home.

What is sometimes difficult for older women to live with is the loss of whatever power and influence we have had in our work.

Eva continues to struggle with making peace about no longer being in the forefront of Toronto family therapy circles, and having to accept young upstarts whom she trained years ago becoming the teachers and trainers of family therapy. She feels that she has gradually lost much of her influence in the social work profession. In her old age, she has developed into more of a maverick who thinks to herself "No one is going to tell me who I am or should be." For Eva, the loss of power and influence has been traumatic. Despite this, work remains central to her existence. As a freelancer, she thrives on challenging projects in social agencies and enjoys her private practice which includes supervision and training in the field of family therapy.

Helen's transition into retirement was, for a few months, painful and disorienting. However, since then, she has thoroughly enjoyed working in different ways at a different pace, without organizational restrictions and responsibilities. She continues her active involvement in feminist counselling, groups, workshops, etc.

It is important to note that, despite our very differing approaches, we have enormous respect for one another's ability. We love discussing our work together. It gives us both a heightened sense of mutual appreciation. Helen has always had a passion for ideas that is contagious. Eva credits much of her own creativity at work to her old friend's stimulation and a readiness to share thoughts and ideas.

In fact, work has become the hub around which we most appreciatively connect with one another, intellectually and emotionally. This despite knowing that some topics (like men and feminism) can only be tackled when we are very well rested and consciously prepared to listen respectfully. Then, we learn a lot from one another.

Health
Regarding health, fitness and sport, Eva and Helen inhabit different planets.

Eva feels eternally grateful to her medical doctors for saving her life in 1983 when she had cardiac arrest following a massive coronary. The cardiac rehabilitation program in which she participated enabled her body to work again. And she believes that the continuing care she gets from her doctors makes it possible for her to lead a full life. Eva feels truly nurtured by her doctors, who are mostly men.

Helen distrusts the medical profession and hospitals and searches out alternative approaches to health care. She is currently postponing surgery for cataracts, despite dimming eyesight. Whenever possible, she sees women practitioners. She is grateful to the women's movement for its critique of how conventional health care has damaged and ignored women.

We know that we can no longer take our bodies for granted as we once did. We both casually tell our age and feel comfortable about our bodies (so long as they stay in one piece). In fact, we tend to boast about being in our late 60s and still finding life interesting and challenging. Helen has a sense of achievement about lasting this long. Eva would love to live her life over again.

Our attitudes towards illness differ. Caregiving around illness comes easily to Helen in relation to people she loves. Eva felt she was an angel of mercy when Helen visited her in hospital in the early days following her heart attack. Eva, on the other hand, dislikes physical illness, and too many demands from loved ones when they are sick make her angry. However, Eva is remarkably in tune with emotional problems and has been there for Helen when her world threatened to fall apart.

The danger of being marginalized as older women haunts us both. For example, should we be confined to our homes or in institutions somewhere down the road, we anticipate big trouble. Strong-willed as we are, we could easily be labeled as problems in need of behaviour modification, or "psycho-geriatric" messes of one kind or another.

Helen loves sports. Eva dislikes all physical activities and very reluctantly follows a prescribed exercise regime. Helen is terrified of losing her beloved sports as she ages and of becoming trapped in her body and in her house. Eva's terror has to do with having another heart attack and dropping dead and she sees her exercise regime as the only way to prevent this.

We envy each other in different ways. Eva wishes she could be tuned into her body like Helen. Helen wishes she had Eva's unflagging energy.

We know that what we eat is very much related to women's health and aging.

If you, dear reader, were a fly on the wall when Eva and Helen are together, the conversation might unfold like this:

Eva (with intensity): I'm getting worried. We haven't decided where we're going to eat and we might not be able to get a reservation and what will be do if we can't get in?
Helen (sarcastically): Oh, God, Eva, for sure we're going to starve to death.
Eva (with intensity): Can I help it that you can't be bothered with meals? I've been dreaming about what I'm going to eat ever since I woke up this morning.

And the truth is, Eva does come to consciousness every morning with food and plans for meals at the fore. She loves to eat and she loves to cook. When planning a visit to Helen in Ottawa, she periodically erupts in a state of panic, convinced that she is in danger of being starved and deprived at the Levines. Eva is hungry in the morning, all day long and late into the night.

In an earlier life, Helen managed 25 years of plain cooking, displayed no talent and less interest. She resented the time and energy involved in food preparation and how quickly her hard work disappeared at meals. She disliked being expected to serve and service anyone other than young children. Years later, she abdicated from cooking and grocery shopping and turned into a near-vegetarian.

From time to time, Eva condescends to eat at a vegetarian restaurant with Helen. This, to her, is being magnanimous in the extreme because she loves meat, potatoes, Polish sausage and Diet Pepsi. Eva's relationship with food is linked to wartime hunger in Poland, when her family survived on cabbage and potatoes. She swore then that she would never again trivialize the importance of food.

Our current food restrictions are related only to health. Neither of us pays much attention to the question of beauty and youth prescribed for women by North American culture. We have neither wished nor bothered to submit to societal dictates about trying to stay young and beautiful.

Fun and Freedom

We both glory in an increased sense of freedom and choice as we get older. In contrast to many older women who live at or below the poverty line, we feel lucky to have the money and the health to enjoy our freedom. It was only in the later years of our friendship, as we left behind the personal and social constraints of family life, that we learned how to play again.

For example, we make our annual trek to the Shaw Festival where we live it up in a good hotel and enjoy not sitting in the gods (is that the term still used for cheap theater seats?). When not attending performances, Eva indulges her passion for shopping, Helen often lies around reading. We relax easily as we sink into an old-shoe comfortableness with one another.

We are considered hotel freaks or senior delinquents when we often decide to stay in a hotel overnight in Ottawa or Toronto, instead of visiting together in our perfectly respectable homes.

There is a kind of mischievous quality to what our friends sometimes consider ridiculous or immature behaviour. We delight in it, partly because of the stark contrast with our younger years when we lived on very meagre incomes, and took everything and everybody so seriously. The memory of our rooming house in 1946, with one bathroom for 15 people, and dishes from hot-plate meals washed in the bathtub, heightens the joy of our current indulgences. We love our sometimes childlike enthusiasms, the rich kooky moments we share together.

Neither of us feels guilty about indulging ourselves in our old age. Neither has any sense of obligation about saving money to leave to our children and grandchildren. We prefer to leave them our ideas and our ideals.

Some of our indulgences differ. Eva has a passion for travel which overtakes any sensibility about money and security. She is terrified that she is not going to see the whole world before she dies. One of her deep regrets is Helen's lack of interest in seeing and exploring new territories. Helen leaves her old friend behind when she indulges in singing, dancing, tennis and biking. There is a zany, kooky side to Helen which Eva does not share. Helen laughs more, especially with her daughters. Eva weeps more, from both happiness and sorrow.

We delight in being two feisty old women who have preserved a sense of fun and entitlement.

Troubles And Turning Points

This is a crucial part of our friendship. We turn to one another in the crunch, during major or minor upheavals. We have seen the best and the worst, the strengths and the weaknesses, the fears and the anxieties that have been part and parcel of our lives. We know a great deal about each other, including one another's parents and siblings. There is a great comfort in being known so well for so long. It establishes an historical context for us whenever trouble threatens.

Our friendship has not been all smooth sailing. There have been crises between us, feelings of betrayal and rejection. But we are able to hang in with one another and put words to whatever has gone wrong between us. Some of our closest moments together are spawned by taking hold, openly and directly, of painful differences.

Eva lost her husband five years ago. Helen's is alive and well. We have both lost dear friends. In the midst of sadness, we cling to our belief in life as a process of change, in new directions springing from the very losses we mourn. We both appreciate the importance of learning to live comfortably with contradictory thoughts and feelings, with ambivalence. Thus, even while mourning her husband's death, Eva could, from time to time, feel an incipient sense of freedom and imagine the possibility of a new life in the future. To have an old friend who understood and validated how she truly felt helped Eva through this most traumatic loss in her life. It was Helen — who had not experienced widowhood — who related to the very human mix of grief and possibility.

Helen well remembers lying in bed depressed and lost, a few months after retirement. Her world seemed to have turned upside down, the threat of another breakdown too close for comfort. Eva came to spend the weekend. One afternoon, she was sitting quietly at the side of Helen's bed, after she had puttered around the house and made lunch. The conversation went something like this:

Helen: Oh, Eva, what am I going to do? It's all such a mess again. I'm finished, I can't carry on. I just don't want to move out of this bed.
Eva: I know. It's awful. (She well knew the importance of validating misery, not opposing it. Most people would do the opposite.)
Helen: God, there really is nothing more. I can't even try an overdose. I tried it years ago and was a failure even in that department.

Eva: Helen, you can't end it all because you have to give the eulogy when I die from my second heart attack.

Helen: You have no right to die first. I can't bear the thought of losing my oldest friend. (Here, at 65, we compete again, as we used to in our younger days.)

We look at each other. The house is deadly silent. Suddenly and unexpectedly, we both burst out laughing, grasping the black humour of it all. The laughter builds, tears and smiles emerge, tension eases. This episode proved to be a critical and positive turning point for Helen.

Thoughts and feelings have never been censored for long in our friendship. Part of the bond between us has to do with sharing the crazy mix of outrageous thoughts and feelings that are deemed to be socially unacceptable. We insist upon claiming them, out loud.

Helen's postscript — I don't quite have the words to express my feelings about Eva at moments like this. She inhabits a special place in my world. She knows the very essence of my struggle. She, who is so goddamned opinionated and full of bluster, makes no judgements; she, in the midst of crisis and danger, stays in touch with strength and potential; she connects, fearlessly, when disaster threatens.

When I was a child, my mother took me to a children's comedy, a movie called *When a Feller Needs a Friend*. I sobbed noisily throughout the whole film, likely starved for a very close friendship way back then. Eva represents the very essence of what friendship meant and continues to mean to me, as child, as adult and as aging woman.

On Men

In 1946, we were both involved with our future husbands and we competed as to who had the more meaningful relationship. Even in those days, we differed in our expectations. Helen was much more demanding of men, Eva always gave men the benefit of the doubt. That thread has played itself out over the years.

We see women and men in totally opposite ways. We have agreed, as we write, to say it this way. Helen sees Eva as quick to defend men and critical of women; Eva sees Helen as quick to defend women and critical of men. In a sense, we play a double standard from opposite directions.

From the beginning, Eva remained constant in her belief that a career was just as important as marriage and family. She was able to comfortably combine social work with being a wife and mother. Helen's original driving force was to marry, have children and live happily ever after (classic!). Real-life experience and feminism turned these aspirations upside down over time, resulting in profound personal and political changes. For Helen, feminism now inhabits the core of her life, her work, and her world view. As all this has changed, so too have her views of men.

Helen continues to live with her husband of 43 years. One of her big fears in this relationship is the danger of wasting precious time and energy in the years left to her on the sometimes bizarre trivia of a shared daily existence. One of the strengths with her husband, over time, has been their dogged ability to work hard at changing whatever threatened to become unworkable between them.

Eva lost her husband of 39 years. Eva would like to find another man with whom she could share the rest of her life. For her, women friends do not replace the need for male companionship nor satisfy her yearning for intimacy and sex. Apart from difficulty in meeting single older men, her profound need to be in charge of her own life and not to depend on any man for survival makes her an unlikely candidate for remarriage. Helen cannot imagine looking for or wanting another man in her life, either via divorce or death. She thinks she would work hardest, in relation to aloneness or loneliness, at developing a wider circle of friendships among women.

These differences sometimes play havoc with the friendship. It is interesting to note that we worked on all other topics in this article with warmth and closeness. Not so about men. It became loaded with hurt, anger and tears. At one point we had to question whether it was worth the struggle and the time.

There was a telling moment that occurred in the midst of a working weekend together that vividly illustrates the gulf between us. Helen handed Eva a recently published article of hers to read which was, in large part, about men. She cautioned Eva to tread carefully and respectfully.

Here is what transpired:

Eva: It's beautifully written, but I have to tell you that it's all totally alien to me and I can't identify with any of it.
(Helen pauses for a moment and bursts into tears.)
Eva: What's the matter?
Helen: I didn't expect you to agree with me. But you know

damn well how close to the bone my writing is for me. My God, why do you think it takes me so long to let you read my stuff? Why couldn't you, for once, just appreciate my work in *my* context instead of leaping to where you're at?

Eva: I didn't want to hurt you. You're right that I leap without thinking. I have to control it more.

Helen: It's not just control. It has to do with respecting difference. Remember when you showed me your paper on families and incest? I appreciated what you had done out of your frame of reference. Afterwards we discussed our very basic differences.

Eva: Well, I guess I've been very angry that you've changed so much in your ideas about men. I've changed very little, and what worries me is that any important difference between us creates intolerable walls. So I attack and try to smash those walls.

We ended this painful exchange as we have others in the past, with a hug and an unspoken recognition of conflict and wounding as part of friendship and life.

We both think it obvious that our friendship demands Eva's identification, not with Helen's view of men, but with what feminism and her way of being in the world means to her. Helen has been more comfortable with difference. Ironically, it is the women's movement that taught her how women are in different places for very different reasons, at any given time in their lives. Helen accepts Eva as a person and simply assumes they have disagreements. It is important to note that Helen and the women's movement have to some extent influenced Eva's thinking about men, mainly in relation to power and violence against women.

Conclusion

In the midst of dictating our material, Eva suddenly came downstairs weeping.

Eva: I can't stop crying, every second sentence makes me weep.

(The pages are blotched with her tears.)

Helen: Good Heavens, Eva, which part is getting to you like this?

Eva: (with tears flowing copiously) It's, it's the introduction! (At which point we both burst out laughing at the marvellous madness of this enterprise.)

Here is yet another illustration of the connectedness between two old friends. As we grow older, we become more and more fascinated by the infinite complexities of human behaviour, our own and everyone else's. Like kids, with a kaleidoscope.

Recently, we both realized we were losing that animated capacity we once had to explore and to discuss all kinds of experiences and issues. So, characteristically, we decided to do something about this. Writing the article together represents one aspect of our attempt to recapture and renew that capacity.

This story is about our togetherness and our separateness; about similarities and about differences; about love and about anger; about the vicissitudes of life which shape our thoughts and ideas in our old age; and above all, it is about the process of our friendship. Clear to both of us is the knowledge that in friendship there is no end to searching, exploring, growing and changing. For older women, there can be rich new beginnings.

One of the distinct pleasures of this joint writing project has been the experience of revisiting our history and our friendship. Instead of completing the work as we wrote and talked and remembered, we discovered new nooks and crannies that we wanted desperately to explore further. And the most amazing discovery was that as our story unfolded, even at age 68, we learned new things about one another and about life in general.

"Imagine," we said, looking at one another in stunned appreciation.

Postscript — Eva Kenyon died on August 27th, 1994.

this is the way you visit your mother

Mary Toombs

you put your hands beneath her arms
and pull her into a sitting position
so her muscle-slack abdomen shifts
for a while to the other side

you check her cupboard for supplies
and see she needs denture cream
and face cream   and you must remember
the cream for today's tea

and this is the way you clean those dentures
you brush them and scrub them with fury
then hold the basin close to her mouth
so the rinse water dribbles out safely
and you slide the dentures into their place
and wipe her mouth gently

and this is the way you style her hair
you wet it a little and brush it up
so it falls into the softness
of last summer before the stroke
and you flip up the ends as she observes
herself in the mirror and approves
your efforts with a smile
from the newly cleaned dentures

and this is the way you darken the brows
and colour the lips and blush the cheeks
and hold your hand by the hearing aid
to spray cologne behind each ear

and this is the way you do her nails
push back the cuticle on her dead hand
and you paint the nails
with the clear polish she loves

and blow them dry with your own breath
now you smooth down the front of her dress
and fasten the pearls at the back of her neck
just over that tender roll of flesh

and this is the way you check the level
in the plastic bag which drains her fluids
hiding it under the rug on her lap

then you release the brakes on her chair
and push her out smoothly into her world
of wheelchairs and dressed-up infirmities

and you see her smile
see her blue blue eyes gleaming as she greets
those around her with pleasure

this is the way you visit your mother

My Mother

Beatrice Archer Watson

Dear Zizi,

The other night I thought of my mother. I find I think about her more each day. She is quite a woman. I believe she is the first feminist I ever knew. She has endured a lot.

When Mom visited me five summers ago I wanted her to stay as long as possible. There was so much I wanted to ask her about her life and her personal struggles. These things did not matter to me before, but realizing how women were silenced in the past, I wanted to know my mother's experience. I wanted to hear her words, in her own voice. I wanted to analyze my mother's life from a feminist perspective and to understand my mother, not as a mother, but as a woman. I know my mother's life was hard, as were the lives of many other women in the village. I respect her stoicism, her independence, and I credit my own independence to her example.

But, you know, Zizi, there was a side to Mother that was hollow and unfulfilled. I don't know what it was. There seemed to be a bitter undertone to her life. All she did was look after us children and make sure that we were okay. I remember her drumming into our ears that we should get a good education before marrying, and earn our own money. Well, I'm the only one who listened. My other sisters got married very young and are leading miserable lives.

One day, my mother said to me, "You're the lucky one. You have a good husband, a good education and only two children."

"Why do you say that?" I asked.

"Your sisters are struggling back home, with all sorts of problems. Your oldest sister is married to a jailor. He tells her how to do everything. He gives her a few cents and expects it to move mountains, and he gets more cruel with age. Your other sister is divorced with six children. She's having a real hard time, but you...I watch you...you're the boss," Mother said, quite pleased.

"That's not true, Mom. There's no boss here. Both Dave and I are adults and we respect each other as such. I demand it. I won't have it any other way. The only thing I truly own is my life, and I will do with it as I please."

Mother shook her wise head and smiled approvingly.

"Things are a lot different now", Mother whispered.

"You had a good life, Mom, didn't you? I never saw Dad hit you and you rarely quarreled. You went where you wanted, when you wanted. I never heard Dad stop you ever."

"You're right, he never hit me, but I never wish any of you my luck. No matter what I did, how hard I worked, your father was the one who got the respect. He was the man of the house and I was the woman. I washed, I cooked, I farmed, I sold the goods and brought the food in. I sent you children to school. I did everything because I thought I had to. When other women stayed at home during rain storms, I went to the market because I felt I had to. I was the man and the woman and yet, when any important matter had to be decided, everyone looked to him to make the decision. I was only a woman."

"That's what the feminists are trying to change. I think you are an old feminist, Mom. And it is because of you that I am what I am today."

"I have a lot of anger inside for the things your dad did to me. He never beat me, but he might as well have; the lying, the cheating, the drinking. He never had any money to give me but he had it to give to other women."

"You could have still left him, if you wanted."

"Yes, but where would I go with four children? Nobody was going to take us in. We had a house that your grandfather gave us. It was our property. I couldn't do better than that. You kids would have been punished too much if I'd have moved out."

"Yeah," I said. I understood what she meant, Zizi. It's the problem facing many women today. They're trapped in the marriage/family spiral, from which it is difficult to unwind. Let me share a stream of consciousness poem I wrote. Maybe you can tell me what it means, my philosophical friend.

something ails me
i don't know what
it doesn't feel good
doesn't feel right
i feel poor
yet I'm richer than
i ever was
materially

i don't fetch water
or walk for miles
the bus is there
i make good money
live in a better house
i have it made
or so it seems

what's wrong with me?
why do i feel so...so
i don't know
my soul is gone
my voice is weak
my struggle is complex

i face life
as never before
in ways i've never wanted to
i've grown up quickly
the pieces of the puzzle
are in front of me
i see the whole clearly
a beast of burden
being whipped, kicked,
degraded

a scary picture
i feel smaller, poorer
being minority, ethnic, immigrant,
visible "special" woman
i shrink with each label

my shell is gone
i don't feel very well
and the doctors…
they can't tell
don't have a name for my problem
don't seem to know
what's wrong.

And that, Zi, sums up my feelings tonight. Don't worry. I'll rise again,
for sure, tomorrow.
With much love and friendship,

Beatrice

Sister

Jean Crane

small circle sister
big circle dance
you allowed me
to weep smile sing shout float
soar dream dance
and i allowed you
the Spirit sings

"We Are Stones in the Same River" by Sophia Rosenberg

the telling is my daughter's

Keith Louise Fulton

the bedtime story my daughter told me
last night began, "Once upon
a time there was
a woman named
Keith and
she had
a lover named
Sally
and one night"

(I had stopped right
there — but not my daughter
not even a pause)

       "tap, tap, tap
on the window, just as they
were going to sleep"

                  Skunkel Bunkel

visits at night
looking for friends — the story she tells
was one I'd invented
years ago: children and creatures
slip into the dark together
then back under the covers just
before morning

but this story my daughter tells me
for my own sleeping opens
as my child self had never imagined
and certainly was never told:

once upon a time there were two women
and they were lovers

this way of beginning
I had to find myself
to live — the telling
is my daughter's

Chapter Six

Telling Our Stories

Old Wives' Tales

Raye Anderson

Once upon a time, a queen sat by a window. She was very beautiful, but often alone. She pricked her finger on her needle and a drop of blood fell from her finger onto the snow outside. "I wish," sighed the queen, "that I might have a child, a girl with skin as white as snow, with cheeks as red as blood and hair as black as this ebony window frame."

Her wish was granted and in due course, she was delivered of a daughter. She named her "Snow White."

This same queen possessed a magic mirror. When the king, her husband, was far from home, she would look in the mirror and say,

"Mirror, mirror on the wall,
Who is the fairest one of all?"
And the voice of the king, her husband, would reply,
"My queen, my queen, with golden hair,
In all the land you are most fair."

The queen was reassured and all was well. This continued for many years, 14 to be exact. Then one day, the queen went to her mirror...."

So begins one of the many versions of "Snow White" that the Brothers Grimm heard as they sat at the feet of women, some old, some not so old. Then old stories were passed on from mother to daughter to granddaughter, woman to woman, generation to generation. The queen in this story was not a stepmother but Snow White's real mother, a mother who had longed for a daughter, and whose daughter was her only child. When the queen began to suspect that the King was attracted to her child, what did she do? The story tells us. She sent Snow White off into the woods to be killed by a huntsman. Was it a coincidence that the huntsman she chose was too soft-hearted to do it? When she found out that the child was alive, she made three attempts to kill her. Three times she failed. She always left a margin of error, and because of that, Snow White survived. Nevertheless, when the queen was found out, she was sentenced to a terrible death by the same king who had spoken to her from the mirror.[1]

This is not a pretty story. It is not one you would call a fairy tale. Certainly it is not a child's story. This is an adult women's story. It tells of a woman caught in an almost insurmountable dilemma, using the little power she has to survive, and to help her daughter survive. It poses questions about how women live their lives when power is virtually removed from them. It also tells how strong and decisive women can be when tough action is needed. Did this queen believe that death for her child was better than the incest that the father's words implied? Was she trying to save her own life and her own position at the cost of her daughter? Was she simply jealous? How could she face the king, knowing what she knew? Did she know? Was the voice from the mirror really his, or was it the voice of her own fear? And in that case, was her fear justified?

Women would wonder, discuss and speculate as they sat around the fire on a northern winter's night listening to the sound of their knitting needles.

This changed story is not an isolated example. Many old versions of fairy tales are similar. There are stories of childbirth, sexuality and the fragile power that it brings, stories of lost children, dead babies, and the punishments inflicted on women who do not obey. It's Hansel and Gretel's real mother who loses them in the woods, because if they stay home, everyone will starve. Sleeping Beauty's prince already has a wife at home, who, when she finds out the truth, decides to serve him his new children in a stew as revenge. Infanticide often occurs as the ultimate, final weapon of the woman who has been betrayed.

These are not easy stories. They tell of dark secrets and they carry dire warnings. But they also tell of women who are resourceful, ingenious and humourous in the teeth of disaster. Many versions of "Cinderella," told around the world, are incest stories. They tell of a girl who retreats into the kitchen and makes herself grubby and unattractive to avoid marrying her own father. The girl also knows how to get a fur coat to keep herself warm, and makes excellent soup that will win the heart of a prince. She regains her birthright, on her own terms, and sometimes she forgives the father who betrayed her in the first place. She's a long way removed from the starry-eyed, helpless creature that Walt Disney made familiar.

Few of the women, who told stories as they baked and stirred and sewed and spun, could write. The versions we know were mainly written down by men. The Grimm Brothers traveled around listening to stories told by women and recording them in written form. What they chose to publish and how they edited them radically changed the stories. Gone were sexuality, childbirth, and women making life and death choices. Mothers became saints, dead saints preferably, and cruel deeds were done by stepmothers whose motives were certainly evil. Old women were called witches and were best avoided. Fathers, on the other hand, were kind-hearted, sensible and sometimes wise, although at times beguiled by some wicked sexy woman. Princes, of course, could be absolutely trusted to make everything right, forever.

The Grimms discovered a lucrative market for children's books, and adapted women's tales with this in mind. They stripped the stories of their subtlety and power. They made them sweet and good and delightful, with happy endings. They also pumped up the violence as a cautionary warning to any child who might have ideas about wandering off the prescribed social path.

What subtlety and power did the stories lose? The subtlety of women who imply, insinuate with a word, a smile, a caught breath, knowing that what is implied is understood because it is recognized. Women who know that these things can happen provide warnings to women everywhere. They tell what happens when women's power is limited to the parameters of the family, and also about the depth and effectiveness of that power. They also tell that whatever the circumstances, women still retain the power of resolution, of compassion, forgiveness and understanding. The stories are often rooted in fear, but they are driven by hope. The women in these stories prevail against overwhelming odds.

So why don't we know them? They weren't written in a form we could read and our generation tends to identify with the written word. These stories were told, and they are still told, in places where the storyteller's art is valued. These stories are often designated as folklore and, as such, they are dismissed as cute, amusing or irrelevant. Gossip. Tittle tattle. Old wives' tales.

They are much more than that. They are the cultural record of women's lives through the last two millennia, and beyond. We need to reclaim them and pass them on to our daughters, not as they know them now, but closer to their original telling. Just as male myths support the notion of heroic men, many of these stories tell of heroic women, who survived and took responsibility for their lives under adverse circumstances. They are stories of courage and strength, of endurance and intelligence, of ingenuity and faith. They are ours, as women, to teach, to warn and to console us; to reassure and amuse us, to inspire and to affirm our sense of our female selves. We need them back, as part of our cultural psyche. They tell us who we truly are.

pillar of salt

Carol Rose

you stand resplendent in the sun
an ancient shrine   relic from a cult
like your name   long forgotten
there's mystery in your womanform
cast in crystal or made of tears
when not even ten in His image
could be called worthy   & you were
left shimmering in the sand
witness to a time
when looking back was sacred[1]

The Tin Box

Joan Turner

Once long ago this little tin box contained tea from Holland. Its distinctive blue images have rubbed away, with the touch of women's fingers making tea. Or, at least, that's what I imagine. Yes. That's what I think.

"Think you're right? Don't get too big for your britches," I hear Aunt Ethel say sarcastically, her sharp eyes gleaming. Oh, she could lunge right through us with words sharp as swords. We children watched what we said and did around Aunt Ethel. Except, that is, when she bent over to open the oven door on the wood burning stove, and with one swift motion, brought exactly one dozen perfectly browned rolls into our view. "You make the best buns in all of Saskatchewan!" we'd exclaim with delight. She'd glow with pride. Her crisp exteriored buns were wonderful with fresh farm butter oozing off their soft, delectable interiors. We'd lick our lips and ask for more. The scent is in my nostrils now, the taste on my tongue. I pause, remembering. We experienced Aunt Ethel's love and creativity, in her own unique recipe, formed into buns.

Come to think of it, Aunt Ethel wore a different kind of bun at the nape of her neck. Every night, sitting in front of her bureau, watching herself in the mirror, she'd brush her long white hair one hundred strokes until it shone. Then, in the morning after brushing quickly, for there was work to be done, she'd twist and wrap strands of hair around her fingers very precisely, fastening her creation with long hair pins. She pulled her hair back from her pale, classic face until she became old and frail and they cut off her hair in the nursing home. With a straight face, determination, and sometimes even stubborness, she dealt with life. She lived one hundred years.

But it is Aunt Ethel's hands, not her hair or face, which intrigue me now. Her hands were slim, with long deft fingers. I remember them as they washed clothes by hand, tatted and embroidered, and sometimes quilted too. "A woman's work is never done," she'd say, often working into the night, mending and patching with tiny, precise stitches. Her mends and patches would last for years. Recently, at my mother's, I slept under one of her patchwork quilts, now very frail and worn, so frail it can't be saved, except in pieces and in stories.

I've inherited a tablecloth that she made and which was used less often and is on my table here today, and this tin box. Why did my mother pass the tin box, half-filled with balls of string, on to me, saying very clearly, "this is for you"?

I am puzzled about the significance of the blue tin box. When I brought it from Saskatchewan to Winnipeg, I placed it, not in a cupboard, but in our living room. Sometimes visitors have asked or commented about the box, but mostly it just sits, occasionally receiving a glance, or a dusting.

I rarely open it. When I do, it speaks to me of mystery and memories, and about being frugal, not wasting anything, not even a piece of string.

How old is this string? One hundred years? More? Less? Less is more. More is less. My thoughts twist around, like the string twists around its centre. I remember the agile, circular movement of Aunt Ethel's hands as she wound the string, saving every piece she found. Now I count ten balls of very old string in the blue tin box. Some balls are very little, some are larger.

"Ah, throw it all out," says the voice in my head that wants my home uncluttered. "That string has served its purpose. Throw it all out."

"I can't," I say softly. It's my heart speaking from my aging woman's body, the niece remembering her aunt. "I can't ." Or, is it, "I won't"? This string speaks to me of history, or herstory, in little balls of string saved because everything is precious. Nothing that was useful, or could be, gets thrown out.

"What do I have to do, old little balls of string?" I ask, not knowing what else to do.

"Unravel me, the family stories. You know Aunt Ethel was a storyteller. She remembered the tales of women who came before her and she told their stories vividly. Alas, she never wrote her stories down. You listened. So you be the keeper and the storyteller now. That is your inheritance and your responsibility. Spin and weave. Use words, not string." And this I do, feeling important, feeling foolish.

"Ssh, listen. Do you see her? Do you hear her?"

Aunt Ethel is beside me, looking at our box of string. Now I sense her high above us, on the ceiling. I anticipate the stinging words she might say to her imperfect niece. She bites her tongue, and smiles instead. Tossing back her head, her long white hair drops to her waist. "All's well," she says, and flies away.

The Label

Iris A. Robinson

By and large, women are starving organisms. I realize now that it was my incessant hunger that led me to be labelled. I was a grown woman, but my needs were ravenous. Searching for a nourishing breast, I discovered psychiatry. My intention here is to provide a female perspective on the subject of labelling, not to bash men or psychiatry.

In order to comprehend how I came to be labelled, I suggest we look at what it means to be a woman in a patriarchal world. As a woman, I have been and still am, socialized and defined as an object. Psychological literature describes women's nature as "expressive" and men's as "instrumental."[1] These adjectives define the expectations of normal behaviour. The demarcations are gender specific and any crossover is likely to be seen as deviant.

In psychiatry, women are reduced to component parts. The focus is on the individual, and cultural context is ignored. It is as though we are entities unto ourselves. We are judged and labelled by a system of male design. We are measured by male standards although we have been educated in the "expressive" female school of life. This is where the problem arises.

I am now a middle-aged woman. During my early development, I was taught, overtly and covertly, that power could be obtained vicariously through association with males. The message was "marry well" or to put it more bluntly, submit to the "marry him, save me" mentality. Women were seen as helpless, dependent sexual objects. Our worth was dependent on attracting the right mate. In the event that we "married poorly," it was we women who were considered flawed. It could be said that I "married poorly." I was not selected by a professional: therefore, I was a dandelion, not a rose. I married an ordinary man who worked every day, shared his income and did not beat me. By the standards of my world, he was not a "good catch." He was an unaccomplished male, and as such, he reflected my failure as a woman. My mother always said "marry a doctor." (She never said become a doctor.) There was no question in my mind, my husband had no power in the social world. Each time I looked at him, I was acutely aware that we were at the bottom of the social order. He was supposed to have advantage in this men's world. He was supposed to make a difference. I hated him with a passion for not being my saviour. If he had had social power, I suppose I might have been vicariously satisfied. I could have had a life filled with amenities. If only — if only he had provided.

Add to this equation the knowledge that my mother, my grandmother and all the great-grandmothers I know about, were abused by their spouses. Abuse of women originates in male power and domination. If you also suffer the misfortune, as I did, to be molested as a child, the legacy of the helpless female victim is magnified beyond measure. I grew up in a situation where children and women were objects. Their self-worth and dignity could be stripped bare. This was the rape of souls. The combined effect of all of these factors led me to seek the expertise of a male psychiatrist. As you can see, I was a perfect candidate for labelling.

I recall the day I questioned him about my diagnosis. I had read a book on Borderline Personality (B.P.D.) and I thought it described me in a lot of ways. I also thought it sounded like most North Americans. But being a good patient, I accepted the fact that I was ill and that my problems were in my head. My psychiatrist, playing the role of the "good" doctor, never discussed such things as diagnosis with me. Yes, we seemed to agree, I was a Borderline. Upon confirmation of the diagnosis, I began to vacillate. At one extreme, I felt rage, while on the other hand, I felt passive acceptance of this label. Eventually, I became exhilarated about my new identity. A sense of flattery ensued. For the first time I knew who I was. I was a Borderline. There was an outline for my pathology, a script, if you please, something which could provide me with an identity. I'd failed in all my other roles. This time I would not fail!

The most important benefit to being ill was that, at last, I could associate with a man who, I thought, possessed immense social power. There were "perks" to my patient identity: respect, intellectual stimulation and the "gift" of undivided attention for two hours a week. Being labelled crazy seemed a small sacrifice for so many advantages. This was my fantasy marriage. Each hour spent in the presence of my psychiatrist afforded me an illusory sense of power. The association felt like my sustenance. The label would guarantee me continuing care; however, only in illness was I assured of his attention. The sense of power that I experienced with him was better than no power at all. Although I knew it was a fantasy, fantasy seemed better than reality. I would have done almost anything to maintain this alliance.

The quest for illusory power is a sad testimony. There is no empowerment in being labelled. In fact, it is the antithesis of power. The acceptance of labels represents the acceptance of domination. It is pathological to allow someone else to determine our life. Assuming an assigned role does not constitute living life, it is a kind of living death.

Therapy is a healing process meant to enhance one's life. Yet thousands of women like me see themselves as powerless. In seeking relief from our pain, we become professional patients. I was willing to forfeit finding my own identity by adopting a label. I thought this was the way to become more powerful. How ironic!

I believe now that women must become a cohesive force in the world. We must help each other become independent by providing empathy and mutual support. We need to forfeit the illusory rewards of being trophies for men. Our power comes from within ourselves. Recognizing this we can become a force for change.

I am a woman with an incessant hunger. I am feeding that hunger as I study to become a feminist therapist. I am nurturing and respecting myself. I am empowering myself by refusing to accept the definition and the limitations of a psychiatric label. I am challenged to re-educate men. I am trusting the person I know I am and am becoming. I am Woman! I am Power!

Hockey: Bringing the Body Alive

Susan Zettell

I have, for the most part, ignored my body. It has been a home to thought, daydream, fear, worry, intelligence and, sometimes, love and anger. I have not been particularly active, though I have always been busy. I have never been athletic, but I have loved to play: skating, running, volleyball, twirling, skipping, ball against the wall, baseball (at which I was, at least, never chosen last). Games of Statues, British Bulldog, Mother May I, Dodge Ball, Hide and Seek, and made-up games with arbitrary rules and an ending where someone went home crying, usually Patty Long, or my sister, Anne, after which I would be called home and told I was the oldest, or biggest, or something, and to play fair.

But I cannot recall feeling my body. Though I sensed its potential, I was not good at knowing its limits. I remember daydreaming about what a good skater I was. I could see all the moves in my head, could see me making them, but when I hit the ice, my feet were leaden and slow and I couldn't make the fancy turns or skate backwards or do a figure eight. I still do that: daydream an image of the best I can be, then I disappoint myself with the limitations of my reality, my weariness, inflexibility, clumsiness or fear. Even just a plain lack of practice, that used to seem inconsequential.

Then, last winter, my friend Jan said, "Let's play hockey." "Let's," I said, terrified and thrilled. Jan called friends, rented ice time, recommended a second-hand shop for equipment, and as simple as that, hockey began. Women's hockey on a team called MAMMAH (Middle-Aged Menopausal Mothers Attempt Hockey). Not competitive games, for most of us could hardly skate, and none of us could stop in our new, second-hand hockey skates. We played learning, laughing games of shinny on an outdoor rink. Some of us fell every time we swung our sticks or bumped into another player. All play stopped as we helped the downed player back onto her feet to the repeated polite echo of "Sorry, are you all right?" And laughter, and more laughter.

At our end-of season banquet, we gave out awards and certificates of merit, one for each player. We decided we needed some basic skills, so we signed up for women's hockey camp in the spring. Seven weeks of exhausting drills, exercise routines, and gradually, more and more competitive play. We enjoyed it, but we grumbled and complained, and once, my friend Heather and I went for beer instead of going to practice. Still, we began to improve, and we hoped we wouldn't get too rusty before winter.

Now, I know I am getting better. Last week at our hockey game, I felt like a sturdier person. I blocked goals, felt the pleasant thwack of the puck against my stick, listened to the sound resonate across the ice as it bounced off the boards. And I blocked players, held them off with my body and my stick, felt their resistance, their solidness and determination. I sensed their clear desire to get away from me.

I felt triumph and exhilaration when I got control of the puck and sent it where I wanted it to go. I felt a rush of adrenalin when they got control and I had to go after the puck again, win it back for my team. I even felt a kind of terrified thrill when an offensive player and I collided while skating at full speed. I wasn't injured, but even if I had been, I was ready to skate immediately, shaken but vibrating with stunned energy, itching to get right back into the thick of it.

I am best at defence. I am not sure what that means, but I like to block offensive players, wrestle the puck into the boards, keep it away from my net and protect my goalie. I like to feel the energy from the other players as they rush toward me to score, as we try to keep our heads clear when chaos reigns around the net and we compete as if we were starving for a morsel of food. I like to get the puck, find an opening and shoot it to a teammate, watch the play at the other end of the rink, and wait for my turn to skate like a demon, to sweat and grunt and laugh.

This week I scored two goals and an assist, my best offensive effort to date. It felt great, the strategy and the teamwork were perfect, but I still prefer the thrill of keeping the puck out of the net to that of getting it in.

So maybe I am becoming more aware of the physical me, the body works of Susan Zettell.

And, one more thing. On Tuesday, I got out of my car and yelled at a beer-truck driver who had quite deliberately parked his truck on a one-way street so that it blocked passing traffic. He yelled back and I yelled back and he yelled some more and it didn't do one bit of good. But, damn it, I wasn't afraid, though maybe I should have been. I knew I was a physical presence, could feel my body there, sweating and angry. I knew that he could see me, couldn't ignore my power. And that felt great!

Outside the Sky Waits

M. Joan Baragar

Green finch and linnet bird, nightingale, blackbird,
how is it you sing?
How can you jubilate sitting in cages,
never taking wing?
Outside, the sky waits, beckoning, beckoning,
just beyond the bars;
how can you remain staring at the rain,
maddened by the stars?
How is it you sing — anything? How is it you sing?[1]

She bounced into my counselling office. She was eight years old and bouncy. I heard her tell me she wanted to draw a special picture today of her forefathers. (Within reach on my table was always an assortment of papers and drawing materials.) I've learned that children's pictures are sometimes worth more than words. Especially when a word I interpreted naively as "forefathers" became a picture of "four fathers."

A story took shape with the sketches of each of the four men who had lived, for various lengths of time, in this child's home. One of them, her natural father, had been "kicked out" by Mom, and had gone to live in "another country." Each man was given his due on the page of drawings, but an aura of mystery and a tone of longing was reserved for only one: the natural father this child hardly knew and said she would miss forever. Agreeing that we can miss what we have never really had, we decided that some things were just plain difficult, and it was OK to feel whatever we felt. What struck me was the alchemy of adult sensibility and childish abandon from which this young person managed to distill meaning and keep herself fully alive. Of course, there were times when she felt alone and forgotten. Yet she spoke of her "fathers" with acceptance and even humour, assuring me that no one had been mean or hurtful to her and that, once in a while, she even got treated like a princess. If only she could see her "real dad" again, someday! Perhaps this little bird, restricted by choices not of her making, had made a choice of her own: a kind of peace with the uncertainties of her eight-year-old life.

Children keep me guessing. They are such unique models of

survival. As a school counsellor, I learned to see, even in the most rebellious individual, the persistent attempt to make sense out of a world gone awry. For many of the students who found their way into my office, the world had gone awry. Where I worked, some children seemed to bring with them with them an inordinate amount of emotional baggage. I thought I knew first-hand about life's unfairness until I met little people who came to school inadequately clad, without breakfast, having had neither the comfort of a goodnight kiss nor the impetus of a good morning hug. How did they manage to get up and dressed at all? And why? It seemed that, for many of these children, coming to school felt like coming to a nurturing home, where the care was consistent. So they would arrive, no matter what. Getting them to leave was more of a problem: they could find some very creative excuses for hanging around.

I am referring to that percentage of a school population whose basic childhood needs have not been adequately met, the children who have no assurance of safety or love.

"...How is it you sing — anything? How is it you sing?[2]

At my school, the whole staff was concerned. How could we be a kind of family for these children, at least within the school walls? Did we dare to help them reach beyond the cage bars that circumstance had created for them? Was it even safe for these children to let down their guard in the outside world, to pick up the tools we provided and carve out the personal goals of which they dreamed? Realistically, would these troubled children ever spread their wings and take flight? Distrust and fear, forged over generations, are tough bars to break. Yet the instincts of hope and optimism kept emerging. In all of us. And the children sang.

Again and again, in the course of a work day, I struggled to understand as a child. Gradually, I discovered that I was being assisted to let go, to see without condemning, to dispense small doses of encouragement, and to try something new without putting my self-esteem on the line.

The children were teaching me.

I began to work with groups of the very young on imaginative "survival kits," which included a Circle of Light to be used as a protective shield when a child was feeling unjustly accused and knew that retaliation would make matters worse. One individual added a unique reminder to his kit. He could take a "Pretend trip" to the "Planet X-tra," beaming himself up when his parents started their loud arguments!

Some children put their most inspirational self-talk into writing. One boy, who was the major caregiver in a single-parent home, wrote journals and drew pictures depicting the things he knew about staying hopeful and strong. He loved to write his autobiography and see it "published" in the school library: *Tim Jones — My First Nine Years.* His last story (before his family moved for the 13th time) was a projection of his life into young adulthood, in which he saw himself as a police officer. He said this career would keep him out of trouble and it would let him help others avoid some of the tough things he had experienced. Whatever happens to him, whatever he ultimately chooses, he has in his mind's computer the stimulus of that youthful goal which went beyond survival to a vision of his potential.

Children dare to dream. They dare to draw bright rainbows and make cards that say in big, bold letters, I LOVE YOU. Unless they have been yanked into premature adulthood, they still value play. Their endurance, adaptability and energy keep them going, even if they haven't had a good breakfast. As they grow older, some of them, knowing they are defying the odds, will reach for the beckoning sky. Some of them will fall. And some of them will remain in cages, "staring at the rain, maddened by the stars."[3]

Part of my early learning was that I could offer the children no guarantees. I would not play sheriff in their young lives; I would not play magician, either. An important part of my counselling job involved closing the school door without finishing things, discarding my mental "fix-it" list, recognizing that every individual is ultimately the expert about her or his own self, and a partner in any healing enterprise we might undertake. Resigning as "rescuer" has never been easy for me. I suppose the children made me aware of that, too. Thankfully, my hands were always full of soft reminders of their acceptance and forgiveness: sticky candy, bits of colour on paper, loving words, and my name, often delightfully misspelled.

One of the great mysteries of my life is why I should always be surrounded by children. Not only have I never felt particularly maternal, but my own childhood left me with more memories of responsibility than spontaneous fun. I wasn't very experienced in the crazy-amazing art of being a child. Maybe that's why, from my early days, children have always fascinated me; other children, different from me, doing wild and wonderful things, female children in literature like Pippy Longstocking and Alice in Wonderland. When I became old enough to acknowledge some of the playtime adventures

I might have denied myself, I let the next generation help me fill in the blanks. What great ideas they could hatch, not just as serious problem-solvers but, also, as entertainers and sensitive listeners! I joined them at school, on the playground, in the classroom, in my office, learning to consult with, rather than just talk to them. It was, for some children, a totally new experience to be approached by an adult as "experts" in anything. So they crept closer in curiosity, and later, in trust. Some even dared to give me a push in a new direction.

For example, there was the kindergarten class who invited me to ride their fantastic wooden rocking elephant whenever I visited them. Five-year-olds are fine encouragers of a big person who will enter their world on their terms. This was at a time when my personal life seemed to have caved in on me, and my outlook was very serious indeed. I felt silly on the elephant, at first. Later, I made friends with it, getting a pattern and constructing one just like it, telling myself it was for my grandchildren (who had not yet been born)!

Flashback: I am a seven year-old, watching my father in his woodworking shop. I love to see the magic of his creations. Toys and sleek furniture evolve like natural extensions of his skillful hands. It is called "man's work," not recommended for a female child. I stay out of the way of the saw and hammer, pick up wood chips and nails, imagine whole cities of miniature wooden structures. How I love the sight, the touch, the sawdust smell, this celebratory way of being with my clever dad. There is a comradeship, even in silence. He lets me help a little, but what I really want is to do what this man can do. And more, I want to share the look on his face as he works. Chewing his tongue in fervent concentration, he wipes the sweat from his brow and conveys such sweet satisfaction to me with his grin.

All these years later, I realize what a reach-for-the sky thing it was for me, a female adult with zero expertise, to enroll in an evening woodworking course at a neighbourhood high school. It must have been more than the elephant or the kindergarten class. I sense it was a kind of yearning for the hands-on building buzz I had never experienced as a little girl. It was filling in the blanks, catching up with my youthful self. Table saws, belt sanders, machinery that, with terrifying speed, molded ordinary pieces of wood into myriad shapes;

all of these were new to me. My initial project was a napkin holder. I wondered how I would progress from that to my rocking elephant, but I drove home singing at the end of each class, my hair full of wood shavings and my heart full of hope. Thus, an invitation from children allowed the caged bird, in me, to fly. Although it took most of a year, the day came when that wooden elephant stood proudly in my living room. Perhaps, it was I who stood proudly. The elephant still stands, unlikely symbol of renewal and recovery, enticing me to consider options. The velcroed ears may be on or off, depending on the whim of the last rider, the tail inviting a tug, the trunk ready for a swing. Best of all, there are no gender or age restrictions. Anyone may hop aboard. The natural healers in the kindergarten class taught me that.

Working and playing with children, having my own, are experiences which have kept me realistic about the sweet-and-sour natures that are confusing parts of us all. I know children can be taught to hate, as they can be taught to love. I know that they can be nasty human beings, that they may take off on their own collision courses no matter what we do. But what brightens my memory is the evidence I see of a child's spontaneous capacity for giving. The jaded adult in me is sometimes taken by surprise.

Flashback:
I'm waving my little son and daughters off to school one bone-chilling January morning marvelling at their cheerful energy. Was I ever like that?

All at once
they tumble through the door,
chattering sparrows flailing winter air
through cloudy drifts of freshly-fallen snow.
Goodbye.
Come on!...You Can't catch me!...Goodbye!

When I walk back inside to the cluttered breakfast table, something catches my eye:

Focus: bright balloon. I sense a gift
before I claim it from my six-year-old.
Orange globe. Red-ribboned to her chair.

Her pen has etched a face,
brighter by a grin than any other of its kind.
And underneath, her printing, bold and clear
MOM! GOOD MORNING! LOVE AND X AND O!

Children who know they're loved, and even some who don't, may give back love with stunning generosity. Never could I imagine a greater child-gift than that of a ten-year-old boy I heard about once. He was asked to contribute a kidney to his younger brother. Doctors and family discussed the procedure with the older boy and were satisfied that he understood. He asked no other questions, and did not hesitate to agree to the surgery. It wasn't until he was wheeled into the operating room that he asked, "Will I die right away, or do you think I'll wake up for a little while first?" Suddenly, the surgeon realized that no one had informed the boy that he had two kidneys and was only being asked to part with one! Willing to spend his life for a brother without so much as a whimper, that child took a flight of the spirit that removed him from fear. As an adult, I am awed and humbled by love like that.

At a much less exceptional level, children seem to have the knack of living many "no-strings" moments, of giving themselves to people and events with a freedom adults often lack. Over time, life's damaging experiences obviously tempt us to trade in our trust for caution, or even bitterness. Childhood's natural instinct is toward spontaneity and celebration. The world outside, whatever "outside" means, has never really been safe for children. Yet, if I must ground them by teaching them to watch their step, I also want to remember how to fly with them sometimes, no-strings attached.

For they do long to fly. They cry out against real or imagined injustices: "It's not fair!" Then they bound into a new day without carrying old grudges, hoping to heal. Over and over, they trust the next moment, the chance to begin again. If life puts dangers and other obstacles in their way, they do their best to get over or through them, "ring around a rosie." If someone opens a door, they fling themselves singing, into the air, at a moment's notice. "You can't catch me!" is the shout of those confident, resilient ones, who believe that childhood means the sky's the limit.

Children have taught me that for all of us, at any age, the sky awaits and beckons.

"me and my shadow" by Heather Spears

Daily Assaults

Beatrice Archer Watson

Barbara was having one of her migraine headaches when Anisha came home from school looking rather downtrodden. Barbara forced herself to smile and to give Anisha a reassuring hug.

"How was your day today, love?" Barbara asked.

"Okay." Anisha shrugged and walked off towards her room.

"Come here, honey." Barbara sat Anisha down on her lap and passed her rough hands over the child's face in a loving gesture. "What's wrong with my baby? You're not your usual womanly self. Tell Mommy what happened."

"Oh, nothing."

"Now, now, c'mon," her mother coaxed.

"Some kids were teasing me… I hate it here… I hate all of them." She burst into tears. "They were calling me nigger and black poop and all kinds of mean things."

"Oh, honey." Barbara hugged her daughter as tightly as she could without hurting her, her own headache seeming to disappear with the poignant heartache she was now experiencing.

"They are just a bunch of foolish, ignorant, mean kids. I'm going to see the Principal tomorrow."

"No, Mom, please don't."

"Why? Don't you want me to put an end to this nonsense?"

"It won't do any good. They can still call me names outside of school. Besides, I don't want to draw attention to myself."

Barbara felt sorry for her child with a sadness that can only be felt by someone who has known this pain. Memories of her own childhood, living in the shadows of the Massa plantation, surfaced. How very sad and lonely a child can feel when degraded. It's a wound that never completely heals, but is exacerbated at times like these. Barbara cried her eyes out. She was crying for the daily assaults of racism, sexism and classism she encountered. She had hoped to protect her baby from these feelings of helplessness, isolation and worthlessness.

Fresh memories of the time when she had just moved here from Nova Scotia and was looking for an apartment surfaced. She remembered finding a beautiful apartment, perfect for Anisha, then seven. Barbara wanted it badly. She had her money in hand, ready to sign the deal. Ruth, her Jewish girlfriend, remained in the car with Anisha while Barbara went in. A friendly middle-aged white woman answered the doorbell. The woman surveyed her from top to bottom as if she was taking measurements for a suit. "Wait," she said. She called her husband. A short, stocky, balding man with a thick moustache emerged. There was a mixture of frown and curiosity in his expression. Barbara told him she came about the apartment.

"The apartment is gone. Someone took it about an hour ago," he said brusquely. He turned his back, ready to go.

"But I called an hour ago and you told me it was available", Barbara protested.

"I didn't talk to you an hour ago, lady. I'd know your people's accent anytime," he said confidently.

Humiliated and hurt, Barbara fought back tears that were on the brink of spilling. She did not want to give him the satisfaction of hurting her. She left holding her head high. The facade fell as soon as she got into the car. She cradled her face in the palm of her hands, sniffing and crying. She knew she was facing the ugliness of racism again. Ruth was silent. Anisha was asleep. "Thank God," Barbara thought.

"Let's go," she said to Ruth.

"You want to tell me what's going on here?"

"Nothing."

"Okay...nothing. Want to tell me why you're crying?"

"The apartment is taken. I'm just disappointed."

"Did those people say something?"

"No, he just looked at me and said the apartment's taken."

"You think they're lying. You think it's because you're black, don't you?"

"It hurts to think that."

"I know," Ruth gritted her teeth. She continued, her lower jaws pulsating, "At times like these I'm ashamed to have the colour I have."

"Don't be. I happen to like your colour and you, just the way you are." Barbara managed to smile. "Hey, c'est la vie."

Ruth was very angry. She circled the block for about twenty minutes. Barbara could not calm her down. Ruth had to find out. One hour later she knocked on the manager's door and asked for the apartment. It was available. She was furious. She blasted the couple.

"You bastard," Ruth said, "didn't you just tell my friend that the apartment was gone?"

"Sorry, but now it's gone for you, too," he said, shaking his head with a mocking grin.

"Do you know racism is a crime? Do you know what you are doing is against the law?"

"Perhaps your laws, not mine. I worked hard for what I have and no government is gonna make me wreck it with people like them. My apartment is for a certain type and class of people. I'm not a racist, just a practical businessman."

"Burr," Ruth shook her jaws, "You make me want to throw up."

"Do that on your way out. Wouldn't bother me one bit."

"You haven't heard the last of me. Bigot!"

He shrugged his shoulders and grinned.

She took the matter to the Human Rights Commission. The process of proving that someone was violating the Human Rights Code was exhausting and humiliating.

Ultimately, Barbara decided to drop the case. She did not have the luxury of time off. She had to find food for the table and she had to work to keep the roof over her child's head.

Barbara's head throbbed badly. She was always thinking and worrying about the future of her child. She often wondered how Anisha felt. Anisha did not think she was beautiful. The child wanted to look like the white children. It must be low self-esteem. Barbara had read about it in a book. Anisha showed all the symptoms. Anisha always said she was ugly, that her hair was too short and curly, her clothes never fit her the way she wanted. She plagued Barbara for stylish clothes to wear to school, but she never seemed quite content, even with the best. That put pressure on Barbara's meagre salary. She tried to accommodate her daughter's wishes, knowing full well that she was indulging her. Anisha was her pride and joy, her only child. She loved her. She loved her a lot. She prayed for the day when Anisha would acknowledge how naturally pretty she was, with her big brown eyes, sapodilla brown skin and shiny woolly locks that felt richly textured. She ought to be proud to be so blessed.

Barbara sometimes shared her concern with other black mothers who had children attending the same school. There were a lot of similarities in the children's behaviour. Their children also experienced racial abuse at the school, particularly from their peers.

Anisha said she felt excluded. She said she didn't have any "real" friends. Barbara understood.

"I wish everyone was the same colour. I feel so different and ugly and stupid sometimes. I know I shouldn't, Mom, but I can't help myself," Anisha said to her mother one day.

"It must be awful."

"It is awful to be called names."

"Names, what names?"

"Nigger, whatever is not white."

"I am going to see the Principal about this."

"No, please don't. It'll only make things worse."

"How will they know what they're doing is wrong?"

"Trust me, they know." She gave a faint smile. "I'll handle it. It's not as bad as I am making it sound. I guess I am just depressed."

"Can I tell you something, Anisha?" Barbara said with a twinkle of discovery in her eyes.

Anisha shook her head up and down.

"I think you have a lot going for you. You're smart, you're beautiful and you're very talented. Don't let those kids get to you, honey. Keep your head high and be proud of who you are. Our history, African history and Caribbean history, is rich. We have a lot to be proud of. The only reason those kids put you down is because inside they feel very small."

"You're just saying that because you're my mom." Anisha smiled indulgingly.

"Maybe. But make no mistake, every word is true."

"I love you, Mom. You're just the best there is."

"Now, isn't that because I am your mom?"

"Moooom," she droned.

The feeling of self pity crippled Barbara at times. It made her wonder why she stayed in Canada. She had a choice. She could return to her country. She was not a refugee. She made a choice, an economic choice, to be in Canada. If she returned, she would return to a life of poverty. The wages would be low, very low. She'd be poor, perhaps unemployed, relegated to the lowest class and looked down upon by the upper class. Barbara realized she was in a no-win situation. She felt she had to choose on the side of economics, but the price seemed so high. Like parents before her, she lived in hope that things would be better for her daughter. Now she wasn't sure about the wisdom of that thinking. Why do children have to have it better than their parents? Is it more important to have a "highfalutin" lifestyle than a simple one with friends and family around you, people who care about you? Barbara was not sure anymore. However, she was sure that she did not want her daughter to fight the same battles that impacted so negatively on her own health. She was thankful for her friend, Ruth, who always seemed to be able to put things in perspective.

"The way I see it, you're doomed if you do, and you're doomed if you don't. How much respect do you get in your country if you are poor?"

"Not a lot. People are very class conscious. We'd have been living in real poverty. Not a pretty picture, I can tell you that."

"We have to fight racism, classism and sexism."

"There's a lot of good things about being here. We won't starve. The welfare system is generous. In my country, we have no such thing. You have to beg in the streets."

"You came for a better life for yourself and your daughter."

"Yes, is that wrong? Am I being greedy and selfish? Sometimes I feel that I am selling my soul, especially when I see the pain in my baby's eyes."

"You're not selfish. You're a human being. We all want our lives to be better, and we've been migrating throughout history in search of greener pastures. It's okay. What is not okay is you being discriminated against because you're black."

"Thank you for saying that. It feels like a soothing poultice on my sore heart," Barbara said, hugging Ruth close to her.

George[1]

Kathryn Countryman

(The scene takes place on a ship; the characters are on an overseas "field trip.")

Last year, I started calling my period george, cuz I don't like saying, "Oh, I have my period." A period is something you put at the end of a sentence, george is something you mock. Well, at least I do. George is all mine. A guy could try to rationalize it. But I can do whatever I want. It's my way of reminding all those other girls that it's something that only we have.

Anyways, about an hour later, I knew it was time, so I pulled out that bulky sanitary napkin, made my way to the bathroom. After I peed, I put the woman companion on my gotch, and left. With all this inventing, you would think that someone would come up with a napkin that does not go squish, squish, squish. It always feels like people can hear me coming before I arrive.

I crawled back up onto the bunk, laid down. I pulled my legs up to my chest, tucked the blankets tightly around my neck. For me, the first day is crampy. I only got george two years ago, and the Doctor told my Mom I cramp so bad, cuz I'm so old. Now that I'm on the PILL, I just have little spasms. That's another thing, the Doctor put me on the PILL so that it would stop my cramps.

I like being by myself on the first day, just relaxing, thinking, daydreaming. I was happy to finally get george. All my girlfriends had her, and I felt kinda like a weirdo for not. Not only that, when I have her I get my own space. It's important to me, having time and space to myself.

When I awoke, Elisabeth was staring me in the face. "You've gobbed on yourself."

So I had. Spittle was on my cheek, and the pillow was, in fact, wet.

"Gross. I hate when that happens. Don't you?"

"Yeah."

"What's up? Why are you in bed?"

"George."

"Oh."

As I pulled myself out of the covers, I saw Ruth and Hanna walking in.

"What's with you?"

Elisabeth answered, "She's got GEORGE."

"Oh."

Not skipping a beat, Ruth starts telling us about when she first got george. "I guess I was around twelve or so. My Mom came in with this blue box. She sat down on my bed, pulling at the comforter, telling me that soon I would be a woman."

"No kidding."

"Yep, she came in, told me it would last for about four to five days, every month for the rest of my life. She told me that it was a very special and private moment for me. Then she pulled out a napkin, got up and pulled out underwear from the drawer. She proceeded to show me where the pad goes and how to adjust the belt."

"Didn't happen like that for me," Elisabeth says with her eyes down. "I was at school, scared that I was bleeding to death, thought, 'Jesus Christ, what the hell is happening?' I stuffed a bunch of toilet paper into my gotch, and told the teacher I was sick. I never said anything, just kept using toilet paper. I would hide my soiled gotch in the garbage can, inside empty milk cartons. A few months later," says Elisabeth, laughing, "I found a BLUE BOX in my gotch drawer."

We all laugh.

They look at me. We look at one another. I start telling them about my experience.

"I only got george when I was fifteen. I was away in Thunder Bay, and walking around with some girls. I was wearing my white Lee shorts and my favourite yellow T-shirt with the number 13 on the back."

Hanna butts in, "I remember that shirt. You wore it all the time."

Elisabeth and Ruth look at Hanna, "Shud up."

"Anyways, we were walking around, checking out the park, and we walked to a corner grocery store. It was warm, the trees were in full bloom. Large oak trees reached up into the sky. They looked so strong, compared to the poplars back home, the skinny pencil poplars. I felt great, so important and special. Boys were whistling at us, waving. We walked through the steel gates to the community pool. The water was so blue, like peacock blue from Crayola crayons. We stopped and talked about the water. Gerda told us that it was so blue because of all the chlorine they put in it. I even scooped some of the water into my hand and I could smell the chemical. As we were standing by the water a boy come up to us. He told Gerda, 'Better tell your friend she needs to go home,' pointing at my shorts. I was confused, wondering what he was talking about, Gerda walked behind me. My shorts were full of blood. I had ignored the crampy feeling. I thought it was gas. Well, Gerda gave me her sweater, I wrapped it around my waist and headed for the billet."

Elisabeth comes up to the bunk and holds my hand. She rubs her hand on mine. I felt chokey, the lump in my throat about to explode.

"It's okay, Rebekah, you're here with friends. It's okay."

I try to talk, the words choking in my throat.

"When I got back to the billet the woman with the grey hair and pointy chin asked me what was wrong. I told her that I got my period."

"Oh, you're MENSTRUATING. Where did you pack your sanitary napkins?"

"I didn't know if I had any. I didn't know what to do or what was happening."

"You DO have sanitary napkins. You DO know what they are?"

"While she asked me that, she kept pushing her glasses back up onto her nose. I stood, paralyzed, blood dripping down my legs, feeling uneasy. Yes, yes, I know what they are."

"I asked a question. Do you have any? Did your mother pack any SANITARY NAPKINS for you?"

"I shrugged my shoulders and followed her downstairs. Her shoes clipped, sounding like a dog's nails on linoleum. We rummaged through my suitcase. Sure enough there was a blue box in the corner. She left the room, slamming the door. I took the box and a change of clothes and went to the bathroom. I undressed and put the bloody clothes in the sink. I turned on the cold water. The sink filled with red water. I pushed my hand into the shorts, trying to get rid of the stain. My nails were coated and gooey with blood. The last thing I put into the porcelain basin was my gotch. I didn't think they would ever come clean. While I showered, I rubbed my belly. It seemed to help my stomach ache. When I got out, I put on the belt and pulled on jeans and a sweater. I stayed in the basement for the rest of the night.

The next day, the woman called my mom inconsiderate and selfish for not explaining menstruation. While she babbled on, I ran my finger around the yellow veined table, tracing around the margarine and peanut butter tubs. As she slammed down my plate of toast, she mumbled, 'You're too old to just be getting your menstrual period. There must be something wrong with you.'"

I took a deep breath, wiped my eyes, and blew my nose.

"So, that's my first experience with george. That was also my last year at volleyball camp. After that, Mom couldn't afford to send me."

I crawled off the bed, made my way to the washroom, and cleaned up my face.

When I returned, all three girls were sitting at the bottom of the bunk. Ruth spoke, "Rebekah, it's okay. It's good to talk. We're your friends." Then she stood up, opened her arms, and hugged me.

"The Flow" by Veronica G. Green

Threading My Way

Katherine Martens

For the first nine years I attended a one-room country school. Over time, I read every book in the library. The images in a children's adaptation of *Pilgrim's Progress* by Bunyan made a lasting impression on me.[1] I liked the idea of progress through life as a journey or quest, but there were also discouraging images in it: the Slough of Despond and the Valley of the Shadow of Death. I hoped I would be spared the many false turns the pilgrim, Christian, made. Following a fearful, gloomy path through life, Christian had many narrow escapes.

I, like Christian, arrived where I am, not via a straight line, but by a series of loops and spirals, rather like the loops we made in penmanship class in grade school. Though I often felt I was going backward, in truth, I was not. I remember my father's voice demanding to know what I was reading as a child. If it was a novel (and usually it was), he called it lies and asked why I didn't read something that was true. He was also fond of saying, "Tell the whole truth and nothing but the truth," but what was true for him was not necessarily true for me. What did he find so threatening about imagination? I tried to avoid conflict and retreated into silence just as my father did when he and my mother had differences, and my mother would scold him. Her stories were almost always stream of consciousness. When I was a young girl I did not want to identify with her at all. Whatever the cause, the effect was that I worked scrupulously to keep my writing grounded in fact, and rarely let my imagination go.

My personal image to describe my quest is the red line of menstruation which we used to call "falling off the roof." It runs through my life like a series of periods and commas, marking the waning of each moon. When menstruation ended, the red line became an exclamation mark, in the form of inflammation. When I looked for causes of the inflammation the road led back to childhood.

My first positive acknowledgment of the red thread was in university courses, which I started in my late 30s. I did a research project about women's attitudes to menstruation and self-esteem, and gained a new slant on the subject. Through my discussions with other women I learned that our feelings about menstruation were as valid as those of the experts. I had seen "falling off the roof" negatively, and I valued my fertility more than my period until after I had borne three children. Then I felt a shift and I viewed menstruation as a source of strength. Earlier, I thought of menstruation as a badge of inferiority. By listening to my own body, I began to see menstruation as a source of energy and creativity rather than a nuisance and an interruption. I began to see life as cyclical.

I recognized that I was ashamed of my desire to withdraw from the world once a month and began, instead, to honour that desire. Rather than letting experts tell me that ovulation was the most sexual time of the month (note I did not say responsive time), I listened to my body. Reading male authors on sexuality, I gathered that intercourse during the menstrual period was frowned upon. When sexual activity during menstruation was discussed, it was suggested that intercourse might reduce the discomfort of menstruation. The possibility that a woman might find it more pleasurable was not mentioned. (Female sexual feeling during the menstrual period is more intense and active and therefore less feminine and submissive.)[2]

When I was 38 years old, our youngest daughter was learning to swim. When she urged me to join her at the deep end I took swimming lessons for the "absolutely terrified." I thought I had mastered drownproofing but when the instructor announced a pre-test, I had a panic attack. Crippling anxiety was the reason for going into three months of therapy with David Martin. There I first uncovered a repressed childhood secret. I rationalized that the sexual part of the incident had not hurt me, only the secrecy had.

My insights helped me to turn inward and I decided to write rather than pursue a post graduate academic degree. I chose to write about my family, based on oral interviews. After my book *All in A Row: The Klassens of Homewood,* was published, I was asked to read from it at the Mennonite Centre in Toronto, in the winter of 1990.[3] Someone asked, "Why are you not as angry in your writing as some of the younger Mennonite women writers are?" My immediate response was to say, "I don't know," but I sensed that my anger had simply not yet made it into print. A volcanic anger had roared inside me while rewriting a part of the book but I had not known how to incorporate that anger into my prose. Unpunctuated prose allowed my anger to flow through my journal entries and became part of my next manuscript, the story of my physical and spiritual pilgrimage.[4]

When I returned home I tried writing fiction. I had recently completed an oral history project about Mennonite childbirth stories, and now I felt I could write whatever I wanted.[5] Years before, when I was about 12, I had written novels modeled on the popular books by Grace Livingstone Hill.[6] Two older brothers teased me about my stories and when I refused to let them read them, they chased me through the house. In desperation I dashed downstairs and threw my writing into the flames of the coal furnace.

Now, decades later, I tried to write fiction, but I got stuck whenever I began to write from my unconscious. For example, I tried to describe a birth scene from the perspective of the infant and came up against a brick wall. At the same time I suddenly had a painful genital inflammation. Medication alleviated the symptoms but did nothing to address the root causes. The red thread of menstruation disappeared and now I had an inflammation. Menopause, *Wechseljahre* (change years), which I had hoped would lead me to calmer shoals of wise old age, seemed to have launched me into a stormy sea instead. I went to see Joan, whose massage therapy skills had previously helped me with writer's block. Her hands found where the tension was stored in the body, and in her peaceful room I learned to breathe and relax. I did not move in a straight line to the insights that are obvious to me now. It took weeks of steady hard work, of slipping back into the state of mind of my child self and forward into the present where I had adult problems to solve. The child I had abandoned was not easy to find. Christa Wolf says, "Anyone who stirs up his [her] childhood can't expect to make rapid progress."[7] Paradoxically, the harder I tried to find my childhood self, the more she evaded me, but the more I let myself play, or do nothing, the easier my access to her became.[8] The anger and fear that the young girl could not express was embodied, stored at the base of her groin. Now they surfaced in physical symptoms.

I used crayons to draw myself at age seven or eight, and I gave a pencil to the left hand of the child in me to help her write from the unconscious. When I opened the Pandora's box of childhood I had to overcome strong taboos and resistance called FEAR. I had not acknowledged or lived through the fear and anger that was repressed in my body. I had not recognized the patterns of behaviour that affected every intimate relationship I had. Now I knew that I must defy the command: DON'T TELL. The strong injunction against telling my parents was lifted by their death. One by one I told my brothers and sisters what had been a shameful secret for more than 50 years. Many times I felt sheer terror at my chosen course of action, but I knew my soul would die if I kept silent.

In therapy with Joan I gave the young girl, hidden in an airless room all these years, permission to come out into the open. Each time I went to see Joan for therapy I felt as if I was coming to play in a sacred sunlit garden. I had to overcome a lifelong fear of reprisal. Sometimes I felt paralyzed. I could not turn back but neither could I go forward. This was similar to the way I feel when I am on a diving board.

Once the door to childhood was opened, other memories followed. Twenty-five years after the birth and death of my first child, I relived that experience with Joan, in a massage session. I felt my feet go numb and tingly as if with anesthesia in labour. On the massage table I cried out in anger. Anger at the way my hands had been tied down and anger at having had to lie in a passive position to labour alone. Then my mind slipped back to my own childhood.

I (or is it my two-and-a-half year-old self) am lying on the surface of a still pond with my eyes closed. I have heard the story of my near drowning many times, but I never put myself back in that place. I am in white water of the pond close to our house. The adults are at the Faspa table.[9] I have seen one of my older sisters walk out on the plank that goes into the pond to get a drink of water. I do the same but i lose my balance and fall head first   The murky water parts smoothly for me   the frogs and tadpoles dart in every direction   my mouth opens with surprise   i close it after the first gulp of water   i reach out to grab something anything   but there is nothing   i am spinning in space   my head feels as if i am turning round and round like the jrettre[10] we children do in the kitchen   the world is blurring i am turning   faster   faster soon i am as liquid as the element i am in   my mind and body seem to be separating with one part of me hovering over the rest   water has no hard edges no solid surface no form   only fluidity and at last the bottom   but the ground is so soft squishy i sink in but still there is this pressing element water entering my mouth   my ears   my nose filling all the empty spaces   trickling into my throat   down into my stomach   spluttering   gurgling   i will suffocate   my feet push off   my arms push the water away   i am screaming "mame halp me" but no sound comes out   only more water

pushing in i'm invaded   mouth full of water   ears   chest
pounding   stomach lurching   thinking is useless here   survival depends on rules i never heard of   keep my mouth
shut   when i see the light of the sun i turn my face to it   my
exhausted body   wants only to rest   my arms at my side   the
sun too bright   i close my eyes to shield them   i no longer
resist or fight but give myself to the water and the warmth

Jake, the hired man, saw the family standing around the dugout
wringing their hands. No one knew how to swim and neither did he,
but he didn't hesitate. Jumping in, he found the water came only to
his waist and he had no difficulty bringing me to solid ground. I had
gone down three times by the time he rescued me. My mother carried
me into the house and until I opened my eyes she feared that I was
dead. Mother conscientiously kept her eye on her children, but she
had too many to watch. My father and mother thanked God for
having spared my life. My older sister, Henrietta, held me and
comforted me in her arms all evening.

Did my curiosity cause my near-drowning? Do I plunge into
things too quickly and without caution? When anxiety overwhelms
me I feel as if I am drowning. When I am sad I feel that I am drowning
in tears. To dispel the cool wetness of that state I have to feel blazing
anger.

The *New World Dictionary* says: "Drowning — to die under water
or other liquid because of lack of air to breathe." Now I have learned
to breathe with Joan. I have recreated the same conditions over and
over so I can feel the relief of saving my own life. Jake carried me out
of the pond but I had already turned my face up out of the water so
I wouldn't swallow any more.

In 1993 I packed up all my journals and diaries for a year in
Germany. Once there I read them all. It had taken almost two decades
for me to see the connection between my physical symptoms and the
secret which had affected me like a poison. While I guarded it I had
control over it, but I had limited access to my body and mind. I had
recurring dreams of being undressed in a public place. Sometimes I
looked in vain for a place to sit in a church. Often I woke hot with
shame. When I read all my journals I saw how many times I had
expressed a wish to die rather than confront the conflict I needed to
face. The journals represented the hidden side of me where I expressed
thoughts and feelings I could not talk about. I noted dreams that had

common themes and provided the red thread to my young self. It was time to write the story based on my journals and diaries.

Earlier written versions of my near drowning were simply rote recordings of the story as it was told to me. Only after seeing the movie *The Piano* did I begin to recognize and relive the emotions connected with my experience, and in time I also saw the connection to my birth.[11] In writing my story I found the conflicting parts of myself.

My near-drowning connected to the fear I had during my own birth, and similarly, to my anxiety when I had a bleeding ulcer. When my mother was in labour with me she held me back so she and my father could drive 60 miles to Winnipeg. I was to be the first of their children born in a hospital. My fear about going into hospital for my ulcer was way out of proportion to reality. I asked myself, "What was that all about?" and I recognized the many parallels between my own birth experience and my ulcer, the sense of being out of control and being kept back from acting. I do not blame past experiences for my ulcer. I simply ask, is there a link? When and where have I felt this way before? I believe that my fear of the hospital comes from before I was born, and perhaps after, when I heard other infants and myself crying for our mothers. Whenever I hear babies crying I become quite helpless.[12] It was this scene that I tried to write as fiction and which my anxiety blocked me from finishing. My journal entries provided the thread and helped me to recognize that the fear began with my birth.

At first I was ashamed of being sick, or being dependent on drugs. When I simply observed myself without judgment I began to get better. I follow the principle of taking as few drugs as possible, and realize that I can decide when it is wise to take them and when it is not.[13] In my work with Joan, I have learned that my ulcer was not a failure, or a punishment, but simply a continuation of a learning path. Lessons not learned are repeated.

The red line of body awareness includes passion. Growing older was associated with the fear that Eros would disappear. Certainly there are changes, but the fire of Eros is intimately connected to finding my voice and using it. Honest recording of my dreams helped me see connections. Writing is survival for me. I write first to create myself from the darkness, to save myself from drowning, to remember, to understand and to be understood. Writing and consciousness are two intertwined skeins of thread. I stay alive to write, but in order to write I struggle to understand and express whatever gives my life meaning and purpose.

I recovered my childhood memories and took ownership of them. Now I can laugh and play again and be a silly child.[14] I first learned to trust my body to tell me what to eat and what not to eat. When I abandoned the role of victim in one area it was easier to recognize the pattern in another. Pain has been the most dramatic and reliable guide. It tells me in unmistakable terms to pay attention. Now that I consult not only my head, but all of my body as well, I find myself open to new experiences such as tai chi, circle dancing, belly dancing, giving and receiving massage, Reiki, meditation, and rituals celebrating the seasons. I am thankful to my therapists, my friends, and persons I encounter on my life's journey for staying with me and guiding me through pleasure and pain. The fear that accompanies the recognition of an unknown aspect of myself transforms into excitement and anticipation. My quest will take me back to the Mother, the labyrinth and the void. Sometimes a dream connects different parts of my life, and when I face my fear, I move forward.

Δ

mezzaluna

Sylvia Legris

uses same rocking movement
as cook's knife

mezza
luna

halfmoon

          (there's a girl cuts her food
          into thin circles
          slices each circle in half

              carrot

                  zucchini

                      english

                  cucumber

              halfmoons

          half-

    crazy

goes to bed hungry
rocks herself to sleep

same rocking movement rocking movement same
rocking movement
night
after night[1]

hey diddle diddle The COW writes a poem

Sylvia Legris

this poem
is about pigs:

one little piggy went to market
pork bellies up that week

this piggy's belly was CONcave (con: trick

this little piggy weighed 78 pounds
she heard numbers don't lie but mirrors
play tricks

one morning she stood sideways
saw a skeleton
next morning a pig

this little piggy went to superstore
spent 52 dollars

> [EATING ATTITUDES TEST: *describe a typical*
> *binge (do not exceed allotted space)*
>
> 4 litres homogenized milk
> 2 litres neopolitan ice cream
> family size can chef-boy-ardee ravioli
> 12 hotdogs / 12 hotdog buns
> 6 chocolate bars 1 bag chips ahoy 3 ba...

....

....
...]

(this little piggy ran[1]

Chapter Seven

Singing Our Songs

Singing a Spider Woman's Song

Women Spinning Songs of Healing and Creativity

Victoria Moon Joyce

Introduction

Singing in aural/oral traditions has become an uncommon experience in a highly technological world of professionalism and industrial music. Yet it is, and always has been, a healthy recreational practice, with numerous benefits for mental, emotional, physical, and spiritual health. What I propose in this paper is the revival of singing and music-making as a grassroots, everyday practice in which everyone can participate. Singing is a particularly effective tool for enabling healing processes, sparking creativity, and as a way of promoting a sense of well-being.

As a tool, singing is very practical and portable. At the risk of sounding obvious, the beauty of singing, as a health practice and as a healing intervention, is its naturalness. While it is a complex process to describe, it is also simple and accessible. Songs are found in every culture. Singing is inclusive, easily accessed, requires minimal resources, is life-affirming, stimulating, and enjoyable. Leading people in song requires some skill, but it is not beyond anyone's ability if the leader is comfortable singing.

Singing and music deserve a more central role in pedagogic,

therapeutic, and political practices. Singing holds particular promise for women who have been silenced, since it provides the tools with which to be heard.

For this chapter, I draw from prior research in which I asked seven women (who facilitate singing with other women) to speak about the process of singing and its effects on learning, healing, and political struggles, for themselves and those with whom they sing.[1] I also draw upon my own history as a singer, particularly where I have integrated singing into educational and therapeutic activities.

Background

In North America, during this century, singing has moved from being a normal part of community life to professionalization, and to music as an industry. This has caused a societal shift in what gets valued as cultural production and what is seen as "real" culture. Singing has come to be perceived as a talent or gift that only some are blessed with, and that is "best left to the professionals." As a result, for many, singing has become an isolated or specialized activity, either left for the "talented" or to be enjoyed more passively through listening. Our confidence as makers of music has been undermined. To counter this, our cultural expectations need to shift to make room for everyone to exercise her/his musical abilities without fear of performance evaluation. (e.g. "If I can't be great at this, I won't even try.")

Singing is a natural function, like laughing. But for many people, that natural ability and desire to sing has been dampened or discouraged. Unless we have lost the physical means to make a sound, we all have a voice. Singing is an ability that every voice possesses, and like any motor skill, it requires exercise to develop. For the vast majority who label themselves non-singers, I believe their lack of comfort or skill comes from an earlier event which caused them to stop singing, arresting their confidence to further develop this natural capability.

Singing in a Wilderness Context as Part of a Therapeutic Plan

My experiences as an Outward Bound instructor, working and learning with the Women of Courage program over a five-year period, showed me that singing was an important component in the courses I co-instructed.[2] I became aware of this over time, not because I planned to use singing as an official component but because I witnessed significant changes in the women and in their use of voice when singing.

Singing started out as a way of bringing the women to a place where they were ready to sleep, on their first night, in the intimidating wilderness. I taught them Chris Williamson's "Lullabye" — a simple song to learn and to sing.[3] Singing it became a popular bedtime practice. Based on this experience, I introduced "sing-songs" whenever it seemed that a shift in energy was needed. I remember that we sang some dreadful 50's songs of "love gone wrong," but we laughed and hooted and sang with full voices. The more we laughed, the louder we sang. It was at this point that I realized the significance of the context in which we were singing. No men were present and there was something deliciously permissive about singing into the night sky and the open air. Our voices had a place to expand without bounds. The women talked about feeling a kind of "abandon" that they had long forgotten. A few said they had never felt this way. Energy was raised in these moments, and was put to good use helping the group stay present with one another, and with the work they were engaged in as a group.[4]

For female survivors, the "wilderness" is a place of contradictions: a frightening, unfamiliar place, possibly a place of past danger, but also a place of safety, and/or possibilities and adventure. To sleep on the ground and feel all its curves and bumps, to smell its life and feel its temperature and texture, is often a sensual awakening, especially for those who have not had the opportunity or safe space to intimately and viscerally connect with the earth. What may have been the context of painful or dangerous experiences (many women and children have been abused in outdoor settings), can potentially be shifted to one of pleasure. For such a shift to occur, an environment of emotional and physical safety must be created and maintained by the group. After days and nights in intimate contact with the earth, most survivors begin to open emotionally and physically to the natural environment, to themselves, and often to one another, in very powerful ways.

One of the main goals of this program is to help female survivors re-establish or reinforce a sense of self that has been damaged by violence. This sense of self includes the establishment of healthier personal boundaries. Most survivors have either learned to distrust other women or to trust indiscriminately. Part of the work for survivors is to develop a balanced and realistic approach to trusting themselves and others.

Hopefully, as a stronger sense of self emerges, a growing awareness and an outrage at having been silenced also can emerge. Once a woman finds that she has a right to her voice, she can begin to move towards reclaiming it. This can be understood as "coming to voice." It constitutes a radical shift in consciousness, from which a woman can begin to act in her own best interests. Frankie Armstrong, a singer and leader of singing workshops, speaks of this shift through the practice of singing:

> I believe that the feeling that we have a *right* to be heard is very closely related to our ability to *make* ourselves heard. For many women, so much anxiety and inhibition has come to surround our voices, particularly when it comes to raising them in volume — really letting it rip — that it is truly difficult for us to make ourselves heard in group settings or public meetings. Hence, although the [singing] workshops started as a way of helping people to sing, it soon became very clear that much, much more was being released than the singing voice... And if so many of us feel robbed of our voices and the right to be heard, it must follow that this has implications collectively and politically.[5]

Another important theme in this program is for participants to ask for what they need in terms of support. I have often witnessed survivors struggling with the process of asking for support, and thinking through what that support would best look like. In one instance, I saw a woman use singing as her support in a very dramatic way. She was stuck in a difficult spot on a rock climb. She became more and more frightened, frustrated, and frozen, unable to go further, yet unwilling to come down. Emotions were very high. After asking her what she wanted in the way of support, she made a request for anyone who was within earshot to sing the lullaby she had learned during the course. Her companions were more than happy to oblige. I witnessed a powerful exchange of energy between the woman on the cliff and the women below as they supported her with song. I don't think I'd ever heard a lullaby sung with such gusto! In a debriefing of the event, she thanked the group and talked of the impact that the singing had on her, and how it calmed and "grounded" her so she had the presence and confidence to carry on. The women all shared a sense of accomplishment with her. The singing didn't get her to the top, but it provided something that enabled her to do it for herself.

This event indicates that some healing took place. It is this potential of singing to enable healing (for individuals and groups) that I wish to highlight.

The Healing Effects of Singing

> Singing has always seemed to me the most perfect means of communication... Since I cannot sing, I paint.
> —Georgia O'Keefe (1922)[6]

Through my study of "what happens" when women sing, I found that singing is holistic and exercises all our human capabilities. As a tool for healing work, it can help us stay present and grounded when the degree of risk increases. It can help us stay connected to others, while opening both the senses and the imagination to intuitive knowledge.[7]

At the individual level, singing is making music with the body as instrument. As such, it is a form of "body work" that has the potential to do what all therapeutic body work does. It can release tensions, loosen blockages of cellular energy, and access emotions and memories that may be locked in various locations in the body.

Most therapeutic practices incorporate techniques that help their subjects to "get their feelings out" and "express their anger." However, the prospect may be paralyzing for those of us who are either disconnected from our voices (and bodies), unfamiliar with our own emotions, or terrified to really let go with unstructured sound. For survivors of trauma or violence, singing is a contained and structured way to begin making sounds where the ability to make any sound has been constricted. The playful use of singing can help survivors move through the terror of making sounds or of losing control vocally. In many cases, the process of singing is a doorway to expressing "taboo" or terrifying emotions.

Even though singing *itself* may seem like a risky endeavor, each song has its own way of containing itself. (In terms of risk, participants should always be encouraged to decide for themselves what they want to take on.) Unlike speech, a song is an entity that has clear boundaries, a structure in which to participate, and a definite end or resolution. Bernice Johnson Reagon, founder and director of the singing group Sweet Honey in the Rock, states that "The song is what you use to get you to the singing."[8] Because of its structure, a concrete feeling of success and satisfaction can be felt upon completion of a song.

The playfulness of singing also offers survivors, who are heavily cocooned in themselves, a way to give themselves some pleasure. It is a simple pleasure, not artificially induced by drugs or other stimulants, which can offer a taste of life-affirming joy, and possibly, hope.

The process of "giving voice" is sacred work and singing allows us to express ourselves as spiritual beings. It connects us to our humanity and to our sacredness; it grounds us and centres us in our power. Singing can be a sublime experience, eliciting joy, awe, wonder, and reverence, even in the midst of despair and sadness. It moves and transforms energy. (Evangelists have used this knowledge extensively in musical and pedagogical practices.) Singing can also inspire our individual and collective will to act in the world.

When a group of individuals sing *en masse*, each member contributes to building a synergistic spiral of collective energy, insight and creativity. Singing creates an opportunity for us to open up to one another in order to hear each other in a deep and integral way. Singing crosses differences of class, race, religion, sexuality and age. It creates a space where differences can be seen and acknowledged in a positive and powerful way. There are countless stories of the ways that music has acted as a bridge between people in the midst of war and conflict, returning a sense of humanity to those dehumanizing proceedings.

For women throughout time, singing has been used as a tool of resistance, a survival strategy, a comfort, a companion, a guide to self, a way to strengthen identity and purpose. It has also been a weapon against despair and alienation, and a means to communicate "subversive" information to others.[9] Within society's expectations of what it means to be a woman, there are very strong prescriptions about what uses of "voice" are appropriate. In contexts where female children are instructed that "little" girls should be seen and not heard, the idea and the expectation for women to be *silent* is planted.

Like speech, singing is a gendered activity. In the face of pervasive misogyny, it has tremendous potential to assist women in integrating what fragments us internally and seeks to isolate us collectively. For women, singing is a way to be powerful ("in our power"). It allows us to be in our bodies in a way often considered unacceptable in a male-dominated society.

By engaging in an activity that is transformative, individuals and groups have the potential to be transformed. When all of a person's capabilities are exercised by an activity like singing, collective change is potentially increased. In reference to the vital role of singing in the 1960's civil rights movement in the southern USA and other movements for liberation, Johnson Reagon states that, "you cannot sing a song and not change your condition."[10]

There is political value to women speaking up and out — to being *respectfully* heard. However, this is a difficult thing to do for at least three reasons: 1) Women acting in our own interests — especially for pleasure, is seen by mainstream North American society as selfish, even sinful and destructive. 2) Homophobia, as on offspring of heterosexism, is used as a device for regulating female behaviour and for discouraging women from taking pleasure with other women. 3) Internalized woman-hating manifests itself in very insidious and ugly ways: self-hatred, women targeting and scapegoating other women, disrespect, suspicion, envy, devaluation as well as fear of other women's (and one's own) power. Again, Johnson Reagon asserts that "when we sing, we announce our existence."[11] It is a very self-loving, and therefore subversive, act for women to sing for themselves, with other women, and for other women. It is one way to reconfigure the economics of power, pleasure, and desire.

Singing Our Way "Home"

Singing, particularly in a context of struggle or transition, has the capacity to enable us to do very difficult things. When we act on our own behalf and are successful, we may experience this as a holistic "peak experience," or what I refer to as "home." Such events are rare, momentary, and usually transformative, changing the way we see the world. The experience of coming home to oneself occurs in such moments. It feels right and it feels good. Most significantly, such a regenerative act is also creative. Home is the place where one feels safe. Home is also about connection, relationship and about a sense of "being-ness." Home is about being at home in the self, of truly knowing who you are. Home is an ideal, a mythical place and a focal point of desire. Miriam Therese Winter refers to coming home as a very common need for spiritual, emotional and even physical healing:

> It has been said that all real sickness is homesickness... We are homesick for wholeness, for at-homeness with ourselves, God, the human family, and all of creation on and beyond

what we call planet Earth. We are in need of healing, and healing means coming home.[12]

If home is "the ability to be who you are wherever you are,"[13] then women have a particular stake in "coming home," for the oppression of women keeps us all in a state of exile.[14] The opposite to exile is "home." Louise Karch identifies what we, as women in a world of normalized violation of femaleness, often fail to see.

> There is a myth of "home" for women. In a woman-hating context, they don't have a home. They may have a dwelling place that may act more as a cage as much to keep danger out as to live in. Women don't have the freedom to walk out the door. Women don't have the freedom to make decisions about their lives. Women don't have the means to prevent the rape of ourselves.[15]

Karch and Sandra Butler both point to the idea that the experience of home is always a pursuit for women. It is a pursuit that is about life and creation, and about survival. While one could argue that some women are highly privileged and don't appear to suffer the oppression of sexism, that is illusory. The threat of violence may be subtle, but it is always there. It causes all women to live in a state of fragmentation and exile. Security and safety are always conditional. Therefore, any process that inspires courage and endurance, and contributes toward reintegration and healing of our fragmented and alienated selves, is welcome. First directed toward survival, the process is then turned toward the development of our full human selves. Singing is one process that contributes both to survival and to creativity.

There is a special connection to "home" for women who are engaged in movements of growth, learning, change, transition, or struggle. Women acting on our own behalf are a disruption to the normalization of male domination. Women's strength *as women*, autonomous and independent from men, is a threat to structures and systems. As we become stronger, we ourselves may feel threatened by the loss of what has been our familiar, albeit oppressive or unsatisfactory relationships. As Michele George says, "Who will there be to play with?"[16] As a woman changes the context in which she lives, the context must make room for the changes.

Singing can help us cope with the difficult struggles of change in ourselves and in the world. In creating "home" for ourselves, we are connecting intensely with our own capabilities and with our *femaleness*.

Some Important Considerations for Facilitating Singing

There are no formulas or recipes for singing with groups or individuals. The primary consideration for facilitating purposeful singing is to create and maintain a space that is as safe as possible. This is essential to help women take the risks that may be inherent in singing.

The holistic potential of singing should not be underestimated or misused. Even when it is not the purpose or intention, the effects of singing can be very deep, mystical, and may overlap into the therapeutic domain.[17] Singing must be used respectfully and responsibly, with the understanding that there may be unanticipated responses. Facilitators of singing should be explicit about the intent of using music (as with any exercise or activity), sensitive to context and to the identities of the participants, and accountable for the results of its use. While group singing has historically been used for purposes of good, it has also been used for ill.

Attention must be paid to content. Picking the right song, or at least one that will not "trigger" an unwelcome response, is important to maintain a level of emotional safety. I might select challenging material to set people thinking or feeling, but I would do so aware of the emotional climate at the time, and I'd select accordingly. For example, I have led singing with a group of "Women of Courage" participants who were tired, stressed and feeling particularly saddened by the impending end of their intimate and powerful course together. Not being attentive to where they were at, I chose to sing a song that was emotionally challenging to listen to. It sent at least three people into crisis at a time when they were vulnerable. This caused me to re-examine my empathic ability, to accurately sense a group's readiness, and to choose the direction that a singing activity will take. (I've also learned it is better to avoid singing sometimes.) This is largely an intuitive process. But it is not necessary for a facilitator to rely on intuition alone. So, if I don't have great radar in the moment, I do an energy check-in before suggesting a song. (e.g. "Where are you at right now? What do you sense would be helpful for us to do?) Hopefully, I will receive clues about whether singing would be useful and, if so, what material might be appropriate. If energy is low, I go for a familiar, non-demanding kind of song, slow to moderately paced, and reflective. If energy is high, frazzled, or unfocused, I teach a song as a way of refocusing, grounding and reconnecting the group. In some sense, the feel of the songs I choose mirrors the energy and emotional pitch of the group. It is a way of acknowledging externally what is going on inwardly. Participants usually experience this as relaxing, refreshing, and connecting.

As mentioned earlier, it is part of the therapeutic process to ensure that participants have permission to calibrate the intensity of their own experience. This means they can always decline or participate in ways that are most comfortable for them. Because singing enables the healing process, it is much less goal-oriented than some other forms of healing. I respect the choices of those who choose not to sing, recognizing that they may also fully participate as listeners (i.e. they are not "resistant" or "non-singers"). Through painful experience I have learned that any efforts to force or manipulate an individual or a group to sing is disrespectful of personal boundaries. I would strongly caution against it.

I am most successful when I am well-grounded in my own power and in touch with what's going on for *me*. If I'm feeling low, chances are the group I'm working with is, too. If my "felt sense"[18] is accurate, I may choose a song that says something that I sense the group is thinking but that no one is saying, or a song that captures what we are all saying and celebrates the work that we've done to get there.

Every facilitator has their own personality, values and styles that are integral to their performance as a leader. There is no right "way" to lead singing. I would suggest that you rely on your own leadership skills and style, and develop a comfort with singing. Amass a repertoire of songs that you like to sing. It is important that the activity be sincerely presented. Be yourself, relaxed and present. I only sing songs that reflect what I believe.

Using music with women requires a sensitivity to women's ways of seeing and some understanding of the issues that women contend with. Songs also reflect cultural identities and histories. It is very important to recognize the culture of participants and to ensure that the content chosen is respectful and non-appropriating.[19]

Songs are most effectively used when we connect to the song's context, and appreciate its historical, cultural, and political significance. This helps participants identify with what they are singing and derive a deeper personal meaning. In choosing content, attention must be given to who will be singing and listening, and to what that might mean for them. The highly metaphoric, symbolic and affective nature of songs presents limitless possibilities for meaning, but it also presents a responsibility for interpretation and respectful representation. I often give some information about a song's origins, before or after using it, as a way of framing and giving context for appreciation.

Conclusion

> It is a Pueblo belief that each human being is connected to the Creator, who is Spider Woman, by a strand of Her web attached to the tops of our heads. It is our doorway to Her and we have free choice as to whether we keep our doorway open to Her or close it. The teaching tells us that it is "only when we keep [this] door open by chanting through it, that we may draw upon this link to the creative wisdom of Spider Woman."[20]

To sing a spider woman's song is to trust in our abilities to weave our webs of connection, home, and creativity. It is to trust the strength of the strands of our efforts. It is to maintain a link to our higher and deeper selves. Like the tough silk of a spider's web, singing has tenacious strength, and elastic resilience. It can support us to do the work we need to do in the world.

And, finally, singing enables us to keep going. We sing to connect with one another, to spin ideas, to communicate the stories and images of our internal and external worlds, to generate and move our energy, and to keep the loom shuttling with the threads of our lives.

We Are Whole and We Are Holy

V.M. Joyce (music), Carole Ann Burris (transcription)

2. We are here and we are living
   We are here and we are living
   Walking in the shadow
   Or walking in the light.
   We are here and we are living.

3. We are sad and we are grieving
4. We have loves that we remember
5. We are strong and we are healing

LAST VERSE: repeat first verse

To end the song, sing the last line 4 times in honour of the four directions.

SUGGESTED ALTERNATIVE VERSES:

We are women and we remember (for memorials of women who have died from violence)
We are strong, we are resisting
We are healers for ourselves and others
We have just one world to live on
We are all mind, body, and spirit
We must plan for our childrens' children
We can learn to live together
We are listening with a heart that's open
We must speak and we must listen
We are both inside and outside
We are speaking from our spirit's centre
We are planning for generations
We are warriors and we are lovers

This song is designed as a multi-purpose chant. Verses for special occasions can be substituted or individuals may be invited to create verses spontaneously during the singing.

(this song was originally written for the AIDS Vigil, Toronto, October, 1990)

Making Connections

Karen Howe (words and music), Rowan Wolf (score)

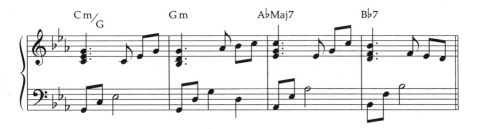

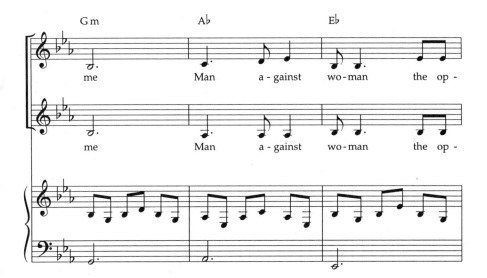

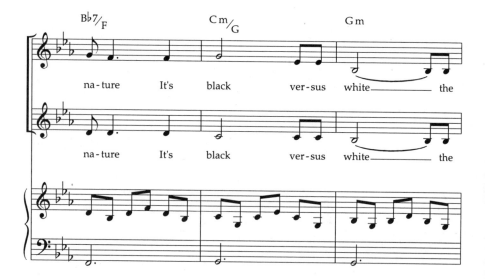

se - pa - rate I'll ne - ver feel my - self whole.

se - pa - rate I'll ne - ver feel my - self whole.

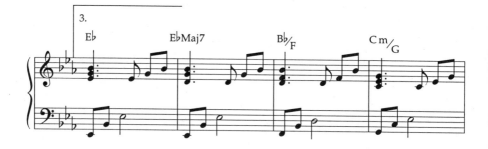

Wind Through the Garden
Trish Gould (words and music)

1. Ooo...
2. The Life Force is mov-ing like wind through the
3. On the tail of a co-met I jour-ney with-

gar - den whis-per-ing voi - ces speak soft-ly
in___ where sha-dows are bright-ened tight pla-ces ex-

to me of long a-go pla-ces through
pan-ded though my heart___ is quak-ing the

time and great dis - tance sing-ing___ songs of
bree-zes are blow - ing mak-ing___ room for new

Bridge
(after verse 3)

home___
being___
with a

deep crack of thun-der and the skies thick and black in my

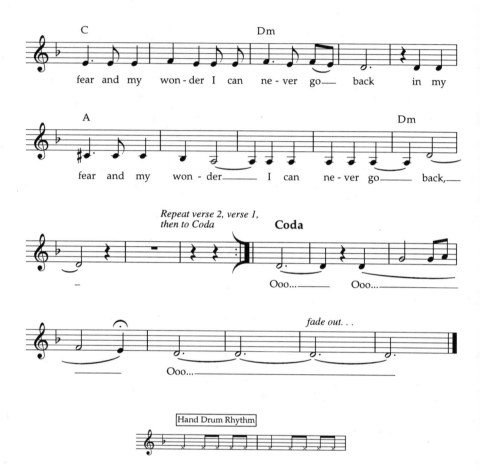

Clear Heart

Nancy Reinhold (words and music), Rowan Wolf (score)

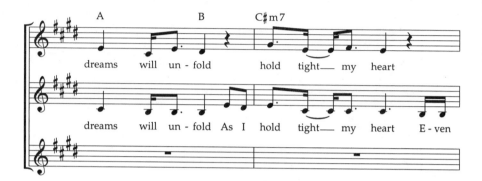

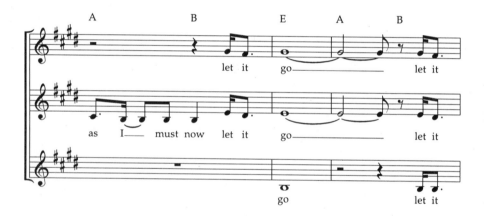

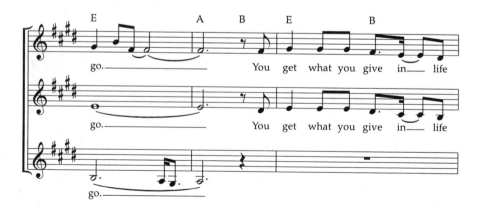

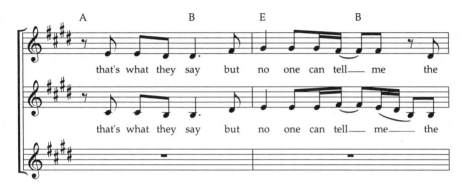

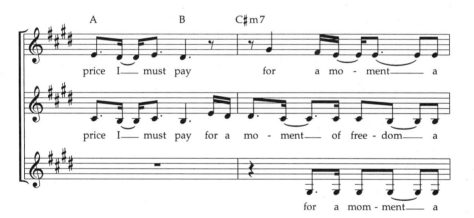

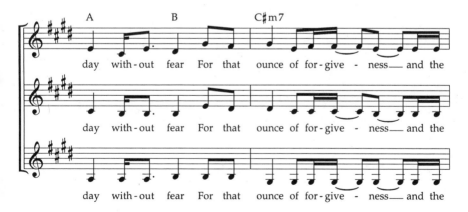

My Mother's Eyes

Deborah Romeyn (words and music), Rowan Wolf (score)

Woman Healing for Change

Esther Kathryn (Klassen) (words and music)
Karen Toole-Mitchell (words)

Chorus:

Wo - man, wo-man Hea - ler, Wo-man heal-ing for change;— We are wo-men to - ge - ther, Sis-ters sing-ing for change.——

Verse:

Wo - man as mo-ther, lift - ing, touch-ing, calm - ing and hold - ing; Wo-man— birth - ing, risk - ing new life, Wo - men cre-a - ting our world.

1. Woman as mother, lifting, touching,
   calming and holding;
   Woman birthing, risking new life,
   Women creating our world.

2. Woman as worker weaving, toiling,
   straining and striving,
   Woman laboring, shaping freedom,
   Women reclaiming our world.

3. Woman as singer, speaker, writer,
   voicing, proclaiming
   Woman knowing, naming, wailing;
   Women transforming our world.

4. Woman as mentor, teacher, elder,
   listening, affirming;
   Woman befriending, daughters, sisters,
   Women as soul of our world.

5. Woman as wild one, shouting, sighing,
   silences breaking,
   Woman passionate, fiercely tender,
   Women as womb of our world.

6. Woman as spider, artist, goddess
   making connections
   Woman weaving, spinning, dancing
   Women as web of our world.

Song of Surrender

Deborah Gabinet (words and music)

I guess— it's been a long time com - in'—

I sure re - sis - ted all the way.

But now— I a - wait the sweet sur - ren - der.—

want the love the light and the sound— take your

torch di-vine Spi-rit— lead the way;— so I can be found.

2. When I go deep inside the temple
   When I find the love within that's real
   Angels and Guides are there to show me
   The love of God; the only love that can heal.

CHORUS
   Now I want the peace God granted her child
   I've been worn down by illusion; and I've been runnin' wild
   I want the love; the light and the sound
   Take your torch Divine Spirit lead the way so I can be found.

Goddess Trinity

Barbara Yussack (words and music)
Esther Kathryn Klassen) (transcription)

To the Earth that is Our Mother

Karen Howe (words and music), Rowan Wolf (score)

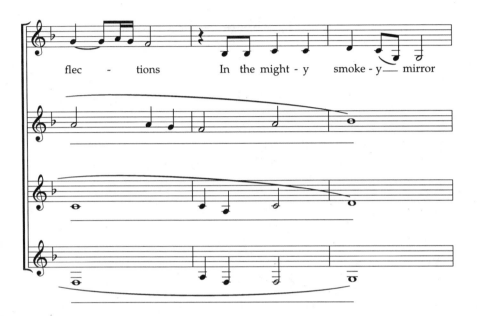

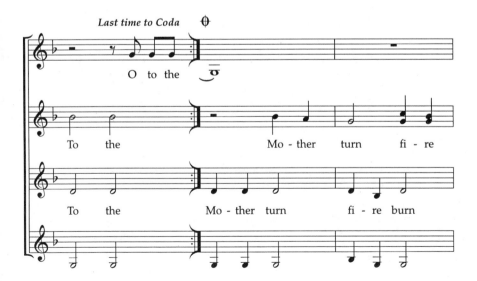

2. We give thanks for all the seasons and the lessons that they bring.
   We give thanks for all connections to the greatness we do sing.

3. We give thanks for many colours. For the gifts of choice and chance
   We give thanks for tears and laughter and for hearts that yearn to dance.

Goddess Trinity: Sacred Circle Dance

Barbara Yussack

See music to "Goddess Trinity." Participants face into circle and join hands: left hand (feminine side) is palm up, to receive energy and right hand (masculine side) is palm down, to transmit energy. Two positions of hand-holding are used: V-HOLD with hands held down by the hips, elbows straight; and W-HOLD with elbows bent so that hands are positioned by the shoulders.

With hands in V-HOLD, the body sways R. L. R. L. R. With L foot leading, step forward into circle; L. R. L. R. and bend elbows so hands are in W-HOLD. Body sways L. R. L. R. Raise arms up so hands are above the head. Participants circle around themselves in counterclockwise direction, i.e., L. R. L. R. until they once again face into the circle. Extend arms into centre of circle and use scooping motion towards the body (thereby taking the Goddess Energy from the centre within) and step backwards out of circle L. R. L. R. Pause for two beats.

Verses two, three and four are identical. Movement of the circle is to the left, honouring the feminine side of the body. The basic step is the grapevine: L foot steps L and R foot crosses behind or in front of it for three bars. The body is left in a "twist" position, wanting to turn outwards from the circle. In the last bar, the participants circle around themselves in five steps, L. R. L. R. L. using the fifth step to rejoin hands so they will be ready to begin swaying to the R as the next verse begins.

Hands are in V-HOLD. Body sways R. L. R. L. R. Grapevine begins: **step L, cross R foot behind L, step L, cross R foot in front of L**. Repeat sequence twice more, ending with R foot crossed over L. The body is "twisted" and wants to turn outwards, so let it! With hands over the heart to acknowledge the sacredness of the Elder within, participants turn around themselves, stepping L. R. L. R. L and rejoin hands in V-HOLD. Repeat for verse three, honouring the Mother within. Repeat for verse four, honouring the Daughter within.

With hands in V-HOLD, body sways R. L. R. L. R. Step forward into centre of circle (eight steps): L. R. L. R. L. R. L. R. and bend elbows so hands are in W-HOLD. Body sways eight times: L. R. L. R. R. L. R.

Conclusion: Turning L shoulder outwards, join R hands in centre of circle, symbolizing the connection of the Goddess from within each to the other, and step forward L. R. L. R. etc., until the music ends.

Alternate Ending: If more than 10 participants are in the circle, the integrity of the Goddess Wheel cannot be maintained. Use alternate ending below:

Place L hand on L shoulder in front and extend R arm towards centre of circle. Step L. R. L. R. etc., until the music ends.

Chapter Eight

Women and Spirituality

Imagination Life's Heartbeat

Karen Toole-Mitchell

Every so often we go to an event, a lecture, workshop, a play, even a movie and we're ready to be changed, open to receive, or perhaps even surprised into a new way of conceiving.

I went to the Spider Women Retreat, and I'd like to share what happened for me at the workshops I attended. I want to share these workshops because they have stayed with me, pushing, probing, calling me into a renewed spirit of awareness.

The first workshop was titled, "Writing Your Heartbeat," and was facilitated by the Jamaican-born Toronto author, Lillian Allen. I went because I thought I should. After all, I am writing, and often I feel like I'm charging into the dark blindfolded, pen in hand! I thought it would be a good practical workshop with some handy tips on creative writing. So, 15 of us gathered in a fairly small room and Lillian asked us to "find our heartbeats." Really, literally. We were a rather lifeless bunch. Hardly any of us could locate a heartbeat.

So, she gave that up. She asked us then to sit for a moment and remember a time when we did something right. Remember a time we felt empowered. A time we felt that it was all worth it. That felt wonderful! I was amazed at how little time we give ourselves to reflect on the good, the moments of "Right on. Yes, I did that well!" Then she said, "Make the sound of your power!" Right then I felt my heart beat. It was panic. Sound of my power? No words? How about we talk about it? But she was clear; make the sound of your power. In a one-liner she said, "Sound comes before words. We have our sound before we use words. Make your sound." By the time we were done the room was full of sounds which ranged from grunts to sighs to cheers. The power in the room was palpable. Then we returned to the heartbeat, and every single one of us had no trouble finding a heartbeat. We were then to make the sound of heartbeat. No two heartbeats sounded alike in that room! Perhaps no two hearts ever sound alike? Perhaps all our hearts have a unique special beat that belongs only to us?

After we made the sound of our heartbeat, Lillian had the women echo it around us, while we made the sound of our power. It's an incredible risk to write about this experience because it truly is beyond words. I don't have the words to describe a room filled with the sound of my heartbeat while I felt my power, but I know it was a spiritually awesome and transforming experience. I felt it from head to foot, from inside out, from outside in.

Mystics, prophets, artists, visionaries, have been speaking, writing, teaching and creatively expressing the truth of such moments since the beginning of time. These are the moments when we "know" not with our head or through the intellect, but we "know" with heart and soul who we are, why we are, and that we are connected to the power of creation.

Now I can already hear the skeptics saying, "Aren't you making a bit much of some sounds? After all, it was just a workshop. Some people sure have a good imagination!"

My response to that is, "Yes, I am making much of it." The alternative is to choose to belittle it, and we've all been, at times, belittled to irrelevance. Yet, it was just a workshop. That's what made it so awesome. I went expecting what I knew and left in awe of what I didn't know. And finally, yes, some people sure have a good imagination. Thank God. I mean that; thank God, thank God or the holy, or the source of divine awe in any way you image her, him or it! Imagination is the essence that connects us to the creative power of the spirit. Some days it's like a superhighway with flashing images streaking by; other days it's a marvellous country road, or a walk along the water's edge. Some days it's a thin fragile thread ready to break.

Folk singer Harry Chapin has a song in one of his collections called "Flowers are red and green."[1] It's a song about a little boy who wanted to paint flowers in "all the colours of the rainbow" and a very unimaginative teacher who was threatened by his imagination. So she tells him, "Flowers are red, green leaves are green, there's no need to see flowers any other way than the way they have always been seen."

There's a need for every one of us to be able to hear and see and connect to the image inside us, the image beyond us, for there is what we name God. There, in the image-in-action. There, listening to your heartbeat and writing it, dancing it, painting it. Which brings me to another workshop.[2]

I like to draw. I always have. As long as I can remember I've been fascinated when something is created by a pencil in my hand. So, the other workshop I attended was conducted by Heather Spears, an artist, poet, court illustrator, of Copenhagen, originally from British Columbia. I went to her workshop because I didn't want to do anything heavy or difficult. I'm not sure when I last worked as hard. I walked in the large room, and all around were big newsprint sheets, pastels, crayons and gym mats.

Heather asked us to begin by conceptualizing the periphery of our vision. She asked us to "fill in the edges." In other words, don't aim at filling the centre of the page with a subject. Stare at an object in the middle of the room but try to image, on the paper, the furthest edge of your vision.

My inner reaction was, "What in the world are we doing?" I have never paid much attention to the edge of my vision. What does it matter what is out on the edge anyway?

She kept pushing at this, pushing further and further out till we were almost seeing our own ears and eyebrows. Then she moved to the centre of the room and sat down. She asked us to stare fixedly at her face. She began to speak of a "moral way" to see, a way to see that's not fantasy but reality, a reality that is not merely accurate but a reality of image and likeness.

She said things like: "The brain loves line. Don't draw a line; draw the space between the lines." Now maybe every art student knows this, but I didn't! I also thought I had two choices in art, the creation of an accurate image, or the creation of my fantasy.

Most of us can't do the accurate image because we're not technically skilled enough, and most of us put down fantasy because it's "just my imagination." No one had ever told me there was a middle place of creation between those two polarities.

No one had ever told me that there was a middle place between the precise technical (true) reproduction and the unfettered release of my fantasy. No one told me about the way of creating an image or likeness that comes out of the dialogue between me and the other.

As Heather put it, "It takes incredible respect to draw the human face. We have to stop seeing what's in our heads already, and take the time to see what's really there. And if we do, we can see in every face the face of God."

I was stopped in my tracks. She said, "God." This was a workshop on art! But she was talking about respect, awe, image and God! The other (little) guidance she gave us was, "Don't move your eyes from the face in front of you. Keep them fixed, and let your hand work by itself. Try to keep your eyes fixed. Keep looking until you see what you've never seen before."

This wasn't a workshop merely on art or drawing; this was a workshop on vision and the divine. It was a workshop on how to see with a whole new set of eyes — eyes that are not interested in lines of distinction, eyes that are unprejudiced by what had been assumed to be there. Imagine if we looked at life like that all the time. Imagine if our brains could stop loving lines. Imagine if we stopped seeing what we expect to see, and started to see what is really there. Imagine if we took the time to do that!

I remember a resource book I once had for youth groups. On one page it had a sketch of two fantastic creatures. One had horns and armour. The other was flat, with pricklies all over it. Underneath the picture was the caption, "I don't know who you are, but I hate you!" The brain loves lines of limit, exclusion, separation (especially in relation to the unfamiliar).

As I stared into the face of the person I was sketching that day, I saw what I never expected to see. I saw small lights in eyes, muscles that move the nose, the cheeks, the mouth, and I began to see a shimmering essence. And just as I was about to rub my eyes and look again, Heather said, "Don't be surprised if the edges begin to soften and light begins to form. Don't try to make it go away. Go with it."

Usually we don't look at anyone long enough to see that light. Usually we think we know what our partner looks like, what our children look like, what the hairdresser, waitress, sales clerk, doctor look like — but look again.

Look without the judgment of expectation and assumption. Look long and look deep, and you may see the light of another living soul. What a morally marvellous way to see what could be! What an art! The art of finding God's image in every face. Go ahead, sketch it, but remember to look in the face and not at the paper. The creation is in front of you, waiting for your art to image it.[3]

The Motherpath Cards

Judy Bancroft

I recently experienced a major transition in my life, moving from one city to another. I moved 850 miles, leaving behind two daughters, family, and many close friends. I had lived in Winnipeg for 38 years. One friend, in particular, had journeyed with me for 37 of those years, and is truly a friend, a sister, and a soulmate.

When we came to our new city, which is gradually becoming home, we had no extended family or friends. Bringing three teenagers there meant that we had much parenting to do, helping the children to adjust. We dealt with the many issues involved in settling into a new home and community. I missed my dear friend terribly. I missed having her to talk things over with, for we had always supported each other on our spiritual journey. We tried to visit each other, and I returned to Winnipeg two or three times during that first year. Now telephone calls and letters sustain our friendship.

One tool that I turned to, and found really helpful on my journey alone, was my Motherpath cards. They became my daily companions and my support. I was in need of guidance, and I felt that I needed a backup for trusting in my own intuition and inner wisdom. The cards were always there for me, they never let me down. I trust and believe that what they invoke in me is my truth, for the moment.

I am grateful for this gift that comes through Carol Rose and Lu-Ann Lynde. They are a set of poetry and visuals designed to use the Biblical mothers as models for growth and transformation.[1] I am grateful, also, for Carol and Lu-Ann's work in bringing this treasure up out of their beings, to gift our world.

I believe the blessings from them go on and on, as others are guided, blessed, and aided in doing the work of their own lives, with the help of the Motherpath cards.

"Leah: Motherpath Card" by Carol Rose and Lu-Ann Lynde

Earth Woman

Robyn Maharaj

She wakes me with stale breath
praying for tears and the troubled sea
my profile etched in copper
coins cover her tired eyes

she emerges from cracked soil
hair tangles with tree roots
fingertips eroded
from sawdust and coal

she feeds on wild rice
cooling in ceramic bowls
her limbs warm and pale
as the bleached bark of a maple

bits of broken shell cascade
down a wooden staircase that
leads her to desert solitude
her stone lips mute
as the air fills
with the rain of white ash

I am frightened by the curve
of her spine

oh woman

Di Brandt

oh you
who are coming to me
through darkness
having risked everything
how you wept over your
shattered child
her bones scattered
everywhere
your hands holding now
branch & stone

your voice shines for me
your face half in shadow
half in light
how you dance up into
my green world, yes!
how it is suddenly green!
snow melting
the dark receding
the tree roots in my head
sprouting leaves
& blossoms!

how you balance right & left
your feet caress the ground
how you sing
your voice deep & soft & low
your song cuts me open
like a knife flaying me
here
there is where i am reborn
you

the croning

Carol Rose

she imagines
fear leaving her body
on long strands of silvery
hair, a light
           under her scalp
she dreams
an old hag, moon-stones
& candles, a wreath
in blue flames
           her body translucent
she hears
drum songs & chanting
whispers of prayer
the feet of women
           spiraling in dance
she sees
gossamered maidens
fresh garlands, a staff
& crude twisted copper
           sized to her head
she knows
magic & ritual
the rites marking change
her place in the circle
           crown worn in pride

Healing Toward Spiritual Wholeness

Carol Rose

Women's groups have been meeting for years, providing a safe place for women to express feelings, and to voice political and family concerns. Recently a new type of women's group has emerged, one that brings women of different faith backgrounds together to explore questions of spirituality. Sparked by what they believe is a lack of interest, or an insensitivity to the spiritual experiences of women, in their own faith communities, these groups help women articulate and validate their experiences. They act as laboratories, places in which women can "experiment" with the sacred and feel empowered by it. Groups may create new rituals, write prayers or sing women-authored hymns. They may honour special events, like the birth of a child, a mid-life celebration, or a death. They may encourage study and the development of teachings that become part of a collective oral transmission known as "women's wisdom." In the company of others, women sense that they are not alone in their quest. Together they lament the loneliness and estrangement they have felt, while at the same time, they work toward building a community that is reflective of their inner needs.

They encourage each other to question, to unravel what is missing for them. They ask questions like, What is women's spirituality? How does women's prayer and meditation differ from traditional prayer? How do women integrate experiences of loss, of change or of joy into their spirituality? How do women talk about their unique needs, recognizing that there is both pain and healing in admitting those needs?

Some choose to reflect on their dreams, sensing that dreams are part of the spiritual work they need to do together. They recognize that dreams are, and always have been, significant tools in understanding both Spirit and waking life.

Many women realize that their experiences of the numinous are so different that they have either been devalued or, at best tolerated in their home communities. For example, their strong desire to celebrate birth and call it holy is often dismissed as "charming." Their awareness of the cycles of nature and their connection to the earth are often labeled "pagan," especially by those in religious institutions.

Many speak of a sense of disequilibrium that develops, a sense of being "out of sorts" with (so-called) normative religious practice. Some become fearful, afraid to name what they actually need for their own spiritual well-being. Some feel censored, unable to speak about meeting the Divine in the midst of their own lives, in the reality of their own bodies. They are silent, afraid of how different their experiences sound from those described by conventional spiritual teachers or religious authorities.

However, in women's spirituality groups they do talk. They talk openly about meeting the holy in the midst of ordinary living — in their interactions with loved ones and with nature. They talk about Spirit immanent, the Divine One who dwells within everything. They share how they have come to know holiness in their pain, as well as in their healing. They talk to gain confidence, to feel less bifurcated from their own inner experiences. They talk to each other so that they can feel a sense of "sameness," a sense of being less strange and (possibly) less mad. They know from the past that it's dangerous to voice opinions, especially when their perceptions are so different from those in power. They keep their sense of holiness private, sharing it only with each other.

As a result, many feel divided between the spiritual life they share with their family, and the celebrations they've developed in their woman centred communities. Some experience this as a terribly un-healthy condition, much like the dissociative states described by sur-vivors who are in one place and yet not really there at all. Many have had to leave the old religious teachings and the institutions in order to feel healthy and sane.

Others remain and, despite the pain, they struggle from within. They challenge us to look at Scripture suspiciously, to expose the ways in which women have been "written out" of that narrative (by not being named or acknowledged for their contributions). They re-define the lives of Biblical women from a woman centred perspec-tive, and they claim them as role models, ancient wise ones who guide them on their journey. They show us that women's lives are sacred, that their insights are valued. They encourage women to recreate the language and imagery of prayer, and to reinterpret sacred text. They remind women (and men) of the vision of the Prophets, of the need to protest against injustice and to continue to dream of universal peace. They see the sacred realm as elastic (like the womb), as an ever-expanding set of truths. They are the bringers of the "good news." They teach us that women's spirituality is inclusive, and that it can grow to accommodate new life, new insight, new ritual. They inspire us to hang on to our vision, affirming that women's understanding of the sacred is a necessary component in the evolution toward spiritual wholeness and peace.

I have had the privilege of participating in various groups of this sort, both in Canada and in the United States. Some groups form themselves around a theme, or a time of year. Often they are composed of individuals who are strangers to each other. Women may come together because they have a vague sense of "something missing" in their spiritual lives (whether they attend synagogue or church, or whether they have lost their sense of "belonging" to any faith community). They come hungry for opportunities to share their feelings of emptiness and isolation. And they come with a belief that, together, they will be able to sort through the isolation.

One such group began in the cloistered walls of a Winnipeg monastery. Simply called Women Journey, it was facilitated by a nun who helped us examine what women call "holy." As it turned out, several sessions had to be devoted to that topic alone. The consensus was that music, song, movement, dance and dreams were very much a part of women's spiritual reality. During those weekly sessions women learned new songs (often authored by women), experimented with movement exercises, and practiced circle dancing. They brought dream journals, and they shared insights gleaned from their dreams, from what they called their "soul stories." They talked about birth and death, and about the ways in which these were doorways to a greater awareness of the sacred. They spoke of how they knew the Divine "from the inside out," from their bodies, as well as their minds. When the weekly meetings ended, the participants felt that they had found a community of like-minded, like-spirited sisters. What they had intuited about spirituality had been confirmed, and they left the monastery with renewed energy and conviction.

Annually, I attend a Jewish feminist retreat, called *Achyot Or*. These "sisters of light" come together from various North American cities every Memorial Day weekend. For four days we struggle to reconnect to our religious and spiritual roots. We locate ourselves in a physically beautiful setting, inviting the natural world into our process. Our sense of "creatureliness" (of being one among many life forms) is reinforced as we study sacred text, pray, sing, meditate and dance together in nature. Nothing is incidental; the chirping of birds, the rustle of leaves, the swish of wind, the scent of flowers, the rain drenched mountains, and the calm sunlight on natural lakes, all get woven together and contribute to our sense of "being in the presence of mystery." In this idyllic setting we seek to find our own unique forms of spiritual expression. Based on a Chassidic belief that humans are gifted with speech only to articulate the awe and wonder of creation, I wrote the following chant to the glorious music of Pachelbel's Canon:

> I am holy
> you are holy
> we are holy
> all is holy...
> Holy Presence lives among us
> dwells within us
> and surrounds us.

These words were inspired by the Kabbalistic image of the Divine Feminine, the Shekinah, the holy immanent who wanders with us in our exile. The women who sang this chant felt exiled too. They felt exiled from their tradition and exiled from a Scripture that often disregards or minimalizes the importance of women. For a moment we all felt Her presence, and we rejoiced.

After the chanting was over, three women led a Torah study session about Miriam the prophetess. The Torah is the embodied wisdom teaching of our people, written on parchment and rolled into a sacred scroll. The story we were working with dealt with Miriam speaking her feelings about Moses' mate, and becoming leprous as a consequence of voicing her opinion. Before the actual study began, one of the facilitators asked the other two to identify where in the body they experience "prophesy." I answered "my back." The other two also sensed that a great deal of what they "receive" gets processed in their back, especially when what they know does not get expressed, or is not fully understood. We used this information to create an exercise. The three of us stood back to back, and one member of the threesome began making sound,; sounds that came from deep inside. The other two interpreted the sounds and turned them into language. We wrote down the words. Next the second member of the team made her sounds, and then the third. After all three sound messages had been recorded, we read "the prophesy."

We took this exercise back to the group. Before we began, however, we unrolled the Torah and we all stood inside the sacred circle of parchment it created. Each of the women held onto a portion of the scroll, wanting to connect with it.

One of the facilitators took a goblet, filled with honeyed water, and she named it "Miriam's cup." She held up the cup and said "we are here to read this story in our own voice. May our words sweeten the tale. May we be able to understand Miriam and all of her prophetic words." Then we talked about how men had been telling the stories of women, and how we now wanted to tell our own tales, from our own perspective. We shared our desire to experience our own prophetic voice and to add it to the body of wisdom we call Torah. The women rolled back the scroll, reverently dressing it in its velvet garment. They placed it gently on an altar, under a cluster of trees. We broke into groups of three, going into a wooded area to perform the exercise we had designed earlier. When all of the groups had performed the exercise and had recorded the words that they had "received," we gathered together in front of the Torah. Each group took a sip from Miriam's cup and then recited the traditional blessing over the Torah. The original story was read. Then each group added its prophetic words. This type of Torah study will probably never find its way into synagogue practice. However, the women who participated in it will always remember the ways in which their words, their prophesy, their insight had been added to the ongoing flow of oral tradition.

Another Winnipeg group searching for authentic expressions of women's spirituality is The Asherah Project. This collective has as its goal the reclamation of women's wisdom and spirituality. In its brochure, it describes itself as follows:

> We come from different spiritual traditions and backgrounds. As wise women, we seek to bring forward women's, knowledge and ways of learning. As spiritual women, we seek to reclaim the female divine in our lives and in our world. In the month of October, the Asherah Project sponsors a Performing Arts evening, a full day Wisdom School, and a closing ritual.

The group endeavours to blend the wisdom, ritual and culture of many faith groups, including Christian, Jewish, Wiccan, Islamic and

Aboriginal. For several months, women meet together to respectfully learn from each other, and to plan for the annual event. It is in the planning that much of the wisdom is shared. The Wisdom School includes workshops and seminars on Midwifery, The History of Tarot, Drumming, Holistic Politics, Menarche to Menopause, Healing Herbs, Journal Writing, Reflexology, Storytelling, Heroines from our Past, Healing Touch, Discovering the Goddess Within, Welcoming Children into the World, and Building Ritual. What makes this group unique is that it provides an opportunity for women to learn from each other, and from the diverse cultures and spiritual traditions that inform us. It also creates a forum for women to celebrate their spiritual and cultural differences, publicly. The event culminates in an interreligious ritual, open to all women.

Woman Healing for Change, which originated in 1992, is another organization that is working to create balance in women's lives, physically, spiritually and emotionally. Although it is Winnipeg-based, this organization has touched the lives and hearts of many women in Manitoba and across Canada, as is evident from some of the contributions to this anthology. Some women have found a safe haven in which to explore and experiment with their sense of the sacred. They have found strength in the company of others who are also searching for ways in which to heal and to change. They have brought their wisdom and their pain, their sense of spiritual isolation and their creativity. They have seen the beauty in each other's traditions, and they have learned to appreciate the various life paths that have led them to where they are in their own struggle toward wholeness. Together they are building a sense of community, a community that transcends differences in education, economics, culture and location. Together they are working toward a new vision of what it means to be whole, to be healed, to be holy.

I am delighted that women are meeting and talking about what is, possibly, the last bastion of inequality, the last stronghold of the patriarchy — the realm of the sacred. I am confident that these efforts will bring about great change, change in how women view their own spirituality, and change in how their faith communities will adapt to these new insights.

I Want Your Voice

Carmelita McGrath

Silence
can be,
be broken

old woman
I cannot speak
the things that coil
like serpents inside me
that build webs
spider-spit-spawn
tangling the cogs of fate

but I have heard

you slip
(I listened by your bed)
say untenable things
last week it was doubt
in all your saints
fist bunched around a rosary,
meaning only in its shape,
the circlet
from the beginning of life
before these times

old woman —
sibyl?
seer? Could I bend close,
translate these things
I cannot speak
into your voice, scarred
but unscared

you say, "I'm going
soon. I don't give a damn!"

Then set free my troubles,
take them and let them loose;
yours is a freedom I will not have
until I am old and they say
I'm childish.

your voice, yes
your voice
speaking the doubts of youth and age
around the circlet, not helpless prayers
but spinning rage
at the mad fervour
of rampant, pandering ideologues,
our mistrust of pallid gods,
politicos, written truths,
laws man-given
trusting nothing but hunger and instinct
trusting nothing but our bones

see how the circlet slips,
these blackened beads grow darker still
with the rage of your youth,
disillusionment of your age.
You hurl it all out
at a world
that will let you say anything now —
with your plastic cards in a file drawer
and you in the last room of life,
speaking for me,
and I, through you,
breaking the silence made of fear
sibyl?
seer?
are we set free?[1]

AIDS Cemetery

Mary Toombs

quilts are stapled to the railing
quilts are pasted on the floor
from narrow walkways sombre viewers
uneasily attend the laid out dead

quilted tombstones count the years
one is for a little girl of three

the designs were born in the lives of the dead
       a trumpeter heralds a jazz triumph
       a police badge claims its lawful space
       a sheet of music sings the moments
       champagne toasts a principal dancer
the small girl's dress is green

names are there   pet names   full names
and some have   no name   here
friends have stitched the memorial
embroidered sadness still rejoicing
"we're glad you died in a loving embrace"
the family weeps at home in silence

their lives are beating upon us
       in the stillness

900 quilts warm the sleep of the dead

Chapter Nine

Working for Change

finding words

Keith Louise Fulton

finding words to loosen what the mother tongue ties
is like learning the spells
unbinding our vows and breasts and feet and eyes
cutting the knots

        we reach out human hands
and I imagine us like paper dolls
scissored into sisterhood
by our dark births

First Mourn, Then Work for Change

Penni Mitchell

The story didn't begin with the shooting at the University of Montreal Polytechnique, yet that is how this story, and thousands of others to come, will begin.

Fourteen women gunned down by a would-be engineer dressed in battle fatigues who failed to make the grade and blamed feminists for his misfortune. The story cut to the bone. Few stories in the news feature women so centrally in their focus, yet it is the name of the man, Marc Lepine, that remains most prominent in our minds.

The women killed were: Geneviève Bergnon, Hélène Colgan, Nathalie Croteau, Barbara Daigneault, Anne-Marie Edward, Maud Haviernick, Barbara Kleuznick, Anne Turcotte, Annie Saint-Arneault, Michèlle Richard, Sonia Pelletier, Maryse Leclair, Anne-Marie Lemay and Maryse Laganière.

Canada became a different place on December 6, 1989. The Montreal Massacre — as the shooting deaths of 14 female engineering students at École Polytechnique has come to be known — marks a juncture in our history. Nothing will be the same again. And as the impact of the event is revisited each year on the anniverary, it becomes more and more difficult to remember what it felt like before it happened.

Though it has been called an isolated tragedy as well as an everyday act of misogyny, December 6 has grown from a public awareness reference point into a chorus for justice that seems to get louder with each passing year.

It is in the names of these women that December 6 is marked each year, yet for those of us still walking and breathing, the anniversary strikes a personal chord.

For me, it's as if their battle wounds have an analogous place in my flesh. I didn't know these women, but through the resonance of their lives, I discover each year a renewed focus on my own work as a feminist. As the saying goes: first mourn, then work for change.

Why do many women feel a personal connection to December 6th? Maybe it's because in a thousand small ways, we have all felt the gun pointed at us. Whether we've been threatened and intimidated on the street or at work, experienced date rape, survived sexual abuse, wife abuse or endured verbal threats, we know how it feels to be targeted.

Many women became adept at ducking the bullets, or making a game out of survival. For others, their sanity demands that they deny the guns are there at all.

Change, real change, happens when women refuse to make do. The "click" in consciousness happens when the significance of one event hooks up with hundreds of others.

In the case of violence against women it wasn't that anyone was in favour of a woman being killed nearly every day in Canada by a boyfriend, ex-boyfriend, spouse or ex-spouse, it was just that the Montreal Massacre made the connections impossible to ignore.

For many women who had felt safe ducking the bullets, the Montreal Massacre taught them that ducking the issue of violence wouldn't stop it from happening to them. Like the tougher scar tissue that grows over a wound, their grief grew into rage. Anger flowed into action as gun control became their issue.

Suzanne Laplante Edward was, in her own words, a "typical complacent, suburban, middle-class Canadian," before her 21-year-old daughter Anne-Marie's bullet-ridden body appeared on the front page of newspapers, slumped over a chair in the cafeteria at the university, one of 27 victims shot by Marc Lepine with his semi-automatic rifle.

Today, Ms. Laplante Edward is a hero. She is unmistakably one of the reasons that the federal government's latest gun control bill was successfully passed. The renewed movement for gun control would likely not have happened without the rage and determination of women like her, as mothers and peers of slain women turned into outspoken activists for gun control.

Heidi Rathjen is a hero too. She was an engineering student at the École Polytechnique when the shooting took place. Rathjen organized the memorial service for her 14 peers that was attended by thousands, including the prime minister. Rathjen also immersed herself in the gun control issue in the aftermath of the massacre, quitting an engineering job to become executive director of the Canadian Coalition for Gun Control.

The victory of Canada's new gun control bill against the powerful and well-funded gun lobby belongs largely to women who took up arms and won.

Manitoba Senator Sharon Carstairs also deserves credit. She

shepherded the bill through the Senate. Manitoba Senators Mira Spivak and Janis Johnson broke party rank and supported the bill. Seventy-five percent of women senators voted in favour of the bill; while 55 percent of male senators supported the bill.

Maybe it's no accident that the largest massacre in Canadian history has become a symbol of gender justice. Mourning is, after all, a stage of transformation. And having the faith to act out of a belief that one can make change possible is an act of courage that women are demonstrating every day.

Feminist and anthropologist Margaret Mead described it best:

"Never doubt that a small group of thoughtful, committed citizens can change the world. Indeed it is the only thing that ever has."[1]

"The Women's Monument." Photo by Donna F. Johnson

The Women's Monument:
In Memory of *Our* Fallen Comrades

Donna F. Johnson

Monument (from Latin monere, to remind), n. Anything by which the memory of persons or things is preserved, esp. a building or permanent structure; anything that serves as a memorial of a person, event or of past times; a document, a record.[1]

When I think of monuments I think, primarily, of war. Conquerors and conquistadors, men on horseback, brandishing weapons triumphantly. I think of military power.

Monuments take up space in parks and squares, plazas and intersections in cities and towns all over the world, solemnly reminding us of the ultimate cost of war. But there is a double message, for monuments also solemnly reinforce patriarchal notions of masculinity and manhood, nationalism, dominance, force, and cultural supremacy. In the war monument patriarchy honours itself in stone and steel, cement and iron, copper and marble and granite, lest we forget that this way of ordering and protecting life must and will endure. Sadly, in the patriarchal state, society does not benefit from the transformative power of memory.

In the centre of a tiny heritage park in Ottawa a different kind of monument has been erected. "The Women's Monument" was unveiled in 1992 to commemorate women who have been murdered by men. It was the dream of a handful of women who work with battered women in shelters and agencies in and around Ottawa.

It began in June 1990 with the murder of 55-year-old Pamela Behrendt by her husband in Ottawa South. Pamela was hacked to death with a chainsaw. The women organized a vigil in Minto Park. A tree was planted and a small plaque was laid in the ground, dedicated "to all women suffering from abuse, and to those who have died."

In April 1991, Reva Bowers, 30, was slain by her estranged husband outside her Gloucester home. A vigil was held and another tree was planted in Minto Park.

In June 1991, Sharon Mohamed, 14, was scalded and stabbed to death by her mother's boyfriend. In August 1991, Charmaine Thompson, 23, was stabbed to death, and Rachel Favreau, 20, was shot to death. In November 1991, Patricia Allen, 31, was slain by a cross-bow. After each of these slayings women gathered, six times in less than 18 months. The handful of women who organized the gatherings now called themselves "Women's Urgent Action." Their mandate was to respond swiftly and in an organized fashion to injustices against women, and when a woman was murdered, to hold a vigil within a week of her death.

The vigils were an act of resistance, a public sign of our refusal to allow violence to have the last word. Through speeches, music, prayer and poetry we sought to make explicit the connections between the individual murders and the conditions of women's lives. Huddled together in freezing temperatures, in searing heat, and under darkened skies, we found courage to carry on. Tree planting symbolized life and hope for the future. Each time we gathered we prayed it would be the last. But the violence seemed to be escalating.

The planting of further trees in Minto Park was prohibited due to "Heritage Park" restrictions. This restriction fired our imagination. Minto Park was recognized in the community as the place where women come together to grieve and protest. The idea for a Women's Monument was conceived.

It would be a monument large enough to contain our pain, to represent the enormity of the problem of intimate femicide. It would be inscribed with words that described accurately what is happening to women rather than disguising in acceptable terms who is doing what to whom. It would have us remember the individual women who have been killed. It would provide a rallying point for the community and stand as a permanent reminder of our commitment to zero tolerance of violence against women. It would give strength and hope to those women who are living with abuse.

It would not be a static record but a dynamic and energizing piece of art. It would be designed to acknowledge anger and sadness and to inspire a vision of what the world could be. It would be a memorial on our terms, and it would document the violence done to women in a way that would be difficult to erase.

In November 1991, "The Women's Monument Fund" was struck as a result of a joint meeting between Women's Urgent Action and local community groups. Money to cover capital expenses was raised through volunteer efforts, two female artists were commissioned, and at the December 6th memorial service the following year, the Women's Monument was unveiled in Minto Park.

The centre of the monument is a magnificent oval boulder situated at the end of an accessible red spiral path. The face of the stone is polished and engraved with ancient symbols of passage, rebirth and continuity. Along the path are stone markers, each one bearing the name of a woman who was murdered. The central boulder is inscribed with the following words:

À la mémoire de toutes les femmes qui ont subi jusqu'à la mort la violence des hommes. Imaginons un monde où les femmes libérées de l'emprise de la violence s'épanouissent dans le respect et la liberté. To honour and to grieve all women abused and murdered by men. Envision a world without violence, where women are respected and free.

I have been to the monument more times than I can count. Each time I am struck by its beauty. The space is sacred, evoking deep emotion, inviting all who stand before it into the transformative power of memory. Not just to remember. To remember and be changed.

There is something going on in this moment in history that we do not want forgotten or erased. The Women's Monument documents in stone the murder of women by men in the latter part of the twentieth century. It provides a permanent record of women's efforts to organize against these murders.

It will be left to our daughters and granddaughters to carry this work forward. To the extent that we take up space, to the extent that we leave behind solid and permanent documentation of our efforts to eradicate violence, we will make their task that much easier.

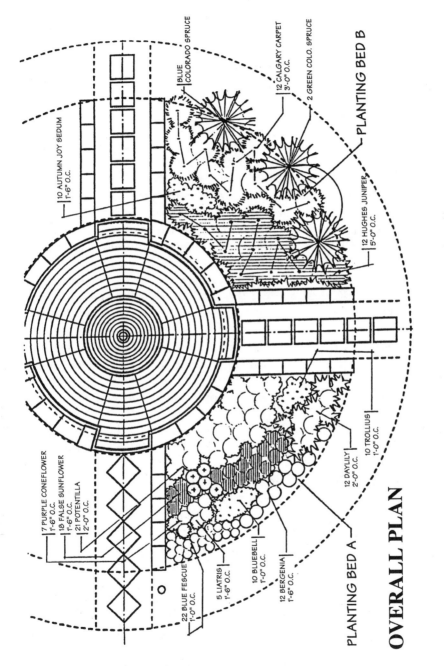

10 AUTUMN JOY SEDUM
1'-6" O.C.

BLUE
COLORADO SPRUCE

12 CALGARY CARPET
3'-0" O.C.

2 GREEN COLO. SPRUCE

12 HUGHES JUNIPER
5'-0" O.C.

PLANTING BED B

7 PURPLE CONEFLOWER
1'-6" O.C.

18 FALSE SUNFLOWER
1'-6" O.C.

21 POTENTILLA
2'-0" O.C.

22 BLUE FESCUE
1'-0" O.C.

5 LIATRIS
1'-6" O.C.

10 BLUEBELL
1'-0" O.C.

12 BERGENIA
1'-6" O.C.

12 DAYLILY
2'-0" O.C.

10 TROLLIUS
1'-0" O.C.

PLANTING BED A

OVERALL PLAN

Landscape design of Women's Grove Memorial by Cynthia Cohlmeyer

317

A Living Commitment:
The December 6th Women's Grove Memorial
Dedicated September 24, 1995

Keith Louise Fulton[1]

The December 6th Women's Grove Memorial, on the grounds of the Manitoba Legislature, blessed by Myra Laramee in 1992, is a sacred place, a place of honour and responsibility, a place where we remember ourselves, each other, and the earth.

The Women's Grove Memorial commemorates women's lives and the worth and dignity of those lives. Here we honour women who have been humiliated by violence. Here we celebrate the work of creating equality and justice for *all* women. Feminism is the belief that we can have the society democracy promises us — where all women are equal with all men, not just some women with some men. *All* women with *all* men. Since this work of transforming our society will take many generations, it is important to remember where we are going, individually and as a people together.

Today we affirm our living commitment to honouring the lives of women: to those who struggle to make those lives better and to those women whose lives are stolen from them. And we promise to them and to ourselves a living commitment to end violence against women.

The idea of this garden memorial began with a small group of women, in response to the December 6th, 1989 killings in Montreal. We had a vigil for those women in the rotunda of the Manitoba Legislature, but the building could not hold the large numbers who gathered. We decided we needed a place where we could continue to explore the thoughts and feelings shared that night, a place of permanence, growth, resilience, and continuity.

And we needed to do something positive with our tremendous anger and with the energy it gave us. Newspapers were not telling our stories. They had their own stories of gore and grief. We had rage, political insights, memories, sorrow, fear and plans for the future. The women who were killed "could have been our sisters," our daughters, our mothers, our lovers and our leaders — they could have been "you or me."[2]

We notified women's groups in the city and we called a meeting in one of the rooms at Evolve, Klinic's program for battered women. From there we wrote women's groups all over the province, and some 40 responded immediately. The late Gerrie Hammond, Minister Responsible for the Status of Women, and the Manitoba Advisory Council gave political support to our plans. And we began educating, fundraising, and organizing. The garden you see here today has been paid for through the gifts of hundreds of people; through funds from the Winnipeg Foundation, the United Way, and anonymous contributors as well as concerts by Manitoba songwriter Deborah Romeyn and friends; and, through the sales of many buttons and T-shirts. This garden, designed by Cynthia Cohlmeyer, was not built by public money. The Government of Manitoba gave permission for the site and provided the lighting, engineering and the excellent services of Roger Brown, the legislative grounds gardener, and the greenhouse staff.[3]

In the six years we have worked on this garden, we have consolidated our strategies for change and we have firmed our resolve to create a community of power, respect and entitlement for women.

That respect is written into this Memorial Grove in the public symbols of a garden welling up from our earth, raised like a burial mound, encircled by the limestone of Manitoba's deep sea past. The circle is open, for the garden is not a fortress. Its paths lead from the four directions to a sacred space where all may enter. Our determination is solid as a rock, our goal engraved in stone, our presence a claim on the highest goals of democratic government and public purpose. The flowers are prairie perennials whose life span includes many winters; time in the sun must nourish them for time under snow. From their roots in the earth, they return again in the spring. And so it is for us. Those who stand here today, those who visit, can do the work to end violence against women in places that we come from. But, we don't have forever, so we had better get to work.

In the process of doing the work, we learn. For example, we considered commemorating the names of women, but where would the list begin and end? There are many ways to die from violence, some immediate, some over many years. The forms of violence may be the gun, the fist, the knife; or daily battering, blows, words, images, closed doors, overwork, poor food, exhaustion of hope, public policy or community disregard. Poverty kills. Systemic lack of opportunity kills. Learned self-hatred kills. A damaged and polluted environment kills. Contempt of our society is connected to the cancer in our breasts. And certainly, the ways men and women learn "to do" intimate relationships and sexuality can kill.

In Winnipeg, as in other cities in the 1980's, feminists began holding vigils for women killed by their partners. The repeated gatherings made the number of deaths and the presence of violence in our society visible. The misogyny people learned in public institutions like the education system and the military, the media, in family life and in the local pubs — the treatment of women as "different from" and "worth less" than the humanity of men — was present in each of the killings. So when a man with a gun walked into École Polytechnique on the night of December 6th, 1989, and began shooting women for being where he thought they did not belong, women and men across the country were horrified — but not surprised. The values, beliefs and attitudes he acted on were those which we meet everyday. Is it so different for 14 women to die in one evening instead of one year? To die in one place instead of 14 separate places? To die together in terror instead of alone in terror?

The 14 women were killed that night of December 6th because they were women who were in school, studying to become engineers — builders and planners of society. Their killer called them "feminists." They were strong, intelligent, determined, hard-working women. That night of killing in the halls and classrooms of one of Canada's universities is a painful landmark in the history of Canadian women. It marks not so much a violence unlike anything that came before or followed, but a time of consciousness for Canadians. After December 6th, 1989, we knew, collectively, as we may never have acknowledged before, the reality that there is violence against women in our society and that it is linked to misogyny.

From December, 1989 to September, 1995, in Manitoba alone, 59 women have been killed by male violence, often by men the women knew and trusted, sometimes by men they have conceived children with and have loved.

Violence affects us all. We all know family members, neighbours, friends or co-workers hurt by violence against women. As women, we know the fear of this violence: our hearts speed up, we plan where we will walk or park our cars, what we will or will not wear, we defy or ignore our fears, we deny the dangers or we stay inside, and within those walls too often we live with the terror and with the violence. It all gets mixed up with our families, our dreams, our unbearable memories.

Two weeks ago we stood in vigil on this spot for a woman who was apparently killed by a man she had taken into her home. She died, not because she was generous, but because this man decided her life did not matter, and that he could use his power to take it from her.

Sandra Butler has said that the problem is not just that some men abuse their power, but that they have so much power to abuse.[4] How do we change that? There are no easy answers to ending violence against women. But one thing is clear — violence against women will not be eliminated until the social climate is changed, until *all* women are honoured as full and equal members of society, until *all* of our lives matter, and our futures and our bodies belong to us.

First Mourn, Then Work for Change
This garden marks a place of mourning and of commitment, of memory and of determination, of reflection and of action. Here we celebrate and honour women, dishonoured in their deaths. Here we claim with pride our history of social activism in Manitoba. We remember that on September 24, 1995, we stood together to affirm and celebrate:

a living commitment to end violence against women
a living commitment honouring the lives of Manitoba women

There is a story in those words. Over ten years ago, when many women and men were working for the equality provision in the Canadian Charter of Rights and Freedoms, there was another struggle going on to create shelters for battered women and to do analyses of the violence in women's lives. Then, we couldn't get people to talk about violence against women; to Canada's shame, when the subject was first raised in the House of Commons in May of 1982, it was greeted with laughter. Now we have the words written in stone on the grounds of the Manitoba Legislature. Violence against women is an equality issue; inequality is socially sanctioned misogyny.

In our paid, underpaid, and unpaid work, in our daily lives as mothers, partners, and daughters, we see that the undervaluing of women's efforts, talents, and contributions results in abuse, poverty and violence. When we talked about the idea of a Women's Grove

Memorial, we spoke of honouring the struggle for the rights and lives of Manitoba women. We knew that rights and lives went together, that you could not honour a woman's life and deny her rights. But when the stone carvers were placing the words on the stone, we decided that the words, "honouring the lives of Manitoba women" included a recognition of women's rights. I hope we were not wrong. Our trust is never to let women's lives be so diminished in our understanding and our public policies that they can be separated from women's rights. This garden stands for that shared trust and commitment.

But make no mistake. This project began as an affirmation of women's lives and marks a public commitment to work for change. While this garden represents grief and determination, it has sprung from the energy of our anger, from our productive, sustained, and sustaining anger: the stones of our convictions, the words of our analyses, the flowers of our passionate love for our lives, the lives of women, and the design from all the dreams in our hearts. With this garden we commit ourselves to a fair, just and non-violent society.

Designed by Sally Papso, Cynthia Cohlmeyer and Anne Belanger

Creating a New Politic for a Global Village

Marianne Cerilli

In a global village, the world is our neighbourhood. If we believe this, then our politics, our relationships, and our decision-making must reflect it. I believe that as we become more whole and healthy, more conscious and empowered, we can become creators of positive change. As women, our personal experience has shown that we can heal ourselves, recreate ourselves, and act out of our deepest convictions. This knowledge is crucial, especially for those of us in positions of power or influence. An understanding of how we effect our own healing can be applied to our work in organizations, the community and the world. I believe that it is necessary to transform our global village from one that is plagued by inequality, violence, and destruction, to one of sustainability, cooperation and sharing.

Many people are not psychologically prepared to take on the enormity of this work. They live in what Helen Caldicott calls "manic denial," where they cocoon and focus exclusively on their own lives, ignoring larger issues.[1] Others immerse themselves in worthy causes, driving themselves without regard for their own health. However, when the connection between personal health and the health of the planet is made, I believe that manic denial can be replaced with a compassionate activism, one that leads to a generous and forgiving egalitarianism. The link between our own health, the health of our communities, and of the planet is key: the personal *is* political. This balance requires the wisdom to know when to focus on our own inner life, and when to act in the world.

One of the things that helps me make this connection is artistic expression. When all else fails, I write poetry. When the outer world becomes difficult, I go inside and sort things out. Art helps me pay attention to my inner world, my inner life. We can all take comfort in artistic expression, be it drawing, writing, weaving or music. Becoming a creator allows us to acknowledge our need for beauty and order. It allows us to affirm our values and to regain a sense of personal power. With renewed strength and creativity, we can forge a new reality. The kind of power I am referring to is "creative power," using the gift of imagination. In fact, Einstein said that imagination is even more important than knowledge.[2] Art, creativity, and the use of imagination can help activate new ways of thinking and problem solving. In his book *Earth in the Balance*, Al Gore, Vice-President of the United States, talks about developing a new spiritual consciousness, a new imaginative approach to help avert environmental destruction.[3] From the women's movement we have learned how political action helps us to move from victim to survivor. Texts such as *The Courage to Heal*, by Ellen Bass and Laura Davis, have shown us that acting on the courage of our convictions can be both healing and cathartic.[4] Now we must expand on this and, drawing from other resources like the teachings of indigenous peoples, we must learn to work collectively, pooling ideas and energy to bring about systemic change.[5]

Applying what we know to change political and socio-economic relationships is a challenge, especially in our highly individualistic society. Yet, in order to work for the greater good, in order to create a global community (in its truest sense), it is essential that we face these challenges. The concept of collectivism must not be abandoned. Even though the current notion of competitive markets is favoured, and everything else is feared as being part of the failed communist ideology, it might be helpful to examine other socio-economic models, models that function well in other parts of the world. We also need to recognize that technologically-driven capitalism (a kind of corporate colonialism) has become a new form of totalitarianism. The global trade agreements developed in this era need to be seen for what they are, declarations of corporate rights over human rights, with little regard for the protection of the environment. Corporations have hunted out nations with the lowest pay, weakest environmental and labour laws, and the poorest enforcement practices. Current trade arrangements may have brought monetary returns for investors, but have culminated in few benefits for most citizens. If we are to survive as a global village, we must seek a common, safe, and equitable means of sharing resources and wealth.

At the beginning of the new millennium we have the opportunity to enter into a wiser form of global democracy, one based on mutual respect and ecological integrity. Learning how to listen to the "dissenting voice," work toward consensus and conflict resolution are tasks that we must set for ourselves. No longer can we function out of a "power-over" or a "majority-rules" mentality. All those affected should be equal partners in decision-making and in planning. As I envision it, the new global democracy will be about inclusion and diversity, and about creating non-hierarchical political structures. Probably our young people, especially those who are currently learning schoolyard mediation, peer counselling and support, are our greatest hope. May we teach them well so that they may find a way.

Tears and Stones

Anne Szumigalski

When the stars threw down their spears
And watr'd Heaven with their tears

—William Blake

My sister, Ruth, the gentle and complaisant one, the dear one whom everybody loves, how often she weeps for the wrongs of the innocent, the dogs and cats, and snakes and spiders, and so on and on. (About horses, however, she's more cautious. She's always been rather afraid of them.)

Most of her tears, though, are reserved for her fellow humans. She has only to read in the newspaper of some lost child or mistreated old man and she's off again, ruining her make-up, and giving herself red-rimmed eyes.

When I spoke to her last year, she was jokingly threatening to make a career of all this crying. She was, she said, going to call her business RENT-A-TEAR. She would get in a good supply of lace-trimmed handkerchiefs, suitable hats, and flowing garments and rent herself out to weep at weddings, funerals, farewell parties or other suitably sad, or happy occasions. Her motherly figure and slightly pathetic stance would help her in this enterprise, she was sure.

So far as I know, this is still only a threat. But how comforting for the people of the world, her small world, indeed the world at large, to know that even if she has never met them, she weeps for their hardships, for their bereavements, their disappointments and for their injustices.

In these times, when we are so often encouraged to weep for ourselves, and this applies particularly to women, it's surely a relief to find someone who weeps for others so readily, so purely, so warmly.

Not, of course, that we should be prevented from seeing our oppressions for what they are, admitting them, getting angry, confronting our oppressors and so on. Not that we shouldn't come to the rescue of the Hurt Child Within (or whatever the current expression is). After all, we must somehow find a way to come to terms with our lives, our miseries, unfairnesses, our bad dreams — don't we all have them, small and passing, or large and looming?

Scene: A road on which I meet my Hurt Child Within

SELF: Who are you?

H.C.W.:   That part of you that has always been suppressed, oppressed, abused and treated unfairly.

SELF: Yes, I remember that time Mama spanked me for something John did to the kitten.

H.C.W.:   Hanged her from a tree, didn't he? Anything more?

SELF: Now that you mention it, I have always been aware of the fact that Mother and Father didn't really care for me the way they did for the other six. I've had to live with that fact all my life. For example, there was that time Mary got a new dress with three lacy ruffles and I...

H.C.W.:   What colour was it?

SELF: Blue, I think. Or it could have been that lovely peachy pink colour...

H.C.W.:   And...?

SELF: My brothers always said our parents neglected my education.

H.C.W.:   Go on. This is getting interesting.

SELF: I can't. All I want to do is cry for all the awful things they did to me.

H.C.W.:   Go ahead. Cry all you like; it's good for you.

SELF: Oh, boo-hoo-hoo.

H.C.W.:   Splendid. Go for it. I'm beginning to enjoy this.

SELF: Oh, boo hoo hoo, so am I.

H.C.W.:   Your nose is getting awfully red.

SELF: It's sore too, sniff, sniff.

H.C.W.:   There, there, I'll lend you a hankie, the one with forget-me-nots and TUESDAY embroidered on the corner.

H.C.W.:   My favourite. I think I lost it in the playground when I fell off the swing that time.

H.C.W.:   (priggishly) Nothing is ever truly lost. Nothing is truly forgotten.

Enter GOD(DESS) L.

GD: What's with all the weeping and wailing?

H.C.W. & SELF: It's us, O Deity, bemoaning all the pain that we have endured in this life...it's just not fair....

GD: I did warn you, but you still insisted on being born.

SELF: I thought it would be fun and interesting. But...

GD: I don't remember saying anything about fun. Anyway, you ignored my advice.

SELF: What advice?

GD: "DON'T WHINE, KICK."

SELF: You mean, get angry?

GD: Precisely. Get angry and tell people off to their faces.

SELF: I could never do that. After all, I am a lady.

GD: Then there is no help, no hope at all for you. Goodbye.

Exit GOD(DESS). The SELF and H.C.W. are left to their wailing.

And what has all this to do with Carrying the Stone? Everything and nothing. Perhaps these rituals of tears and recriminations do help some people to put down their personal burdens. Such waterworks are not for me, are not, in fact, for many of us, oppressed and abused though we may have been.

ANNE: It doesn't really matter how many years have passed. It doesn't fade off. It is still present as the present. I've always felt that this was a kind of stone in my breast, and when I was writing Z I hoped to put this down and not carry it with me...

TOM: I'd like to ask Anne about carrying the stone.

ANNE: It didn't get rid of the stone. Now I could take it out of my chest and put it down and look at it. But I still have to carry it around all the time.

TOM: And I feel the weight of that stone in myself and I can't take it out now...[1]

And so, cast away your little personal burdens, dear daughters, dear sisters, and pick up those heavy stones we all must carry, and never put down again until we come to the end of the world. Perhaps by then we shall have expunged all oppression and abuse, not simply from our own lives, but from all those others, the innumerable oppressed. Ah, think what a cairn we shall build between us, to the memory of our species, our gender, our far from perfect lives.

Photo of Raku firing by Sandra Somerville

Chapter Ten

Afterword

A Guide to Well-Being:
The Personal Is Political

Joan Turner

This is a guide to combine care of the self with care of the planet. It is not intended to be a demand for personal behavioural changes, or to overextend ourselves to change the world. If this guide seems overwhelming, write your own list of three or more actions that will be possible for you to accomplish at this time.

1. Develop your strength, your courage and your resources to get out of abusive situations. Resources include friends, crisis lines, shelters, the police, emergency departments, doctors, nurses, social workers, trained staff and volunteers at women's resource centres. Protect your life and the lives of your children.

2. Create a safe place for yourself. No one has the right to abuse, harass or intimidate you. Create healthy personal boundaries for yourself. Learn to say "NO" with conviction. Get counselling, attend a self-help group or attend workshops if you need help to learn how to do this.

3. Breathe fully and deeply. Develop your breathing capacity through conscious intention, practice, exercise, yoga and/or singing. Breath is life.

4. Open a window to fresh air. If you possibly can, go outdoors and connect with the earth on a daily basis. Go for a walk, find a tree,

a rock, a place in a park or by water; garden, bird watch, sit quietly and appreciate the beauty of our world and its inhabitants; cycle, snowshoe, skate or ski. If you can't go outdoors, look at posters or pictures of beautiful places, tend to one or more plants, watch birds, squirrels or spiders, listen to tapes of sounds of nature, hold a stone or a shell, and/or use your imagination to take you to a safe and beautiful place that nurtures your spirit.

5. Eat food that is healthy, nutritious and prepared with awareness. If you are hungry, ask for help. If you have abundance, be thankful and share with others. Reduce your intake of junk food, soft drinks, sugar and coffee. Consider being a vegetarian and consume primarily locally grown foods to be considerate of the earth's resources. Compost to put fruit and vegetable peelings, etc., back into the earth. Read and keep informed about nutrition. Experiment with low-fat recipes. If you are at risk with an eating disorder, get help. Find the best resources available to you in your community or region.

6. Drink lots of water to hydrate and cleanse the body. If you don't have access to clean water, boil it, get yourself an effective filter system, or lobby with others to change the situation.

7. Experiment with activities that you enjoyed or would like to have tried as a child. Try drawing with crayons, painting with poster paint or watercolours, using pastels or markers, knitting, sewing, being creative with crafts, creating a collage, using clay or plasticine, blowing bubbles, moving freely to music, singing, skipping, playing hop-scotch or tag or board games. Give yourself the gift of time, attention and fun.

8. Become aware of negative habits and addictive behaviour, e.g.: addiction to gambling, drugs, alcohol, cigarettes, caffeine, work, sex and/or abusive people. Face your stresses, your truth and your pain. Start today to develop a healthy lifestyle for yourself. Get the help you need from friends, addiction treatment or women's resource centres, and/or from psychologists, social workers, and other professionals who have expertise in helping people to change. Join a self-help group like Alcoholic Anonymous or Al-Anon. There are also classes, books and videos available to help you. If you try to change and don't succeed, try and try again.

9. Create a safe space for yourself and for your inner child. Get the sleep and the rest you need to heal and to stay healthy. Give yourself time and space to feel. Contact your anger, fear, sorrow, rage,

joy and sense of humour. If this isn't safe or possible to do on your own, ask friends, a counsellor, therapist, or support group to assist you.

10. Find at least one person to listen to you and to support you. Go for therapy or counselling when you need to. Find the best resource person(s) available to you in your area and stay with the counselling process as long as you need to. The quality of your life is important. When you arrive at a place of sufficient strength, extend yourself to another person or persons, work for and participate in a women's organization or an ecological organization, or do volunteer work.

11. Develop and maintain close friendships with women and men who are able to listen, support and/or challenge you. Share with your friends and develop ways of helping each other. Along life's pathway be prepared to develop new friendships as you grow and change. If there aren't women's or men's groups available to you, form a group.

12. Learn the art of self-care. Examine your breasts and your skin on a regular basis, schedule medical and dental check-ups at intervals appropriate for you. Exercise several times a week. Choose something that will give you satisfaction and that you can sustain over time. Walking, swimming, cycling, yoga or Tai Chi are activities with which to begin. Get a massage or some form of body work that helps you to get in touch with your body. Find what helps you to reduce stress and promote relaxation. Go on retreats alone or with friends. Take time to nurture your body and learn to love and care for it.

13. Listen to music, sing, play an instrument, and/or chant; participate in drumming, dancing and/or music-making circles. Include music that nurtures, stimulates and/or sustains you in your daily life. Listen to, and appreciate silence and the sounds of nature.

14. Stay tuned to your inner process; write in a journal or draw your thoughts and feelings, your dreams, your images and visions. Learn to appreciate and to hone your intuition. Develop and honour your creativity and the creativity of other people.

15. Learn to meditate. Consider beginning or ending your day with meditation. For some people this may take the form of prayer, sitting in silence, walking or swimming. There are many different forms of meditation and many different spiritual paths. Explore how you can best meet your spiritual needs.

16. Try something like a new game, a recipe, a poem or a song,

different clothes or hair style, new arts or cultural activities, travel, a language, or new skills. Be experimental and playful. Credit yourself with each new step taken. Challenge yourself and take risks in a way that is safe and healthy for you.

17. Reclaim your power. Consider talking to, or writing to, those who have abused you and diminished your sense of self-worth. You may never actually speak in their presence, or send the letters, but the act of imagining and/or writing may give you a sense of release. A counsellor, therapist or lawyer may be important resource people to consult. You don't need to do this alone.

18. Create rituals and celebrations to mark important occasions for yourself and your friends, e.g.: naming of a child, onset or completion of menstruation, change in career or relationship, becoming a crone.

19. Learn about women's herstory. Listen to the life stories of older women. Read about brave and talented people of various traditions. Learn from elders. Listen to the concerns of younger women and assist them if you are able to do so. Encourage consideration of careers in non-traditional work. Work at meaningful paid or unpaid work that is healthy and life-affirming for you.

20. Enjoy your own sensuality. Appreciate your sexuality. Practise safe sex.

21. Fine-tune your senses to find beauty, peace and joy in you, around you, and in the simple things of life. Savour what you find.

22. Learn to pace yourself and keep a sense of balance. Listen to your body, your heart and your spirit. Be kind to yourself. As you age, you will be called upon to make changes, to do less, or more. Only you can really know what is right for you. Weigh well intentioned advice and then make your own decisions.

23. Make every day a blessing. Tune out negativity on the radio, television, in print; go outdoors, look for beauty, bring more light and lightness into your life; read poetry or fiction, watch a comedy; cry, laugh, exercise, participate in a sweat. Ask for help from family, friends, an elder, a professional, or a spiritual counsellor.

24. Recognize the privilege of those who have access to fresh, clean and safe water and to nutritious food. Save your pennies or your loonies to donate to organizations that work with communities in impoverished areas. Or, choose some other form of volunteer work which appeals to you, and contribute what you can without depleting or burning yourself out. You will likely gain even more than you give.

25. Participate in recycling. Support locally owned and operated businesses. Work for an environmentally-friendly project. Learn to use alternative and safe cleaning solutions and avoid toxic chemicals. Be sensitive to those who have sensitivities or allergies to perfumes, dyes, chemicals and smoke.

26. Love a child or children and care for them well. Care for animals. Be conscious that we are all part of an interdependent web and that each of us, including every spider, plays an important part. Reflect on our interdependence as you look at a spider web. Notice and appreciate the uniqueness and the creativity of the spider's work. Creatively support life in all its forms.

27. Use this "Guide to Well-Being," or the parts of it that fit for you at this time, or develop your own self-care guide. Weekly and particularly in times of stress, turn to the guide and choose from it whatever is most useful to you. Add to your "Guide to Well-Being" whatever nurtures you and is healthy for you and the planet. Direct energy and resources towards making this a non-violent world, safer, more caring, for women, children and men, and for all life forms. Take one step towards health and well-being today.[1]

Women's Wisdom

Carol Rose

We hope that the completion of this anthology is not an ending but, rather, the beginning of conversations that will continue long after the final pages are read.

From the beginning, we believed that women had a great deal to say about creativity and healing, both on a personal and universal level. We were certain that, given the opportunity, women could discuss the creative process and identify its similarities to the art of healing. We knew that women could conjure visual images, music, poetry and prose that would speak to and enable others as they journeyed toward wholeness and well-being.

We believed (and still believe) that what women needed was a forum in which to express their ideas, their individual and collective wisdom. Fortunately, we were not alone in that conviction. Many writers, artists, educators, social workers, politicians and feminist therapists, along with organizations such as Woman Healing for Change, shared our beliefs. We all agreed that in order for women to take charge of their lives, in order to really effect change, women needed opportunities to express what they had gleaned from their own life experiences. They needed permission to examine the strategies that had helped them, and they needed to do so in a manner and style that was uniquely their own. In a sense, women needed to create a new cultural reality, a way of naming and identifying the particular modalities that they actually use to give meaning and shape to their lives. Part of this meant finding the right language, the right image. Part of it meant reclaiming the tools of the past, dreams, intuition, dance, ritual, story and song. All of it meant taking a risk...giving voice to that which is considered dangerous, the subjective, the body, the experiential, and often, the experimental. In a world governed by the weight of empirical evidence and statistics, a world based on all that is "provable," these slower, more internal methods, are highly suspect. Yet, they are what women have been using for many years...quietly and often, in secret.

The challenges of writing a book that employs these methods, that gives credence to the intuitive, dreamy, creative side of the brain, have been many. How to weave a whole out of so many individual, idiosyncratic parts? How to translate the personal into the possibility for collective healing? How to share what has been transforming for one woman into a language and metaphor that resonates beyond that woman's experience? These were some of our concerns. We were willing to suspend disbelief, however, to allow the unfolding of what we truly believed to be at the core of this book: a wisdom and knowledge that women have held for years. What you now hold in your hands is the fruit of that belief...a text woven out of the courage and the creativity of countless Canadian women from across the country. Each woman was willing to take a chance, willing to share her own unique story, image or song. Like the ancient Spiderwoman myth, the women in this anthology have created a new reality out of their own bodies, out of their own understanding of what it means to live with integrity, in harmony with the earth and her creatures. They have done so, despite efforts to silence them, to squelch their ways of knowing. As we enter a new millennium, may their wisdom help to shape the destiny and well-being of us all and of our planet.

End Notes

Cassie Williams Aitchison — Spiders in My Life
1. M. Hubert. *Les araignées*. Paris: Société Nouvelle des Editions Boubée, 1979.
2. R.F. Foelix. *Biology of Spiders*. Cambridge and London: Harvard University Press, 1982.
3. F. Wanless. "Spiders of the Family Salticidae from the upper slopes of Everest and Makalu," *British Arachnology Society Bulletin*, vol. 3, no. 5 (1975), pp. 132-136.
4. H.M. Peters. "Fine structure and function of capture threads." In *Ecophysiology of Spiders*, ed. W. Nentwig. Berlin, New York: Springer-Verlag, 1987. pp. 187-202.
5. E.K. Tillinghast and M. Townley. "Chemistry, physical properties and synthesis of Araneidae orb webs." pp. 203-210.
6. H. Levi and L. Levi. *Spiders and Their Kin*. New York: Golden Press, 1990.
7. W.S. Bristowe. *The World of Spiders*. London: Collins, 1976.
8. W. Boericke. *The Pocket Manual of Homeopathic Materia Medica*. Calcutta: National Homeo Lab., 1976. pp. 69-70; 395-396.
Figure 1: *Linyphia* (6mm) under her "bowl and doiley" web (after Bristowe 1976).
Figure 2: a) *Mastophora* hanging to the trapeze line (1) with its viscid ball at the pendulum line (2), b) Ball of Mastophora seen on a glass slide (after Peters 1987).
Figure 3: *Scytodes* sprays gum over its victim (after Bristowe 1947).
Figure 4: A wolf spider female with her egg cocoon attached to her spinnerets (after Bristowe 1976).
Figure 5: A nursery web female with her egg cocoon in her jaws (after Bristowe 1976).

Raye Anderson — Old Wives Tales
1. Readers interested in knowing more about earlier versions of the stories made popular by the Brothers Grimm should consult *The Hard Facts of the Grimms' Fairy Tales* by Maria Tatar (Princeton: Princeton University Press, 1987), the source text for much of the information used in this article.

Joanne Arnott — Healing Circle
1. Previously published in *absinthe*, vol. 7, no. 2 (winter 1994).

Joanne Arnott — Tracing the Healing Process
1. Joanne Arnott. "flatland summer." In *Wiles of Girlhood*. Vancouver: Press Gang Publishers, 1991. p. 18.
2. Arnott. "Change Herself." Ibid. p. 55.
3. Arnott. "The lot of them." Ibid. p. 67.
4. Arnott. "What if." In *My Grass Cradle*. Vancouver: Press Gang Publishers, 1992. p. 65.

Judy Bancroft — The Motherpath Cards
1. Carol Rose and Lu-Ann Lynde, "Walking the Motherpath." Winnipeg: Rose Counselling and Consulting, 1987. For an example of the cards and an explanation of their development, see Carol Rose, "Walking the Motherpath," in *Living the Changes*, Joan Turner, ed. Winnipeg: University of Manitoba Press, 1990. pp. 106-113.

M. Joan Baragar — Outside the Sky Waits
1. Stephen Sondheim. "Green Finch and Linnet Bird." In *Sweeney Todd, The Demon Barber of Fleet Street*. Music and lyrics by Stephen Sondheim, reproduced in part from *The Singer's Musical Theatre Anthology*. Vol. l, Soprano. Milwaukee: Hal Leonard Publishing Corp., 1986. pp. 204-206. Permission requested.
2. Ibid, pp. 205-206.
3. Ibid, p. 205.

M. Joan Baragar — Reflections from the Middle of the Mattress
1. Camp song. Author unknown.
2. Letter written by personal friend and colleague, Marilyn Boyd, Winnipeg.
3. Lewis Carroll. *Alice in Wonderland*. New York: Grosset & Dunlap, 1946.

Elizabeth Carriere — "Word for This"
1. "Word for This" was originally published in *Prairie Fire*, vol. 17. no. 2 (summer 1996). Included with permission.

Marianne Cerilli — Creating a New Politics for a Global Village
1. Helen Caldicott. "Saving the Planet," a speech recorded in Portland, Oregon, November 12, 1989.
2. Albert Einstein. Quoted in Julian Cameron with Mark Bryan. *The Artists Way*. New York: Puttenam & Sons, 1992. p. 131.
3. Al Gore. *Earth in the Balance: Ecology and the Human Spirit*. New York: Houghlin Mifflin Company, 1992.
4. Ellen Bass and Laura Davis. *The Courage to Heal*. New York: Harper and Row, 1988.
5. Ani D'Franco. "pic yer nose." *Puddle Dive*. Buffalo: Righteous Babe Records, 1993.

Kathryn Countryman — George
l. This story is excerpted from Kathryn Countryman's first novel (unpublished), A Trip of Circles.

Keith Louise Fulton — A Living Commitment (Women's Grove Memorial)
1. In writing this Dedication, I have drawn on the language and discussions of the December 6th Women's Memorial Committee, 1989-1995. Members of the Committee: Sally Papso, Diane McGifford, Judith Kearns, Pat Hrabok, Audrhea Lande, Janice Freeman, Vicki Verville, Debra Blair, Bonnie Dickie, Babs Friesen and myself.
2. Nancy Reinhold. "This memory," recorded by The Wyrd Sisters, *Leave a Little Light*, 1992, side one.
3. On behalf of the December 6th Women's Memorial Committee, we acknowledge and thank the many people who helped with the raising of this garden and especially: Cynthia Cohlmeyer, the landscape architect who, with us, designed the garden and oversaw its construction; Roger Brown, Stu Ursel and Cy Howard, the Legislative grounds gardener and government representatives with whom we worked. Also, Gillis Quarries which donated some of the stone and Scouts Canada, who donated and planted the blue spruce.
4. Sandra Butler. *Conspiracy of Silence: The Trauma of Incest*. San Francisco: Volcano Press, 1978. p. 212.

Keith Louise Fulton — Put It in Writing
1. Marilyn Frye. *The Politics of Reality: Essays in Feminist Theory*. Freedom, CA: The Crossing Press, 1983. p. 36.
2. Sonia Johnson. *Going Out of Our Minds: The Metaphysics of Liberation*. Freedom, CA: The Crossing Press, 1987.
3. Natalie Goldberg. *Writing Down the Bones: Freeing the Writer Within*. Boston: Shambhala,

1986. pp. 8-10. *See also* Natalie Goldberg. *Wild Mind: Living the Writer's Life*. New York: Bantam, 1990.

4. Dale Spender, ed. *The Diary of Elizabeth Pepys*. London: Grafton, 1991. p. 71

5. Ibid, p.44.

6. Adrienne Rich. *What is Found There: Notebooks on Poetry and Politics*. New York: Norton, 1993. p. 32.

7. Adrienne Rich. "Poetry and Experience: Statement at a Poetry Reading (1964)." In *Adrienne Rich's Poetry and Prose*. Barbara Charlesworth Gelpi and Albert Gelpi, eds. New York: Norton, 1993. p. 165; *What is Found There*, p. xiv.

8. Adrienne Rich. "North American Time." *Your Native Land, Your Life*. New York: Norton, 1986). pp. 33-36.

9. Audre Lorde. "The Transformation of Silence into Language and Action." In *Sister Outsider*. Trumansburg, NY: The Crossing Press, 1984. p. 41.

Deborah Gabinet — Dad Died This Week

1. Harry Woods. "Side by Side." In *Treasury of Best Loved Songs*. Montreal: Readers Digest, 1972. pp. 119-121.

Donna F. Johnson — From Damage to Power

1. Bronwen Wallace, from a conversation with Janice Williamson taped on February 22, 1989 in Edmonton. This interview first appeared in *Open Letter, Seventh Series*, no. 9, (winter 1991) and later in *Arguments with the World: Essays by Bronwen Wallace*, Joanne Page, ed. Kingston: Quarry Press, 1992. p. 210.

2. J.M. Coetzee. *Age of Iron*. London: Penguin Books, 1991. p. 26.

3. Bronwen Wallace, Ibid.

Donna F. Johnson — The Women's Monument

1. *The New Elizabethan Reference Dictionary*. London: George Newnes Ltd., 1959. p. 941.

Victoria Moon Joyce — Singing a Spider Woman's Song

1. V.M. Joyce. *Singing for our Lives: Women creating home through singing*. Toronto: Master's thesis, Graduate Department of Education, University of Toronto, 1993. I wish to acknowledge the seven women who participated in the original research: Jani Lauzon, Delvina Bernard, Michele George, Fely Villasin, Arlene Mantle, Sheila James and Catherine Glen. As well as performing, these deeply committed women facilitate singing with women in various contexts and within diverse communities. I also wish to thank Karen Howe and Louise Karch, for their influential support of this work and especially Jenny Horsman, for her constant encouragement and editorial suggestions.

2. "Outward Bound" refers to an international network of outdoor adventure-based schools. The Women of Courage course is an experiential education program and is not explicitly intended to be a therapeutic intervention. However, many of its components will have a therapeutic effect. Singing has emerged as one component that enables the healing of women who have been radically silenced. For information about Women of Courage programs in Ontario and British Columbia, contact the Canadian Outward Bound Wilderness School, 150 Laird Drive, Toronto, ON, M4G 3V7. Phone (800) 268-7329.

3. Chris Williamson. "Lullabye," recorded on *Live Dream*, produced by Dream Machine, Bird Ankles Music, 1978.

4. V.M. Joyce. "Turn off the radio and sing for your lives: Women, singing, and experiential education." In *Women and Experiential Education*, K. Warren, ed. Dubuque: Kendall Hunt Publishing, 1996. p. 258.

5. F. Armstrong. "Finding our voices." In *Voices from arts for labour*, N. Jackowska, ed. London: Pluto Press, in association with Arts for Labour, 1985. pp. 22-23.

6. G. O'Keefe. Quoted from a newspaper article in the *New York Sun*, Dec. 5, 1922, p. 22.

7. If one looks at woman-hating as a societal source of trauma, then we are all affected by it. Thus, I use the inclusive term "us" when talking about survivors.

8. Bernice Johnson Reagon. "The Songs are Free," with Bill Moyers. A PBS Video Production. Distributed by Mystic Fire Video, S. Burlington, Vermont.

9. For example, enslaved African-Americans found the details to assist their escape to the North in songs that held coded lyrics referring to safe houses and safe routes along the "underground railway."

10. Reagon. "The Songs are Free."

11. Ibid.

12. M.T. Winter. "Music, the way home." In *Music: Physician for times to come*. D. Campbell, ed. Wheaton, IL: Quest Books, 1991. pp. 255-256.

13. This expression is attributed to a man who speaks from a First Nations' worldview. At the time of writing his name is unknown to me .

14. Sandra Butler, lecture delivered at the Centre for Christian Studies, Toronto, March 24, 1992.

15. Louise Karch, personal communication, March 1993.

16. Michele George. *Singing for our lives: Women creating Home through singing.* p. 57.

17. *Music: Physician for times to come.*

18. Felt sense refers to a particular quality of experience within the focusing technique. *See* Eugene Gendlin, *Focusing* (rev. ed.). New York: Bantam Books, 1978.

19. Sadie Buck (1995) cautions that a song given in performance from a particular historical and cultural context does not mean it is given *away*; it does not become the property of the audience, but remains the property of the people and historical context from which it came. A song is encoded with meanings far deeper than its words and sounds. As a First Nations' singer and teacher, Buck is concerned that removing a song from its context is not only theft, but distorts the meaning of the song when it is sung out of context by non-natives. In her musical tradition, songs are recognized as a form of medicine.

Songs which one wishes to sing but are outside a singer's culture should be negotiated respectfully. Much depends on the purpose and the context in which the songs are used. Ask permission before singing. Better yet, learn songs from your own culture and history!

20. Merlin Stone. *Ancient mirrors of womanhood.* Boston: Beacon Press, 1979. p. 290.

Irene E. Karpiak — The Primary Fibres of our Transitions

1. Klaus Riegel, "The Dialectics of Human Development." In *American Psychologist* (October, 1976), pp. 689-99.

2. Ilya Prigogine and Isabella Stengers. *Order Out of Chaos: Man's New Dialogue with Nature.* New York: Bantam Books, 1984.

3. Erich Jantsch. "Introduction." In *The Evolutionary Vision: Toward a Unifying Paradigm of Physical, Biological, and Sociocultural Evolution.* Boulder, CO: Westview Press, Inc. 1981.

4. Fritjof Capra. *The Turning Point: Science, Society, and the Rising Culture.* New York: Bantam Books, 1983.

5. Ibid. Ilya Prigogine and Isabella Stengers. p. 141.

6. Ibid. Capra. p. 304.

7. Gail Sheehy. *Pathfinders.* New York: Bantam Books, 1981. pp. 127-28 .

8. Jane Loevinger. *Ego Development.* San Francisco: Jossey-Bass, 1976.

9. Lawrence Kohlberg. "Stages and Sequence: The Cognitive Development Approach to Socialization." In *Handbook of Socialization: Theory and Research.* D. Goslin ed. New York: Rand McNally, 1969.

10. Ken Wilber. *Sex, Ecology, and Spirituality: The Spirit of Evolution.* Boston: Shambhala, 1995.

11. Ibid. pp. 258-262.

12. Mihalyi Csikszentmihalyi. *The Evolving Self: A Psychology for the Third Millennium.* New York: Harper Collins Publishers, 1993. pp. 155-156.

13. Sharan Merriam and Carolyn Clark. *Lifelines: Patterns of Work, Love, Learning in Adulthood*. San Francisco: Jossey Bass, 1991. pp. 208-209.
14. J. California Cooper. "The Life You Live (May Not Be Your Own)." In *The Seasons of Women: An Anthology*. Gloria Norris, ed. New York: W.W. Norton and Company, Inc., 1996. p. 13.
15. Lewis Gilbert (Director), John Gilbert and William P. Cartlidge (Co-Producers), *Educating Rita*. Columbia Pictures Industries, Inc., 1983.
16. Bernice Neugarten. "The Awareness of Middle-Age." In *Middle Age and Aging*. Bernice Neugarten, ed. Chicago: University of Chicago Press, 1968. pp. 93-98.
17. Carl Jung. "The Stages of Life." In *Modern Man in Search of a Soul*. New York: Harcourt Brace Jovanovich, Publishers, 1933. pp. 104-108.
18. Ibid. Ken Wilber. p. 68.
19. Ilya Prigogine. "The Reenchantment of Nature." In *Dialogues with Scientists and Sages*, Rene Weber, ed. Markham, ON: Penguin Books, 1986. p. 191.
20. Eduard Lindeman. *The Meaning of Adult Education*. Norman, OK: Oklahoma Research Center for Continuing Professional and Higher Education, 1989. p. 56.
21. Jean Houston. *The Search for the Beloved: Journey in Sacred Psychology*. Los Angeles: J.P. Tarcher, Inc., 1987. pp. 116-117.

Sylvia Legris — hey diddle diddle The COW Writes a Poem
1. Originally published in *CV2*, vol. 18, no. 1 (summer 1995).

Sylvia Legris — mezzaluna
1. Originally published in *The Malahat Review*, no. 115 (summer, 1996).

Helen Levine and Eva Kenyon — Revisiting a Very Old Friendship
1. Helen Levine. "Crones." In *The Health Sharing Book: Resources for Canadian Women*. Kathleen McDonell and Mariane Valerde, eds. Toronto: Women's Press. 1985.

Katherine Martens — Threading My Way
1. John Bunyan. *Pilgrim's Progress*. (Retold and Shortened for Modern Readers by Mary Godolphin.) Illustrated by Robert Lawson. Philadelphia: J.B. Lippincott, 1939.
2. Penelope Shuttleworth and Peter Redgrove. *The Wise Wound, Menstruation and Everywoman*. London: Harper Collins Publishers, 1994.
3. *All in A Row: The Klassens of Homewood*. Winnipeg: Mennonite Literary Society, 1988.
4. Katherine Martens. "This I Know." Unpublished manuscript.
5. Mennonite Childbirth Oral History Project 1988, and *In Her Own Voice: Mennonite Childbirth Stories*. Katherine Martens and Heidi Harms, eds. Winnipeg: University of Manitoba Press, 1997.
6. Grace Livingstone Hill. *Girl of the Woods*. Mattituck, NY: American Reprint Co., 1942.
7. Christa Wolf. *Patterns of Childhood*. New York: Farrar, Straus and Giroux, 1980. p. 25.
8. It would be better for us to refrain from working or "doing" all the time and simply be. We would be less destructive of the environment if we left some things undone. Fewer wars would be waged if we refused to go to war. I am indebted to Luisa Francia, *Die Schmutzige Frau* (The Dirty Woman) ISBN 3-88104-226-1. Munich: Verlag Frauenoffensive, for this thought.
9. Faspa is a Mennonite tea, served about four in the afternoon. It used to consist of buns or bread, jam, butter and perhaps cheese, and on Sundays cookies or cakes.
10. Jrettre means to dance by clasping hands and putting toes together, leaning back and spinning around on one spot. This is generally done by two children. Rempel, Herman, *Kjenn Jie Noch Plautdietsch, A Mennonite Low German Dictionary*. Winnipeg; Mennonite Literary Society, 1984.
11. *The Piano*, produced by Miramax Films, 1993, Director and Screen Play, Jane Campion.

12. David Chamberlain. *Babies Remember Birth and Other Extraordinary Scientific Discoveries about the Mind and Personality of your Newborn.* Los Angeles: Jeremy P. Tarcher, 1988.
13. Susun S. Weed. *Healing Wise, The Wise Woman Herbal.* Woodstock, NY: Ash Tree Publishing, 1989.
14. The word silly and *selig* (blessed) come from the same root.

Carmelita McGrath — I Want Your Voice
Originally published in *poems on land and on water.* St. John's: Killick Press, 1992. p. 17.

Penni Mitchell — First Mourn, then Work for Change
1. This column was originally published in the *Winnipeg Free Press,* December 2, 1995, page 6.

Lynne Mitchell-Pedersen and Susan Curtis — The Art of Therapy: Using an Artist's Tools
1. Greenspan, Miriam. "Out of Bounds." In *Common Boundary,* vol. 13, no. 3 (July/August 1995).
2. For an explanation of my theoretical orientation, see the works of Roberto Assagioli, founder of an approach to helping known as Psychosynthesis. Roberto Assagioli. *Psychosynthesis.* New York: an Esalan Book, 1965. *See also* Assagioli's *The Act of Will.* New York: an Esalen Book, 1973.
3. Further discussion of these domains is found in any books on Psychosynthesis, stemming from the works of Assagioli. Another good reference is M.Y. Brown. *The Unfolding Self: Psychosynthesis and Counselling.* Los Angeles: Psychosynthesis Press, 1983.
4. I distinguish between *feelings* and *emotions* in that *feelings* occur in current awareness; *emotions* are the undercurrents that lie below the level of awareness (from the work of Murray Bowen, described in Gilbert, 1992, p. 39). It helps to distinguish the two because we are often driven by our emotions but are unaware of that driving force. R.M. Gilbert. *Extraordinary Relationships: A New Way of Thinking About Human Interactions.* Minneapolis: Chronemid Publishing, 1992.
5. Greenspan, Miriam. "Out of Bounds." In *Common Boundary,* vol. 13, no. 3 (July/August, 1995). p. 56.
6. Ibid, p. 57
7. Ibid.
8. Ibid.
9. Ibid, p. 58
10. Ibid.

Gloria Norgang — Mandala
1. I started this mandala in Susan Shantz's workshop at the Spider Women Retreat. It is my personal expression of three spiritual traditions which are important to me — Native, Goddess, and Buddhist. The colours of the Medicine Wheel, the four Grandmothers, the Moon phases, and four Boddhisatvas are represented together: Black- East- Full- Manjushri; Red- South- Waning- Samantabhadra; Yellow- West- New- Avalokiteshvara; White- North- Waxing- Ksitigarbha. The text is a shortened version of Thich Nhat Hanh's evocation of the Boddhisatva's names. Thich Nhat Hanh, poet, Zen master, and chairman of the Vietnamese Buddhist Peace Delegation during the war, was nominated by Dr Martin Luther King, Jr, for the Nobel Peace Prize. He has written over 25 books, including *Peace is Every Step, The Miracle of Mindfulness, Touching Peace, Being Peace,* and *For a Future to be Possible.* Thich Nhat Hahn lives in exile in France, where he teaches, writes, gardens, and helps refugees worldwide.

Anna Olson — Writing My Way to Recovery
1. Gabriele Rico. *Writing the Natural Way.* New York: J.P. Tarcher, 1983. p. 8.

2. Ibid, page 44.
3. e.e. cummings. "Portrait VIII." In Rico, *Writing the Natural Way*, p. 19.
4. Rico, p. 187.
5. Lucia Capacchione. *The Power of Your Other Hand*. Hollywood: Newcastle Publishing Co. Inc., 1988. p. 45.
6. Rico. *Pain and Possibility*. Los Angeles: J.P. Tarcher, 1991. p. 198.
7. Ibid, p. viii.
8. Ibid, p. 198.
9. Capacchione, p. 149.

Arlo Raven — i have survived
1. "i have survived" originally appeared in the chapbook *Holdings: Anthology of New Writings*. Winnipeg, 1995. p. 31

Iris A. Robinson, The Label
1. John W. Santroch, and Steven R. Yeissen. *Child Development*. Dubuque: Wm. C. Brown Publishers, 1992. pp. 567-572.

Carol Rose, pillar of salt
1. Originally published in *Prairie Fire*, vol. 14, no. 4 (winter 1994-95), and reprinted in *Behind the Blue Gate*. Vancouver: Beach Holme Publishers, 1997.

Carol Rose — Harnessing the Imagination
1. Dr. J.H. Hertz. *Pentateuch and Haftorahs*. (2nd. ed.) London: Soncina Press, 1971. Genesis I, 15:26, p. 4.

Carol Rose — body images
1. Originally published in *Prairie Fire*, vol. 13, no. 4 (1992) and reprinted in *Behind the Blue Gate*.

Carol Rose — she brings me her dreams
1. Originally published in *Women's Education des Femmes*, vol. 12, no. 4 (winter 1996-97).

Carol Rose — ms
1. Originally published in *Behind the Blue Gate*.

Libby Scheier — White Spider
1. This piece is a composite of two excerpts from the story "Letters to the Family" published in *Saints and Runners*. Stratford: Mercury Press, 1993. pp. 15, 16, 22, 23.

Spider Women: A Story
1. An earlier version of this story appeared in the brochure announcing the Spider Women Retreat. The following sources of inspiration are acknowledged:
Paula Gunn Allen. *Grandmothers of the Light: A Medicine Woman's Sourcebook*. Boston: Beacon Press, 1991.
Brooke Medicine Eagle. In *Shamanic Voices: A Survey of Visionary Narratives*, Joan Halifax, ed. New York: Viking Penguin, 1991.
Ovid. *Metamorphoses* Rolfe Humphries, trans. Bloomington: Indiana University Press, 1964.

Judy Springer — "revisioning heaven"
1. Originally published in *Herizons*, vol. 6, no. 1 (spring 1992).

Carol Stewart — Remembering and Healing
1. Leonard Orr. *Physical Immortality, The Science of Everlasting Life*. Inspiration University, 1988.
2. Pamela Colman Smith and Arthur Edward Waite. *Rider-Waite Tarot Cards*. New York: U.S. Games Systems, Inc., 1971.
3. Ibid, The 5 of Cups.
4. Ibid, The 2 of Cups.
5. Rashani, Tam Tro Graphics. Sausalito: Brush Dance Publishing, 1992. Printed as a post-card.

Anne Szumigalski — Halinka
1. Previously published in *Rapture of the Deep*. Regina: Coteau Books, 1991.

Anne Szumigalski — Tears and Stones
1. The above are extracts from an interview with Tom Bentley-Fisher, which appears with the text of the play *Z: A Meditation On Oppression, Desire And Freedom*. Regina: Coteau Books, 1995.

Karen Toole-Mitchell — Imagination Life's Heartbeat
1. Harry Chapin. "Flowers are Red." *Living Room Suite*. Scarborough: Elektra/Asylum Records, WEA Music of Canada, 1978.
2. This piece first appeared in Karen Toole-Mitchell's column, *Winnipeg Free Press*, Saturday, June 17, 1995, p. C5. It has been slightly modified for this book.
3. This piece first appeared in Karen Toole-Mitchell's column, *Winnipeg Free Press*, Saturday, June 24, 1995, p. A14. It has been slightly modified for this book.

Joan Turner — Art Changes Lives
l. See Gloria Norgang's mandala on page 79.
2. *Lifelines: A Quilted Portrayal of Life: Alvina Jean Pankratz*. Winnipeg: A catalogue of an exhibition at the Mennonite Heritage Village, Steinbach, MB, 1990.
3. *Myfanwy Pavelic Inner Explorations*. Victoria: Art Gallery of Greater Victoria, 1994.

Joan Turner — A Guide to Well-Being: The Personal is Political
1. Thank you to Deborah Gabinet, Carol Rose, Barbara MacKay, Brenda Proctor, Joe Connor, Toni Laidlaw and Cheryl Malmo and to all those who have given me ideas and feedback.

Joan Turner — A Tapestry of Creativity and Healing
1. Susun S. Weed. *Healing Wise*. Woodstock, NY: Ash Tree Publishing, 1989. p. 6.

Joie Zeglinski — Desperately Seeking Self
1. Expressive Arts Therapy, Certification course, summer intensive, California Institute of Integral Studies.

Acknowledgements

We would like to acknowledge the many strong and beautiful strands of creative expression that have gone into weaving this anthology. To all the women who have shared their papers, stories, poetry, music and visual art with us, our sincere appreciation. We are delighted that you agreed to contribute to this book. It is with regret that we also recognize those women whose submissions we received, but whose work could not be included within the confines of this particular book.

We are grateful to Woman Healing for Change Manitoba Inc. for its inspiring vision and for early funding in support of this book. Thank you also to the Endowment Fund, Faculty of Social Work, University of Manitoba, for its grant in support of publishing.

We thank Pat Dowdall, Dawn McCance, Robyn Maharaj and Andris Taskans for supportive letters of reference. Our heartfelt appreciation to Betty Henry for her enthusiasm for this project and for her competence and efficiency in putting the manuscript and its many revisions onto the computer. Many thanks to Pat Dowdall and to Gela Stach-Gaber who read the manuscript and gave us constructive feedback. Thanks to Joan's neighbours Liz and Tom Smith for offering us ready access to their fax machine and to Liz for assisting us with numbering the manuscript. Mindy Lopchuk provided us with excellent legal counsel. Marie Bouchard made it possible for us to include the work of Janet Kigusiuq. Thank you to Rae Harris who provided significant input in the selection of artists' work. We are very grateful to all these women. To our couriers, Lyle Henry, Joe Connor and Neal Rose, we say "many thanks again."

Our publisher J. Gordon Shillingford has been wonderful to work with. We would also like to thank Terry Gallagher (cover designer) and Clayton Halverson (music).

There were many ways in which our personal lives and the lives of our loved ones were disrupted while working on this anthology.

For their love, their patience and understanding we offer our thanks and appreciation to Joe Connor, Neal Rose and Adira Rose.

We would like to acknowledge the opportunities, the challenges and the consequences of working together. We have made fine and intricate connections with many people, their ideas and their creativity. We are very grateful for the ways in which we have benefited and will continue to benefit. In conclusion, we thank you, our readers, for your interest in our book.

Joan Turner and Carol Rose
March, 1999

Editors

Carol Rose is a writer, teacher and counsellor. She has published in Canadian and American literary journals, including: *CV2, Dandelion, Other Voices, Parchment, Prairie Fire, Quarry, The Wascana Review, Vintage '96, Whetstone, Women's Education Des Femmes* and *Zygote*. Carol also appears in the following anthologies: *Consciousness Raising: Women's Stories of Connection and Transformation, Voices and Echoes: Canadian Women's Spirituality, The Therapist's Notebook, A Heart of Wisdom, The Fifty-Eighth Century, Healing Voices, Living the Changes, Worlds of Jewish Prayer,* and *Miriam's Well*. Her first collection of poetry, *Behind the Blue Gate*, was published by Beach Holme Publishing, Ltd. (spring, 1997).

Carol's awards include the Henry Fuerstenberg Award for Poetry, 1998; co-winner in the Sandburg-Livesay poetry competition, 1997; and second prize in the Stephen Leacock International Poetry competition, 1994. She was also nominated for the John Hirsch award for most promising Manitoba writer in 1996 and 1997. She is a member of the board of *Prairie Fire*. In 1995 and 1996 Carol went to Copenhagen to work on a translation of her poems with Danish playwright, Ulla Ryum. She has also lectured for the Folkevirke Arts and Cultural Organization, and the Danish Writers' Guild on "Women and Spirituality." Carol lives in Winnipeg with her husband and daughter, Adira. Her four adult sons live in Toronto, New York, Jerusalem and Japan (where her first granddaughter, Noa, was born).

Joan Turner is a social worker and massage therapist and for 15 years has been in private practice. She is editor of *Living the Changes* (University of Manitoba Press, 1990), co-editor with Lois Emery of *Perspectives on Women* (University of Manitoba Press, 1983) and contributing author to *Healing Voices* (Toni Ann Laidlaw and Cheryl Malmo and Associates, Jossey Bass, 1990). Her writing has appeared in *Pottersfield Portfolio, Motherworker, Backtalk* and *Feminist Bookstore News.* She lives in Winnipeg with her husband, Joe Connor, and Casey, their cat. She is the mother of two adult daughters, Joie and Cathy Zeglinski, who are both physicians, and grandmother to Amy. She was Associate Professor, Faculty of Social Work, University of Manitoba, for almost 20 years, owner of Bold Print, Inc., the Winnipeg women's bookstore, for eight years, and chaplain of the First Unitarian Universalist Church of Winnipeg, 1990-1994. She is a founding member of Woman Healing for Change Manitoba, Inc. Joan likes to sing, play the piano, play tennis, ski and travel and to participate in arts and cultural activities. She often speaks and leads workshops on a variety of subjects including Alternative Therapies and Coping with Stress.

Contributors

Cassie Williams Aitchison was originally educated as a zoologist/ecologist at the University of Manitoba and later trained as a body therapist. She lives in Kamloops, BC, where she does her own unique mixture of osteopathically-based body therapy and teaches other therapists.

Lillian B. Allen's photographs attest to her reverence for nature. Her thousands of photos, taken in her travels all over the world, record the small wonders that many take for granted. Born in Winnipeg, she studied at several universities in Canada and the United States, obtaining degrees and diplomas in fine arts, applied arts, architecture, home economics, science and education. She taught in the Faculty of Home Economics at the University of Manitoba from 1934 until her retirement in 1971. *Frost*, a book of her photos, was published in 1990 through the University of Manitoba Alumni Association. She served as a teacher and design consultant at the Crafts Guild of Manitoba and a board member and founding member of the Volunteer Committee of the Winnipeg Art Gallery. At the time of her death in 1994 she lived in Victoria, BC.

Raye Anderson first became fascinated with old stories as a child growing up in Scotland. She has co-written, with Lora Schroeder, two plays based on fairy tales for young audiences. *The Snow Queen* placed Hans Christian Andersen's story in a contemporary Manitoban context, and *Cinderella Stories* dramatized different versions of Cinderella from around the world. Both were produced at Prairie Theatre Exchange, Winnipeg, where Raye also teaches drama and directs educational programs.

Germaine Arnaktauyok was born in a camp on the mainland near Igloolik in the Northwest Territories and now lives in Yellowknife.

She has been drawing since childhood and making art is a natural and necessary part of her life. She has a continuing interest in traditional myths and stories of her Iglumiut culture and a particular interest in female entities and concerns: the sea goddess Sedna, creation and birth, which are expressed in very personal ways. She has had solo exhibitions in Chicago and Port Townsend and has been part of group exhibitions in Vancouver, Inuvik, Hamilton, Anchorage and Seattle. She has provided illustrations for many publications and her designs have been commissioned for educational and commercial purposes. In 1998 she was artist-in-residence at the Winnipeg Art Gallery where her work was featured in a solo exhibition.

Joanne Arnott is a Métis woman, a writer and a mother. Her publications include a children's book about birth, *Ma MacDonald* (Women's Press); poetry, *Wiles of Girlhood* (Press Gang) and *My Grass Cradle* (Press Gang), and a non-fiction collection, *Breasting the Waves: On Writing and Healing* (Press Gang). Mother to four young sons, Joanne facilitates writing workshops, and is compiling an anthology of Métis writers in Canada. She lives in Richmond, BC.

Aliana Au was born in Guangdong, China. She studied Oriental brush work in Hong Kong. In 1970 she came to Canada and studied fine arts in Manitoba. Her work has been exhibited in Hong Kong, the USA, Canada and Mexico, and is included in the collections of the Winnipeg Art Gallery, the Manitoba Arts Council, the Canada Council Art Bank and numerous corporate and private collections. She lives in Winnipeg.

Judy Bancroft is a mother of five children, a wife and homemaker, formerly of Winnipeg, now residing in Edmonton. She loves to explore and learn about women's psychology and spirituality, be in nature near water, write and create using fresh and dried flowers.

M. Joan Baragar believes she is finally coming "of age." She has helped to raise a family of four to adulthood, has a Master's degree in Education (Psychology), and over twenty years of counselling experience. She is still in private practice, working with individuals, couples and families. Writing and singing have become more vital to her in recent years. Marrying Michael in 1990 lightened her soul. A seasoned grandmother now, she still counts children among her most powerful and positive teachers, learning from them how to grow and how to keep reaching for the mysteries of the universe.

Anne Belanger is a graphic artist who lives and works in Winnipeg.

Pat Borecky is a teacher, quilt maker and fabric artist. She has won many awards for her work. "Wearable Art" is her current most popular line and may be seen in fine stores and in "Sew Much More," the Singer dealership in Calgary which she owns. She is the mother of two adult daughters. Formerly of Winnipeg, Pat now lives in Calgary. In 1998 she was awarded the coveted Award of Excellence in wearables at Quilt Canada '98 Pacific Connections. Her quilts are in the collections of Walt Disney, the Manitoba government and Riverview Municipal Hospital.

Di Brandt is the author of four books of poetry. Her first collection, *questions i asked my mother* (Turnstone Press, 1987), was shortlisted for the Governor General's Award and the Commonwealth Poetry Prize, and received the Gerald Lampert Award. Her second collection, *Agnes in the sky* (Turnstone, 1990), received the McNally Robinson Award for Manitoba Book of the Year. Her most recent collection, *Jerusalem, beloved* (Turnstone, 1995), was shortlisted for the Governor General's Award. One of the poetic sequences in this book also received the Silver National Magazine Award. Di was also a recipient of the Canadian Authors' Association National Poetry Prize. Di Brandt is the author of *Wild Mother Dancing: Maternal Narrative in Canadian Literature* (University of Manitoba Press, 1993). She teaches Canadian literature and creative writing at the University of Windsor.

Carole Ann Burris has been interested in music for as long as she can remember. At age four she cried with her head on the piano until her mother allowed her to take piano lessons. Since then the piano, and later synthesizers and drums, have been her voice and ear to the world. She is inspired by the rhythms of nature and of women's lives and has been composing for the past fifteen years. She is currently working on music about space for planetariums and she often writes for film and dance. She lives in Egbert, ON.

Elizabeth Carriere was involved in founding the Manitoba Writers' Guild and the publication that became *Prairie Fire*. She is currently living and working in Indonesia.

Marianne Cerilli has been the Member of the Manitoba Legislative Assembly for Radisson since 1990. She has also worked as a high school counsellor, youth program consultant/volunteer program manager, recreation leader and coach. She lives in Transcona (Winnipeg) with Glen and their daughter Mira, dreaming of the day when poetry will "earn a living" and politics, as we know it, is passé.

Mary Louise Chown is a visual artist, storyteller and former public school teacher. For several years she has been a visiting artist in the Manitoba Artist in the Schools program, where she combines storytelling and making art with students. She is a partner in Earthstory, a trio of women who work together in the telling of tales, myths and stories.

Cynthia Cohlmeyer is a landscape designer who lives and works in Winnipeg.

Gloe Cormie is a poet and artist who lives in Winnipeg. Her poetry has been published in a number of journals and broadcast on CBC Radio's "Out Front." She was a winner of *Prairie Fire*'s prose poem contest (Winter, 1997-98) where she also received two honourable mentions for her poetry. Her work is in a chapbook, *The Six-Pack from Heaven*. She has completed Si…Sea…Seee, a manuscript of new and selected poems. She is prize winner in a *Contemporary Verse 2* haiku contest, forthcoming in *CV2* (Spring 1999).

Kathryn Countryman grew up in Sioux Lookout, ON. A university graduate, she lives in Winnipeg with her husband Don and son Dylan, and is expecting their second child. An accomplished photographer, this is her first published story.

Jean Crane is an Inuit elder, healer and painter who lives in Happy Valley, Labrador.

Susan Curtis is the pseudonym of a Manitoba woman.

Allyson K. Donnelly is attending Memorial University of Newfoundland (Cornerbrook), taking a B.F.A. in Theatre with plans to pursue a degree in women's studies. She has been writing for many years and has been published in various newspapers and newsletters. She takes her writing seriously, as a personal outlet, a public expression and an opportunity for consciousness-raising.

Keith Louise Fulton has mothered three children, who are now adults. She lives with her daughter, her partner, two dogs, three cats and two gardens. From 1987 to 1992, she was the first Margaret Laurence Chair of Women's Studies at the University of Winnipeg and the University of Manitoba. She teaches English and women's studies at the University of Winnipeg where she focuses on literature written by women and feminist theory.

Deborah Gabinet is a singer/songwriter who lives on a five-acre farm near Armstrong, BC. She currently leads three choirs: Vocal Joy, a large women's choir; Song Bards, a men's choir; and a children's choir. She composes songs for the celebration of Winter Solstice and other special events. A "survivor" and a "thriver," Deborah appreciates and uses music and writing in the healing process.

Trudy Ellen Golley is originally from Revelstoke, BC and received her undergraduate training at the Kootenay School of the Arts, the Alberta College of Art and the University of Calgary. She went on to M.F.A. studies at the University of Tasmania in Hobart, Australia. She has been invited to participate in ceramic residencies and lectures and gives workshops in Canada, Australia, Hong Kong and Malta. She has been an instructor at the Alberta College of Art, University of Calgary, University of Tasmania and the University of Manitoba, and is currently teaching design at the Kootenay School of the Arts, Centre of Craft and Design, in Nelson, BC. Her work is represented in numerous public and private collections including the Winnipeg Art Gallery and the Canada Council Art Bank.

Trish Gould is a kindergarten teacher. She participates in choral groups sings and plays the guitar. She lives in Winnipeg with her husband Jake and their children Aaron and Jocelyn.

Veronica G. Green resides near Beausejour, MB, with her husband and blended family, consisting of three teenaged sons and a teenaged daughter. Besides working in the nursing profession, she is currently pursuing her B.F.A. at the University of Manitoba. Creating art has always been important to her as an avenue to express her innermost feelings. She hopes that other people will look at her art and discover something about themselves.

Cecile Brisebois Guillemot graduated from the University of Manitoba in 1991 with a B.F.A. degree and has been writing since. She has had poetry published in several journals and magazines, including *Prairie Fire, Women's Education des Femmes* and *CV2.* Her chapbook of poetry, *secret conversations,* was published by Moonprint Press of Winnipeg in 1994. She lives in Winnipeg and is the mother of three young sons.

Rae Harris is an artist and art educator, presently in charge of School Programs at the Winnipeg Art Gallery. She has taught in the public school system and has been a consultant in art education and in early years with the Manitoba Department of Education. She studied arts, fine arts and education at Brandon University and the University of Manitoba. Rae's coloured pencil drawings explore the connections between women and the spaces in which they live — and which live within them. Her work has been exhibited in a number of group exhibitions and has been featured in *CV2* magazine.

Irene Heaman is a creative and journalistic writer who grew up on a farm, now lives in Winnipeg and aspires to return to country life. She has worked as a writer, farmer, teacher, administrative assistant and mother. Irene has published in *CV2, Manitoba, Myriad, Dufferin* (a rural Manitoba history book), and in newspapers and newspaper supplements, including "Western People."

Marj Heinrichs was born in 1956 and raised in the small, rural, predominantly Mennonite community of Rosenort, MB. In 1974 she married her high school sweetheart, Jim Heinrichs. In the next ten years, they had five children: Tom, Jennifer, Katie, Sara and Billy. Marj is a freelance journalist and photographer, working out of her home in Rosenort. Her work has been published in Manitoba community and Canadian Mennonite newspapers.

Joan Hibbert is a retired counsellor and a former lay member of the ministry team at Augustine United Church. She currently devotes her time to being and artist. Joan co-founded the Women's Post Treatment Project, now known as the Laurel Centre, in Winnipeg. She is a mother of five and a grandmother of four. Joan lives both in Winnipeg and at her summer home along the eastern shore of Lake Winnipeg, near Riverton, MB.

Karen Howe is a singer/songwriter who works for Lethbridge Family Services in Lethbridge, AB. In summer, she returns to her home in the country, at Woodmore, MB. Her music is recorded on *Prairie Spirit* and *Celebration of Difference*.

Donna F. Johnson works at Lanark County Interval House, a shelter for abused women and their children in rural Ontario. She is a founding member of Women's Urgent Action and is active in lobbying for changes to the criminal justice system. She lives in the village of Ashton, ON.

Victoria Moon Joyce is a life-long singer and a lover of women's voices raised in song. She spent several years songwriting, performing and recording, but her desire to encourage others to sing led her to become a "cultural animator" with groups wishing to integrate the arts into their collaborative work. She currently lives, works and studies in Toronto.

Irene E. Karpiak began her professional life as a social worker, and in mid-life embarked on a second career in adult and continuing education at the University of Manitoba. She pursued doctoral studies in that field. Presently, she is Assistant Professor of Adult and Higher Education at the University of Oklahoma. Her research and writing reflect her abiding desire to understand adult learners and their development and to create learning experiences that promote transformative change.

Eva Kenyon was a highly regarded social worker and family therapist. She held an M.S.W. degree, was a member of the Ontario College of Social Workers and served a term as president of the Ontario Association of Professional Social Workers. She was Director of Social Work at Mt. Sinai Hospital in Toronto for several years and later Director of the Family Therapy Training Centre at Oolagen. She also had a private social work practice. A world traveller, a lover of theatre and the arts, she is remembered above all for her passionate and unswerving belief in human potential.

Janet Kigusiuq is an accomplished artist, best known for her graphics and her fabric art. She was born in 1926 in the Back River area of the Kivalliq region of Nunavut and now lives in Baker Lake. Kigusiuq's prints, drawings and textile art are represented in many private and corporate collections and can be found in the permanent collections of the Winnipeg Art Gallery; the Canadian Museum of Civilization, Hull; the Macdonald Stewart Art Centre, Guelph; the Agnes Etherington Art Centre, Kingston; the Prince of Wales Northern Heritage Centre, Yellowknife; and the Klamer Family Collection, Art Gallery of Ontario, Toronto. Kigusiuq's mother, Jessie Oonark, was one of Baker Lake's — and Canada's — most distinguished artists. At the time of writing, January, 1999, Janet Kigusiuq has eight children, 30 grandchildren and several great-grandchildren.

Esther Kathryn (Klassen)'s work has evolved out of her life experiences, a background of training and work in music and social work, and her own journey of healing. She is a survivor and a feminist. Esther uses her knowledge and understanding of the body and the breath as essential means for healing in therapeutic work with individuals and groups. Esther believes that we need to address our woundedness in order to find spiritual resources for empowerment, healing and change. Esther is the mother of three adult sons, and is a grandmother. She is a partner in Soul Seasons Counselling and Consulting and leads two Winnipeg choirs: WomynSong and the Unitarian Church choir.

Lilita Klavins of Winnipeg is an artist by training (B.F.A.) and a business person by profession. She writes from her life and the lives she sees around her. She possesses first-hand experience about childbirth, motherhood, divorce, single parenting, and about coping with death and illness. Regretfully, she is also familiar with domestic violence.

Sylvia Legris has written two poetry collections, *iridium seeds* (1998) and *circuitry of veins* (1996), both published by Turnstone Press. She has also published two chapbooks and her writing has appeared in numerous journals, among them *The Capilano Review, Descant, Prairie Fire* and *Arc*. She currently lives in Saskatoon, SK.

Helen Levine has been actively involved in the women's movement since the late 1960s. She was a member of the faculty of the Carleton University School of Social Work from the mid-1970s until 1988. Since "retirement", she has been practising feminist counselling. For five years she was a board member with Amethyst Women's Addiction Centre in Ottawa. She is a member of the Crones, a group of older feminists, and of a Freefall Writing group. She was a major participant in *Motherland, Tales of Wonder*, a Studio D film of the National Film Board, directed by Helene Klodawsky (1995). Helen Levine's writing has appeared in *Perspectives on Women*, edited by Joan Turner and Lois Emery, and in *Living the Changes* edited by Joan Turner. In October 1989, Helen was one of six women across Canada to receive the Person's Award in recognition of her contribution to improving the status of Canadian women.

Lu-Ann Lynde studied art fundamentals at Sheridan College in Ontario. She is presently a tactile artist in a program conducted by the Canadian National Institute for the Blind to produce tactile diagrams for use by visually impaired students.

Robyn Maharaj is a poet living in Winnipeg. Her poetry and book reviews have appeared in *CV2, Dandelion, Prairie Fire* and *Zygote* magazines. Her background is in communications and marketing and she has worked as a freelance writer. She is interested in the process of artists' documenting life stories through literature, visual art, theatre and film. She has worked for the Manitoba Writers' Guild since 1992 and was appointed Executive Director in 1995. She is a founding member of Staccato Chapbooks and of the Winnipeg International Writers' Festival. She has worked as a video editor and film production assistant.

Katherine Martens lives in Winnipeg. She has published a family memoir *All in a Row: The Klassens of Homewood*. She has had numerous articles published in the *Mennonite Mirror*. "Giving Birth" was published in *Living the Changes*, edited by Joan Turner, 1990. "Sexuality and Childbirth: One Woman's Search for Emancipation" was published in *Motherwork* (Summer 1995) and "An Encounter with Maria Reimer," co-authored with Heidi Harms, was published in *Prairie Fire* (Fall 1995). Katherine Martens and Heidi Harms have published *In Her Own Voice: Childbirth Stories from Mennonite Women* (University of Manitoba Press, 1997).

Carmelita McGrath is a poet, fiction writer, editor and reviewer in St. John's, NF. Her books include *Poems on Land and on Water* (Killick Press, 1992) and *Walking to Shenak* (Killick Press, 1994). She has worked extensively as an editor, most recently as co-editor of *Their Lives and Times, Women in Newfoundland and Labrador* (Killick Press, 1995). Her poetry, fiction and reviews have appeared in a variety of publications including: *TickleAce, Event, The Fiddlehead, The New Quarterly, The Journey Prize Anthology, Poetry Canada, Books in Canada* and *Room of One's Own.* Her latest book, *To the New World,* was published in 1997 by Killick Press.

Penni Mitchell of Winnipeg has been the co-ordinating editor of *Herizons,* a national feminist magazine, since 1992. She is also a weekly columnist on feminist issues for the *Winnipeg Free Press.*

Lynne Mitchell-Pedersen is a therapist in private practice living in Winnipeg. She is also a teacher and consultant for health care staff working with older people. From 1981 to 1990, Dr. Mitchell-Pedersen worked as a Clinical Nurse Specialist in Geriatric Nursing at St. Boniface Hospital. She was founding president of both the Manitoba and Canadian Gerontological Nursing Associations. Lynne gives workshops and seminars across Western Canada and teaches for the Department of Continuing Education, University of Manitoba. She is currently writing a book called "From Anger to Empathy."

Gloria Norgang of Ottawa has been inspired by those who dream new worlds and is powered by chocolate, sisters, oceans, trees, smiles, garlic, love, water, light and other forms of magic. For all of the years that she can remember, she has been seeking peace (inside and outside) and challenging the status quo.

Anna Olson, formerly of Winnipeg, now of Grand Marais, MB, is an associate editor of *The Aquarian,* a quarterly newspaper which focuses on alternative spirituality, holistic health and environmental concerns. She is also a freelance writer and gives creative writing workshops.

Denise Osted is a prairie-born and prairie-loving writer, survivor and feminist. She tries to make her head, heart and hands work in concert. Her writing has been published in various magazines and anthologies. She is a Canadian who currently lives in The Netherlands.

Sally Papso is a long-time feminist activist in the women's movement, in her community and in the lesbian and gay rights movement. She works as a counsellor for the Manitoba government in juvenile corrections and as a counsellor in private practice. Her self-care and healing is her garden. She has become known as the bus stop gardener on Arlington Street in Winnipeg.

Arlo Raven lives in Winnipeg and is a survivor of incest. Her work has been published in *Common Lives/Lesbian Lives, CV2, Dandelion* and *Room of One's Own*. She has two daughters.

Edith Regier has a particular interest in portraying family/cultural dynamics in her work. Educated in art in Canada, Mexico and the US.A, she has had solo exhibitions in Houston and Winnipeg. She developed and taught a studio program, and currently co-ordinates the mentor-by-mail program at the Portage Correctional Institution for women. She has also taught at the Winnipeg Art Gallery. Edith lives in Winnipeg with her two sons.

Margo Reimer is a Winnipeg writer and musician. Her study of classical piano and voice served as a valuable basis for a wide variety of performing as well as the recording, in 1995, of a cassette entitled *Moment of Light*. She has a degree in social work and has worked as a mediator and family counsellor in the area of separation and divorce, and counselled children of divorce. She is a vocational consultant. She enjoys writing for children as well as adults and is currently working on a manuscript of a book entitled "In Her Image." She is a single parent and has two daughters. Her artistic interests include photography and watercolour painting. She has published in *Herizons, CV2, Canadian Women's Studies Journal, Zygote* and *Healthsharing*.

Nancy Reinhold works as a songwriter and vocalist and is a co-founder of the successful feminist folk band, The Wyrd Sisters. The group has released two recordings to date, *Leave a Little Light* (1993) and the Juno-nominated *Inside the Dreaming* (1995). Members are currently writing songs for their next recording. With her band partner and love, Kim Baryluk, Nancy lives and works in Winnipeg.

Iris A. Robinson was a friend, partner, mother of two sons, an educator, Psychology major, humourist, story-maker, embracer of honesty and lover of life. She was a life-long resident of Winnipeg until her death April 24, 1997, at age 45, from cancer.

Deborah Romeyn is a singer/songwriter whose music has been recorded on *Prairie Spirits* (cassette) and *Distance in Her Eyes* (CD). As a high school teacher and massage therapist, she encourages people to find and to share their gifts. In her own musical performances, Deborah offers a mix of humour, heart, hope, vision and simplicity that encourages us to listen. Her songs have been performed by other Canadian singers including Heather Bishop, Tracey Riley and Jennifer Berezans. Deborah lives in Winnipeg.

Adira Rose is a Winnipeg student, the daughter of Carol Rose and Rabbi Neal Rose. Her short story "Seven Wild Women" was published in *Fireweed* (Winter, 1997-98).

Sophia Rosenberg is an artist, a poet and a teacher. Her own work, and the work she does with others, is concerned with the creative process and healing. She lives in Victoria, BC with her partner, Catherine, and their feline familiars, Mao and Lucy.

Gwen Satran is a writer, educator and mother. She has been teaching in Winnipeg's inner city for many years.

Libby Scheier is co-editor of *Language in Her Eye*, and author of *Saints and Runners — Stories and a Novella*, and three books of poetry. *SKY — A Poem in Four Pieces*, was described by Phyllis Webb as a "powerful and sobering work. The central drama is child rape, but the imaginative range is cosmic." Scheier was a member of the Women's Writing Collective in the late 70s, an Ontario representative to the 1983 Women and Words Conference, and a founding member of the first anti-racism committee of the Writers' Union of Canada. She has long been involved personally and politically in feminist activities, especially around abuse and violence against women. She teaches creative writing, women's studies and Canadian literature at York University and is founder/director of the independent Toronto Writing Workshop.

Sandra Somerville is a holistic therapist in Winnipeg, providing integrative body work and counselling which focuses on the balance and celebration of one's body, mind and spirit. She has travelled to the four corners of the earth to learn different approaches to wellness and healing. Her photography captures the essence and sacredness of our earth's people and places.

Heather Spears's books *How to Read Faces* (1986) and *The Word for Sand* (1988) both won the Pat Lowther Award. *The Word for Sand* also won the Governor General's Award for poetry. Poems collected in *Human Acts* (1991) won the CBC Literary Prize. Heather Spears lives by teaching drawing, has held over 70 solo exhibitions and published 9 collections of poetry, three novels and three books of drawings. Her most recent collection is *Poems Selected and New* (1999). She has lived in Denmark since 1962 and returns to Canada annually for book tours, art workshops and readings.

Sheila Spence is a Winnipeg artist. She was invited to photograph women and their activities at the Spider Women Retreat, Hecla Island.

Judy Springer is a ceramist/artist who lived in Brandon, Manitoba, for 20 years and now lives in Camden East, ON, near Kingston. Two decades ago the spider became part of her signature on her work after it "appeared" through layers of underglazes and glazes beside her name. She is now concentrating on painting.

Maureen Stefaniuk, of Ukrainian heritage, was born and raised in Kamsack, SK, and now lives in the village of Verigin, SK. An artist, her studies include a B.A. Honours (Visual Arts major), University of Saskatchewan, and a Master's degree in Christian Studies, University of British Columbia. Ms. Stefaniuk is currently working on a series of writings and paintings, "Sophia for the Creative Journey: In My Baba's House are Many Mansions." She single parents and home care nurses her young daughter who is on dialysis for chronic renal failure. She paints whenever possible.

Carol Stewart is a teacher who has established an international reputation for her inspirational use of the Tarot symbols. From 1987 through 1991, she lived in Cuzco, Peru. During that time she led trips to sacred sites in Bolivia, Peru and Ecuador. Before Peru, the Tarot was the voice of her Spirit, intuition mixed with psychotherapeutic training. Since Peru, she has found the voice of her Soul, a personal vision that emerges in following 'the call'. She believes in living what she teaches and vise versa. She makes her home in Nelson, BC, where she has established a Mystery School. Recently she completed a manuscript for a book called "Birth of Inkarri."

Anne Szumigalski was born in England but has lived in Saskatoon for about forty years, and has been a major influence behind the vibrant literary activity in Saskatchewan. She is an internationally known and highly respected poet, essayist and editor. The author of twelve books, Szumigalski has been invited to read in venues as diverse as Oxford, Boston and Indonesian locations. Besides serving on the Saskatchewan Arts Board, she has juried for the Canada Council and worked hard to promote the arts, poetry in particular, in Canada. In 1995 she won the Governor General's Award for poetry, for *Voice*, a collaboration with visual artist Marie Elyse St. George. Her play, *Z: A Meditation on Oppression, Desire and Freedom*, won the Saskatchewan Book of the Year Award. She is a mother and a grandmother.

Barbara Taylor is a writer and mother of two daughters. Her work is in the field of communications. Her passionate interests are in the inner and outer journeys of life and in consciousness and transformation. She lives in Winnpeg.

Diana Thorneycroft has exhibited her art work in major cities across Canada as well as in New York, London, Paris, Edinburgh and Moscow. She is a recipient of numerous Manitoba Arts Council and Canada Council awards and has been employed as a teacher at the School of Art, University of Manitoba, since 1984. Her work is featured in *Slytod: Diana Thorneycroft*, Serena Keshavjee, ed. (Winnipeg: University of Manitoba Press, 1999).

Karen Toole-Mitchell is a graduate of the Atlantic School of Theology. For about thirty years she has worked as a minister in the United Church of Canada in Newfoundland, Nova Scotia and Manitoba. She grew up in North End Winnipeg, and is familiar with life in the inner city. She is the mother of two sons. Karen is a survivor, a feminist and a spiritual humanist. Her theology is focused on the holy affirmation of each life as a sacred gift. Her skills include educational design, pastoral counselling, the creation of inclusive worship and faith/abuse analysis. Her vocation finds its focus in writing in spiritual direction work and in the naming of all forms of abuse. She is a partner in Soul Seasons Counselling and Consulting, Winnipeg, and writes for the *Winnipeg Free Press* and the *United Church Observer*.

Mary Toombs is a woman forged out of the gutsy inheritance of prairie pioneers, and the traditional woman's roles of wife, mother, grandmother, nurse, teacher and school counsellor. She was born in Saskatchewan and has lived in Winnipeg since 1963. She has done much volunteer work in drama: directing, teaching and adjudicating. With her husband, Gordon, she has team-taught human sexuality, relationships, meditation, dreams, spiritual growth, and death and dying. She has studied creative writing at the University of Manitoba and at West Words VIII and is a member of the Manitoba Writers' Guild and the Canadian Authors' Association. She won prizes in CAA poetry contests in 1989 and 1993. Now "retired," she is moving along her path with the aid of writing, dreamwork and spiritual work, in a milieu of fun and friendship.

Val T. Vint was born in Winnipegosis, MB, but spent the most meaningful part of her childhood in the bush, chasing foxes and pelicans while with her grandfather who was a conservation officer. She draws from a background in photography, engineering, design, theatre, music, travel and work with indigenous peoples. She says, "My cultural heritage makes me feel like I have a licence to investigate all forms of art. The Métis were fiercely independent by nature; they did everything for themselves, developing a self-sufficient and highly versatile culture. My work is really varied because of that spirit and it would be impossible to nail it down to one medium." Val's present direction is influenced by her Métis heritage. Her various working mediums include willows, feathers, clay, rawhide, watercolours, acrylics and writing. She says that art was, and is, intrinsic to everyday life.

Esther Warkov is a well-known Canadian artist. Her imagery is complex and is inspired by photographs, literature, Jewish culture and her own rich imagination. Her works often reflect her perspective on social and cultural issues. In the early 1990s her two-dimensional drawings slowly evolved into three-dimensional collages, culminating in the "House of Tea," a headless, life-sized female figure suspended over a coffin. This piece was part of a solo exhibit entitled "Esther Warkov: Recent Drawings" which opened at the Winnipeg Art Gallery, November 1, 1998. Esther lives in Winnipeg.

Beatrice Archer Watson is a graduate of the University of Manitoba where she studied anthropology and women's studies. She also studied radio, television and journalism arts at Lambton College in Sarnia, ON. Her first novel, *Poison of My Hate*, was published in Zambia in 1979. Her poetry appeared in *Voices I, II, III*, produced by the Immigrant Women's Association of Manitoba. Her writing has been published in the Canadian Advisory Council on the Status of Women (CACSW) anthology, *Sharing Our Experiences*, and in *Herizons* and *Healthsharing*, "Family Violence Research Centre Bulletin," newspapers and journals. She has studied video production and in 1995 produced *The Story of the Immigrant Women's Association of Manitoba*. She lives in Winnipeg with her family.

Isabel Wendell lives near Roblin, MB. Winter is a time for cross-country ski trails, writers' groups, and piano lessons. Summer brings her three children home from University and the whole family produces honey.

Rowan Wolf is a massage therapist, drum maker and musician who is exploring the connection between the intellectual, emotional and physical with the spiritual. She celebrates life in Winnipeg with her son Jeremy and partner Jamie.

Barbara Yussack uses a variety of creative tools to aid her in her healing journey. Spiritual tools such as the Enneagram, goddess archtypes, chanting, drumming and singing have empowered her to risk an inward journey into self-awareness and to emerge as a confident and strong woman. Barb is a Sacred Circle Dance Instructor. A ber of WomynSong, she has also written her own songs. "Goddess Trinity" reflects the connection between all women and the Feminine Divine. Barb shares her home in Winnipeg with her adult son, two cats and a dog.

Joie Zeglinski was a family physician in a community health centre in Ottawa, and is now a resident in psychiatry, University of Ottawa. She has studied dance, drama, art, music and sports for personal pleasure, performance and/or competition. She has been exploring the use of expressive arts therapy in medicine and is enrolled in the expressive arts therapy summer program for professionals, California Institute of Integral Studies. She is mother to Amy, born June 11, 1998.

Susan Zettell's first novel, *Holy Days of Obligation*, was published by Nuage Editions in 1998. Her stories have been anthologized in *Quintet* (Buschek Books) and have appeared in various magazines and literary journals. She co-edited (with Frances Itani) the posthumously published short story collection *One of the Chosen* by Danuta Gleed. Susan lives in Ottawa where she continues to play women's hockey.